Peter figuratively describes the real estate business as an endurance sport...and if we accept that real estate or any business is indeed an endurance sport, we will have a higher probability of crossing whatever finish lines we choose to cross. This book will surely help both real estate amateurs and professionals overcome valleys and reach peaks in their business journeys. This is a timely written book for the real estate industry, especially in this era of pandemics.

Yong-Nam, KIM, PhD, CCIM, FRICS, SIOR
South Korea CCIM Chapter President
President & CEO, Global PMC Inc.

Pete Frandano's *Endurance Real Estate* is proof that you can find artists, warriors and renaissance men in the most unlikely of places – even CRE. It is full of relevant wisdom for navigating today's black swan event and all the events that are sure to follow.

Cindy Wolfe
Chief Banking Officer, Bank OZK

Thank you for writing *Endurance Real Estate;* the chronical of your journey to success in our industry is a treasure of knowledge and experience for real estate professionals, young and old!

Steven W Moreira CCIM CIPS
Past President CCIM Institute
Managing Broker - RealSource

When I think of Pete, the word *endurance* comes to mind. He does not give up and is always striving for the next level. Pete is a total professional and his years in the corporate world coupled with the level of entrepreneurship he's shown in commercial real estate make him the perfect person to write this true story of *Endurance Real Estate*.

Cindy Chandler, CRE, CCIM – The Chandler Group
Past President, North Carolina Association of REALTORS
Past President, North Carolina Real Estate Educators Association
Director, National Association of REALTORS

Pete Frandano has given us a roadmap to success. Using his own life experiences, he has provided insights and examples that will help us develop the best attitude and the best results in our lives. Pete has long applied his experience and tenacity as a seasoned endurance athlete to his profession, and the results are evident in his successes. This book can help the rest of us do the same…

Jeff Siebold, CCIM, Author and Principal,
Siebold Group Consulting, LLC

Pete Frandano began *Endurance Real Estate*, primarily with the aim of recounting his life experiences in the up and down world of real estate as a window of disclosure to answer for the benefit of his two sons: who am I? …In answering "who am I" Pete shares some universal truths about life and human behavior which children coming of age need to know and we readers need to be (gently) reminded of. *Endurance Real Estate* reminds us to never take anything for granted, especially in the world of business and to be mindful of what may be around the corner. Quick thinking, the relentless will to survive and a bit of luck characterize Pete's business comeback journey. Think *resilience*. Above all else, Pete wanted his sons and all of us to know that no matter how tough things may be, to never, ever, give up.…

Geoffrey Curme, CRE
Principal, Mount Vernon Asset Management, LLC

Having worked closely with Pete on the North Carolina CCIM Board, I've seen his ability to synthesize lessons learned from his considerable experience and bring them to bear on the issue at hand. When you hit hard times, as we all do, you want someone like Pete in your corner. *Endurance Real Estate* brings those experiences and those lessons directly to you, helping you climb whatever mountain you must face.

Robert C. Vaughn III, CCIM
Director – Agency Lending
Grandbridge Real Estate Capital

I have known and worked with Pete on deals and in industry leadership a long time and he is a relentless ambassador for our industry…

Patrick Riley, CCIM
Vice President, Cape Fear Commercial

ENDURANCE REAL ESTATE

ENDURANCE REAL ESTATE

RUNNING FROM PEAK TO PEAK

Gene,
thanks for your friendship
and all you've done to
our industry...
my Best to you & yours
Always!
Pete

BECAUSE REAL ESTATE & LIFE ARE ENDURANCE SPORTS

PETER A. FRANDANO, CCIM, GRI, MBA

First Edition

Paperback ISBN: 978-1-7365877-2-0
eBook ISBN: 978-1-7365877-5-1

Author Coming out of the Banks Channel - Beach to Battleship Triathlon in Wilmington, NC

To my sons, John and Joe. I am grateful for you…

CONTENTS

WELCOME TO THE NEW WORLD

"THERE ARE DECADES WHERE NOTHING HAPPENS, AND
THERE ARE WEEKS WHERE DECADES HAPPEN..."
- VLADIMIR LENIN

"THE MORE THINGS CHANGE, THE MORE THEY STAY THE SAME..."
JEAN-BAPTISTE ALPHONSE KARR

Greetings! I hope you and yours are doing well in these interesting and unprecedented times.

———

When I set out to write this book (almost two years ago now) and submitted the first draft of *Endurance Real Estate* to my editor at 5:27pm Monday, February 17, 2020 (a glorious moment for me!), I obviously had no idea that the COVID-19 pandemic was right around the corner.

Because of this historic event, some close to me have suggested I needed to "write another chapter." Some also have said the world will now be forever delineated as Pre-COVID-19 and Post-COVID-19.

On the latter point, I agree.

I'm not a fan of Marxism but I am a fan of Capitalism and history – military history in particular. And I think Mr. Lenin's quote above applies to our here and now.

When I have taken an introspective look at the past months of this historic pandemic, I am presented with a bit of a paradox because both quotes certainly seem to apply to our "now."

The two periods, The Great Recession and that long period after and what we are going through today are all major valleys. This current valley and its impact are yet to be determined but I believe transformational and exponential change are occurring to our world in this next 'round'.

What we are going through now is what this book is about. *It's what Endurance Real Estate was built for.*

The basics don't change. I have to keep advancing my ball every day and hopefully taking a few others with me on my journey, over my finish line.

Endurance Real Estate started out as a chronicle for my sons and has evolved into something I hope can help others. My life's experiences, boiled down into some lessons learned and those lessons don't change because of a pandemic. In some cases, those lessons are now circled, underlined and highlighted.

This new chapter has yet to be written. In a surreal, almost exciting paradox, its authorship is up to you and me!

COVID-19 hit right when I submitted *Endurance Real Estate* to my editor. In the spirit of taking my own advice to periodically check the relevancy of your business model, you'll find several instances throughout this book where I added bits of information or perspective as it relates to our new post-pandemic world. Today's challenges and those we will be facing in the immediate future have expanded this book's original intent...

Yet even in the midst of our new challenges, our business fundamentals, our basics and true north compass remain unchanged. How we treat our customers and seek to deliver value – our basic business philosophies –remain unchanged.

How we service our customers and seek to deliver value, basic business philosophies, may modify slightly but the need to do so won't cease because of what we are going through now. Some business models may have to change, and yes, some of those models will win and some will lose. Demand for certain goods and services may change, in some cases drastically or cease to exist, new business practices will evolve, new demand for goods and services may crop up or evolve (see Zoom as an early example), the channels in which they are delivered or how they are delivered may change, but that is the business model. We shouldn't confuse the business model for the fundamentals.

Let's look at a few examples of concepts that have not changed and actually, in my opinion have become more important now than ever before:

1. Endurance, (the need to have it!) and related to Endurance, *Agility*.
2. Focusing on our circle of control and running our own race
3. Maintaining Balance in our life > Physical, Mental, Social/ Emotional and Spiritual
4. Maintaining a relevant and sustainable business model

These concepts don't change because of the COVID-19 pandemic. In fact, if The Great Recession put an exclamation point on the concepts I've presented in this book, the COVID-19 pandemic has just put a finer point on them.

There are a lot of people who are going to need a lot of help and guidance. This is a statement I made early on with some of my colleagues when I saw New York City get shut down and the pandemic wave started washing across our great country.

With all of the news and information flying by and at all of us, predictions, projections and the like, I heard a person I respect say during this time of crisis state that: *Nobody knows nothing and I don't believe any of the information out there.*

His point is well taken: *we've never been here before.* No matter how battle hardened or how many hours "logged" in our respective arenas, *this is new territory for all of us.*

The Great Recession was my "cold bucket of water in the face" moment. A *wow, the light switch just got flipped and I never saw it coming* moment. Well, this *Great Shutdown*, this COVID-19 Pandemic is no doubt one of those moments for all of us. Hopefully, this book will help people now and in future generations to accept and understand that the 'switch' can be flipped – anytime, anywhere, at any point in the business cycle, no matter how strong the cycle appears to be. And my hope is this book will also provide you or others you care about with some ideas on how to push through.

In my view, this event will be read about and studied 200 years from now and beyond. This event will change things, shift things, transform and revolutionize things, people, places, systems, business, infrastructure, towns, cities, counties, states, countries, ways of life, and things we knew to be true, in ways many of us cannot even fathom.

How we run through this next valley and onto our next peak to cross our next finish line is up to each one of us. *That's the chapter yet to be written.*

Endurance Real Estate is couched primarily in my experiences, and those I've observed, related to that last historic valley most of us had to run through, to endure: the Great Recession. Many of us survived. Some unfortunately did not, literally and figuratively. In this book, you will see a theme throughout of running from Peak to Peak and crossing finish lines, no matter what or where those finish lines may be.

So, I ask you: Are you ready for the next valley? Well, here it is now, staring us all in the face.

We can't get rid of the valleys; as we all know, the business cycle and life will *always* continue to evolve and cycle. This is what the mountains and the valleys on this book's cover represent: the business cycle, the cycle of life. And the figure charging ever onward and upward? Well, that's you and me, pushing through the valleys and on to the next peak.

True then, True now.

Lives and livelihoods were at stake *then* and they are *now* too.

Then and now are different of course but there are some similarities in what we can do to *attack it.*

Please permit me a small and personal analogy: In marathon speak, a hill is a hill, just a different degree of slope, so when I'm hitting the hill do I completely change my technique? No, I adjust my pace. In a similar vein, with this current valley, I will most likely have to adjust the way I attack the hill. But I better check my pace, my balance or I won't make it to the top. An old trick I learned from seasoned runners and have used over the years when running that is applicable to what we are going through now: when I hit the major hills I need to think *effort, not pace.*

In our math or science classes over the years, we learned about axioms. The definition of an axiom is:

a statement or proposition which is regarded as being established, accepted, or self-evidently true.

In this time of instability and unknowns, there are 3 Things in my opinion we can hold as axioms while traversing this seemingly overwhelming valley. I discuss these in depth in the section: *What are the 3 Things?* In light of the pandemic, I bring these forward now for a moment, to contemplate and for emphasis:

1. **Invest in YOU, INC.** – one of the best investments any of us can make.
2. **CEO of YOU, INC.** – You are the CEO of *You, Inc.*; making the tough decisions, screen out distractions, focusing and meet disruptions head on and turn them into opportunities.
3. **Gratitude and Attitude** – helping people along the way and acknowledging those who have helped us. On a personal note, for me this is both motivating and humbling.

The 3 Things don't change, but how we operate and adjust within their boundaries certainly may change.

Due to the COVID-19 pandemic, the landscape has significantly shifted. The arena, the table that we play the game on is now altered and changed, in some cases, forever. We may have to adjust how we play the game. That means being both agile and built for endurance. What do we do to adapt and adopt, and come out on the other side of this tsunami alive and a winner?

Back to Lenin's quote above... *There are decades where nothing happens, and there are weeks where decades happen...*

It seems we hear the word "disruption" a lot these days. Some say, "*Disruption is coming,*" almost as a fear-inciting tactic. I respectfully disagree. I say that in the real estate industry, and in almost any industry, disruption is not one thing, its three things. Disruption is 1) coming, 2) here at our doorstep and 3) going to keep coming... *and that's okay!*

I recently told my two sons: "Yes, what we are going through together in our world due to this pandemic is tragic, but you should be optimistic; I believe this will prove to be one of the most significant reset buttons pressed in history..."

If someone wanted to reinvent themselves or their business, this could be one the greatest opportunities in history to do just that!

As in any market, business cycle or condition: there will be opportunities for the vigilant.

We can find some insightful and applicable guidance from Albert Einstein in his "Three Rules of Work":

Three Rules of Work: Out of clutter find simplicity. From discord find harmony. In the middle of difficulty lies opportunity.

Albert Einstein

Some individuals and businesses will find themselves in a great position to stand out from the pack because of their business model. If an opportunity opens due to the changing needs of consumers, do you have the courage of your convictions to adjust course, modify your business model and go for it? Some thought I was crazy when I jumped out of the Fortune 500 arena, into the real estate arena to spend more time with my family and pursue my entrepreneurial dreams. You may have to run through the gauntlet; some may call you crazy as you adjust your business model, perhaps going off road, running your own race, moving toward the finish line you now know to be ahead.

Whenever I cross a finish line of any kind, I always look up and give thanks. Yes, of course I had to exert my own energy and effort to cross the finish line but I also realize that with every finish line I've ever crossed I've had help along the way from people, circumstances, seen and unseen, known and unknown. And I'm grateful for it all.

But here's a cold hard fact: *There will be winners and losers.*

In our *everyone gets a trophy society,* (and I love it because I've coached youth sports and it's been a blessing to me, and I love happy shiny smiling faces as much if not more than anyone!) we learned a hard lesson from the Great Recession (I call it *the long war*) and all previous cycles that yes, there will be *winners and losers.* Life is hard; sometimes we get knocked on our backside. How do we bounce back, pick ourselves up, dust ourselves off and keep moving to cross the next finish line?

As during the Great Recession, there won't be enough lifejackets and lifeboats to go around. Why not choose to win and be a lifeboat for others, helping them move on to new frontiers?

I'm proud of our country, I'm proud of what I have seen and how people have stepped up to help one another and I'm more hopeful than ever. Seeing our hero warrior health care workers, police, firefighters, all first responders, grocery store personnel, delivery folks and others who help sustain us has been breathtaking. This world and life changing event is the ultimate lemons-to-lemonade moment for all of us. It can catapult us up our next peak, over our next finish line.

This *historic and complex event* has made me cling more tightly to my faith and the people around me and has reinforced for me that in my world no day or person can be taken for granted. My hope is that this book can help you or someone in your world in their life journey.

Practicing Endurance and Endurance Real Estate during a Great Recession. Practicing Endurance and Endurance Real Estate during a Pandemic. We've never been here before but we are all in it together.

May God Bless You along your way.

The next peak, our summit, is just up ahead...Now let's get there!

Pete Frandano

INTRODUCTION

"I HAVE FOUGHT THE GOOD FIGHT, I HAVE FINISHED
THE RACE, I HAVE KEPT THE FAITH..."
--THE APOSTLE PAUL AS QUOTED IN 2 TIMOTHY 4:7

Let me say right here in the beginning and in no uncertain terms that you have a story to tell, only you can tell it and chances are someone can benefit from your story and your experiences. It's your life and only you can live it; it's your race and only you can run it. I came to this realization when I started out writing this book. We all have a story to tell...so we should tell it and share our experiences so others can benefit from them, good, bad or ugly.

I'll be the first to admit *I didn't have one clue about what I was getting into* when I decided to leave the Fortune 500 world in 2002 and jumped head long into the real estate industry.

2003 to 2006 made me look and feel brilliant and made my decision look likewise; this was due mainly to the insanity rocket ship our industry was on; in looking back, some refer to this period as the "Silly Season", me included.

2007 - 2009 made me look like the Village Idiot after purchasing a real estate company with my partners. The Earthquake, which was the financial crisis, strikes and in rolls the Tsunami aka The Great

Recession and subsequent real estate downturn, the kickoff of what I refer to as "the Long War."..

2010 to 2012 made me learn all about "survival of the fittest" the hard way. I picked up the pieces and myself, dusted off and kept moving to higher ground, to the next peak...

That 2006 to 2012 period is what I call the "long war." I gave up apologizing for calling it *a war* a long time ago. When lives and livelihoods are lost, it officially moves from an "economic cycle" to a war. I realize the severity of the impact varied by region, but in southeastern North Carolina, the length of this valley made it a war.

Many of you have heard and read about the 2% on Wall Street and what happened there: the financial crisis, kicked off by the collapse of Lehman Brothers, what followed was a historic bailout of our major financial institutions (the Big banks) by our government, which means you and I as taxpayers paid for it, which in turn helped those on Wall Street. That's great, but it certainly did not help many of us out here in the field, in the arena, on main street; this is well chronicled. This book is about and for the rest of us, the 98%.

Ultimately, this book is about savings lives and livelihoods and crossing finish lines. My goal is to help you run from Peak to Peak and surf or swim through any tsunami that might come your way...

Thanks for reading and here's to crossing all the finish lines in your life!

———

WHY ENDURANCE REAL ESTATE?

After some prodding from friends, family and colleagues, I decided it was time to write this book. 2020 happened to be my 30th combined anniversary of working in the Fortune 500 and real estate arenas.

So, maybe I should explain, what's with the title, *Endurance Real Estate*?

I chose the title, *Endurance Real Estate*, because long ago I recognized that the real estate business – any business really – is an endurance sport. I also realized the quicker I came to terms with this fact, the better off my family and I would be.

Let me say - right off the bat - that I consider myself an endurance athlete, but not a "pro" endurance athlete. I'm a humble hobbyist, an enthusiast of endurance sports, I've been blessed to be a happy participant in 100 or so events over the years, including marathons, triathlons, 5K – 8K – and 10K runs, and cycle rides of various flavors for different and very worthy causes. Add to the official events, the informal thousands of miles run, all the short, medium and longer non-official runs I've been fortunate to have done quietly around the globe and it's been a fun and rewarding, yet humbling, experience. I have never taken any finish line crossed, no early rainy day run, no wind driven cycle ride, no frigid swim for granted. Not one. I realize they have all been a blessing and a gift given to me. (At this time, I would like to thank, recognize and apologize to my poor feet!)

Yes. I run, cycle and swim for fun, not for money. I placed in a few events early on when I was hitting a goal time, but never won. Today, my goals are simply to finish and to enjoy the journey. I'm no Dean Karnazes, author of *Ultra Marathon Man: Confessions of an All-Night Runner*, multiple winner of the Western States 100 and someone who once did 50 marathons in 50 days – not by a long shot. I admire Dean, but that is not me. If you are familiar with the bell curve, Dean is waaaay out there on the tippity tip of the bell curve, the anomaly for sure...

When it comes to the field of endurance sports, I am seasoned but am an amateur, not a professional doing it for a living. I've been fortunate to have crossed many finish lines in my life in many different places, whether in business or life or endurance sports! I've also been the recipient of a whole lot of help along the way.

Each event taught me something about myself and others. And I am grateful for all these experiences and for all the finish lines I've crossed. I've been fortunate to always cross the finish line in any event I started. Even in 2015, when I had to drag my sorry, broken-hipped self over the Marine Corps Marathon finish line (story later).

I'm also an occasional golfer and my father and I used to play quite a bit of golf together, up until 2008 when we lost him suddenly to a heart attack (ironically, on the golf course, on his birthday!). A couple of years later, my youngest son, who was around 9 years old then, thankfully pulled me back into the game.

One commonality between golf and endurance sports is *mental endurance*. Eighty percent (maybe higher) of what we do or don't do and what we let get in our way or not plays out in that very small yet immensely powerful space between our ears. I've learned a lot about myself and others on a golf course and I've also learned a lot about myself on 5-, 10-, 15- or 26.2-mile runs...

One thing I learned over the years of endurance sports and business dealings is that some people only see the "fun" part of what you do, not the sacrifices you made to get to that point. People usually just see you cross a finish line or get that deal closed, and don't see all of the front work you have put in. They don't see the early morning runs before everyone else is up. They don't see the years spent in building and growing your network, the analysis you have put in.

Most people are unaware of the hard work put in behind the scenes.

Everyone watches and cheers as the great NBA basketball player dunks the basketball or hits the game winning shot, but most of us are simply reacting to the skill being shown, unaware of his countless hours of practicing the moves he needs to perform to make that basket, of being in the gym, of working through plays with his coach and teammates.

Muhammad Ali once said:

"The fight is won or lost far away from witnesses - behind the lines, in the gym, and out there on the road, long before I dance under those lights."

His quote applies to real estate and to the world of endurance sports and I say also applies to our personal lives and any business we may be in.

Throughout this book, you will find true stories of my (and others) experiences in the arenas of business, life or endurance sports. Some are comical, some not so much. The hope is that they can help illustrate what to do, or in some cases, what not to do!

At the end of the day, I have learned that the endurance world has been a tool to help mold me, a way for God to reveal to me who I am and, at times, to break me down, humble me, drop me to my knees, and build me back up. A way for Him to teach me about myself and to show me I could "do it." That I can, with His help and the help of others, overcome any obstacle, with one of the messages being: "Pete, at times you can't do it all by yourself..." He pointed out to me that I can cross whatever finish line I choose to cross. I know these experiences have at a few key times saved my life and taught me about others overcoming adversity; in many cases, much more adversity than I have ever had to face.

This book ties together three of my passions:

- Real Estate
- Endurance sports
- Helping people cross their finish lines, whatever they may be.

The idea here is that if you accept that real estate or any business is indeed an endurance sport, to be treated with respect, and an effort that is more about what you do behind the scenes than at that ever so glorious finish line, you will have a higher probability of crossing whatever finish lines you choose to cross.

———

I'm hoping my sons are proud enough of this book to share it with their children (my future Grandchildren – no rush, sons!). They have been the biggest part of God's greatest gift to me. I gratefully admit that because of my two sons, I have come to know the two best words I've ever been called:

Coach and Dad

Coach Dad quite a few moons ago - Joe on left, John on Right

TEW: ONE OF THE ULTIMATE GIFTS
TIME * EXPERIENCE * WISDOM

In my opinion and experience, not many gifts are greater than TEW, or...

- TIME
- EXPERIENCE
- WISDOM

When I look back over my life and the gifts I have received from others along the way, there are many wonderful things and experiences that come to mind.

But the *things* I cherish most are not necessarily tangible. They aren't necessarily "things." Many times, they put no money directly in my pocket or returned to me anything I could touch, feel or hold. They are the time someone saved me, the experience someone provided to me or the wisdom someone cared enough to impart to me for whatever reason.

Yes, over the years, the gift of TEW has been the ULTIMATE gift anyone has given me.

There is no price tag I can place on someone saving me time, heartache or helping me cross a finish line by sharing their experience or wisdom with me. It is priceless. I cannot think of anything more valuable than that. And when I reflect back over the course of my 30+ year career, I see that every finish line I have crossed, whether business or a marathon or in life, I've had help along the way; and to those persons, things or beings (and I will leave it at that) I am forever grateful. *That is the essence of TEW.*

I have hit several peaks and have run through my share of valleys. I've had a great career, at times brutal, but overall a great life I have at times taken for granted. I've come to know through others that what I often thought were "common experiences" were not quite so common, after all.

We each have our own story to tell, experiences to share. In many cases, those stories will benefit others in some positive way. Why don't you consider telling yours?

Although I started off writing this book for my sons, it has evolved into something I hope will help others, too.

And if it helps one person cross a finish line or at least acts as an extra set of guard rails in life, *it's been worth it for me.*

MY HYPOTHESIS

I'm certainly no king and have never sat on a throne, nor do I intend to, but when I saw Joel's comment, it reminded me of a certain truism that I have come to accept:

WE ARE WHERE WE ARE SUPPOSED TO BE...

We all have obstacles in our lives.

Do we treat the obstacles we encounter with a "woe is me" attitude or do we use them to propel us to the next level?

Do we let the negative people or thoughts get us down or dictate the direction we take?

Do we listen to the negative chatter from others or ourselves or do we push forward, *no matter the chatter?*

Or do we look at obstacles as a motivator to keep pushing through to the next peak?

Obstacles and mistakes in life can actually pivot us toward opportunities. I gave up believing in coincidences a long time ago.

Two life events come to mind that I look back on now with great clarity:

- Losing my cousin Jeff, who was like a brother to me, in the spring of 2001 at the age of 33, and ...
- 9/11, that same year

These two things were my upper cut, followed by a hay maker in terms of my wake-up call that *life is short*. I touch on both of these events and why they were so important to me in the chapter *Right Turns*, because they truly caused me to change or shift direction and take hard right turns in my life.

In 1992, at the age of 23, I was working as a process improvement adviser in Galax, VA, when the Finishing Department Manager position opened up at the new Greenwood Plant in Greenwood, South Carolina. The plant was amazing; the most advanced textile manufacturing plant in the world, with technology never before employed in the textile industry. I applied internally, was accepted as a candidate and invited to Greenwood to interview with the plant manager.

Long story short, I didn't get the job and was crestfallen, thinking I'd never get out of my current position.

A few months later, a department manager position opened at the Stratford Road Plant. Jim D. was the Plant Manager. Department manager level was a big deal as that is where you are actually managing an entire manufacturing department (usually 200 or more employees) and responsible for its performance. I had worked with Jim at the Kimwell Drive operations before I took over as the newly-created Jamaica Logistics Supervisor. I'll note here that the Jamaica Logistics position was a dream job (especially for a then young man not too long out of college) that involved going to Montego Bay Jamaica once a month, staying in the company town home, while coordinating shipments between the States and the Caribbean.

Jim hired me at Stratford Road.

A few months later, he introduced me to my future wife, Pamela French.

I am grateful to have had a bigger and better door swing wide open after the disappointment of not getting the Greenwood plant position and bonus: I eventually got two awesome sons out of the deal!

Example One of being *where I was supposed to be...*

———

When I was wrapping up my master's degree through the evening MBA program at Wake Forest, three and a half of the toughest, most rewarding years of my life, I had a fire lit in my belly and decided to keep my education going. My goal was to become a Professor and consultant, helping companies improve their organizational practices.

After much research, I landed on a program that fit my plan perfectly: the Ph.D. program in Organizational Analysis and Change, at the University of Auburn. I wrote, connected with Auburn Professor, Dr. Stan Harris, applied and got accepted. Acceptance to the program was no doubt due to the letters of recommendations from two of my distinguished Wake Forest Professors, Dr. Bill Davis (Organizational Behavior) and Jack Meredith (Operations).

I was pumped.

However, we got right up to the moment of truth, then decided not to do it. With a young child, we were afraid of trying to make it on a small stipend for five years while I slogged through the doctorate process.

I was down. I thought a dream had ended -- but -- it was just a fork in the road.

At times, who we perceive to be a negative person, or what we see as some negative obstacle put in our path is actually a stepping-stone to greater things, greater opportunities to help others.

Over the course of my life, I have come to understand that we are, for the most part, *where we are supposed to be*. This is not to say that every now and then we don't have a course correction or hit a bump in the road or not follow a dream or a path we feel we should take. It is just to say that I believe in my heart of hearts that we will naturally navigate to our destiny and you will know intuitively if you have gone "off trail." Although sometimes, going off trail is actually the right path and can lead to some of life's deepest blessings and positive outcomes.

Life often throws us curve balls and it's our job to turn those curve balls into base hits. Twists and turns come our way and we have to keep on trucking. Little things, like the greatest real estate downturn in our nation's history, hit hard and we have to overcome. We go through our trials, run through our fires, walk, jog or run through our very own *Valley of the Shadow of Death* and keep going as best we can – sometimes bruised, sometimes battered, but all the better for it.

I started writing this book in an effort to put into context for my two sons just what we had been through during the Great Recession, so hopefully, they could learn from my experience and understand why "dear old dad" almost got wiped out. How, at one point, he was staring into the abyss like so many others. I knew it was historic, but I had no idea until I dove into researching it just HOW historic. When you are in the battle, fighting for survival, you don't have time to look up and blurt out, *"gee whiz, this is historic"* as your life's wealth rapidly dwindles away...

However, I realize I've been lucky.

––––––––––

2004 - MAGIC MACHETE AND SNAKE BOOTS - "RED WING LEADER! LIVE LONG AND PROSPER!"

Early in my real estate career, I was out walking some land and I came upon a pack of snakes. I tell the story about moccasins because I was near water and I hear moccasins are some of the most aggressive snakes there are. These snakes chased me - it felt like they chased me for 2 miles but in all likelihood it was no more than 10 feet.

Regardless, the story has become one of "lore" and probably one of slight embellishment over the years with friends and family as most who know me know that I have a fear of snakes.

Word quickly shot around the office at Southport Realty...No doubt it probably went something like this: "The City boy got chased by snakes..." To be sure, it drew quite a few chuckles and some good hearted ribbing. A few short days later, I came into my little office cubby upstairs at our office. There, on that sunny weekday morning, sitting on my desk was a bright, shiny, brand new machete with a yellow sticky note...that read:

"RED WING LEADER! LIVE LONG AND PROSPER! - BPQ"

My friend and colleague, Brian Quinn and purchased it for me and left it there. When I saw Brian, he had his great wry smile on his face. I loved it. From then on, that machete, along with my newly purchased snake boots went with me everywhere.

A few months later, my youngest son Joe (then four years old or so) and I were walking off a few lots together to mark them for a septic system to be installed for a client prior to them moving ahead with building a home on their land. Machete in hand, Joe was right beside me, my little side kick. We hit a yellow jacket nest in the ground and both of us started getting the fire stung out of us. We both started yelling, I scooped Joe up, dropped machete (not thinking about it) and put Joe under my arm like a football to get him outta there.

Arriving back at my Toyota 4Runner, Joe crying, tears streaming down his face, aside from a few stings on his body, he had even gotten stung on his lip, looked at me in horror and yelled "What about the Macheteeeeeeee!." The magic machete is what we called it because it kept snakes at bay and no doubt in Joe's mind, he knew that magic machete protected Dad as Dad walked across wild and exotic lands.

"Oh brother!" I thought (I actually probably thought a few other, more colorful words then "Oh Brother."). So, I put Joe safely in the back seat of the 4Runner, charged back into the woods, dodging the yellow jackets and retrieved the magic machete.

Mission Accomplished.

I still have my magic machete and snake boots. They have bailed me out a few times over the years and are a sort of good luck charm. In Joe's eyes that day, I like to think "Dad was a hero", albeit probably a lower level hero, but a hero none the less, having charged back into those woods and bringing machete safely back in hand.

Magic machete and snake boots...Life doesn't get much better.

———

Regarding my hypothesis, fast forward with me to 2011.

It was the winter of 2011, and I was being installed as President of the Brunswick County Association of REALTORS® (BCAR). At the time, the sixth largest board in the state, known as the Big Boards and in order of size: Charlotte, Raleigh, Greensboro, Winston-Salem/High Point, Wilmington, and Brunswick.

BCAR membership had reached historic levels at the market's peak, and then, at the height of the downturn, membership was cut almost in half. I won't reveal the specific numbers, but suffice to say, they were significant.

Our area was unique in that there was a significant amount of land speculation occurring, people buying land and betting on future price appreciation, constructing what we in the real estate industry call "spec built homes" -- building a home for no one in particular, but with the hope of selling it to someone upon completion.

Not only was there speculative home building in our area, but entire speculative developments being constructed. This situation was more prevalent in our market than others, thus exacerbating a problem looming in the distance.

In Brunswick County, we were between two growing coastal markets, Wilmington, NC and Myrtle Beach, SC, both pushing toward one another in real estate growth, enlarging the speculation aspect. We had a large influx of people leaving their professional jobs and their careers (similar to what I had done) to get their real estate licenses. In my case, I was a corporate supply chain manager who left the corporate world for real estate; however, the difference was I had done it five years before the market crashed.

Like so many others, our real estate Association was hemorrhaging at the time due to no fault other than timing and the severe downturn in the market. This beautiful part of our great state of North Carolina had an amazing quality of life but was very dependent on the second home/retirement market. We did not have a significant amount of industry. Our tourism business was good, but not like that of our bigger brothers and sisters, Charleston, SC to the south or Wilmington to the north.

During the run up to the Great Recession, southeastern North Carolina is an area I called "the Land of the Modern-Day Gold rush", except the rush wasn't for gold – it was for land. Land purchasers, that is to say, land speculators were pouring into our region by the boat load, competing with one another for the purchase of land and bidding the price up. I thought it was normal.

To further aggravate our dilemma, BCAR had just "gone vertical" and opened a brand new association facility. Some of our members had pitchforks and torches out for those who were at the helm before me, who had decided to construct the new multi-million dollar building. But there was no need to look in the rearview mirror. What was done was done.

No one could have predicted the severity of the Recession. Some on Wall Street did and were smart enough to short the sub-prime market, good for them. (check out the eye-opening book by Michael Lewis, *The Big Short*[i] for a great inside look at this story and a few that made a fortune betting against the mortgage market, essentially placing bets against the housing market.)

At the time, I happened to be the only Certified Commercial Investment Member (CCIM), one of the two highest designations one can achieve in the field of commercial real estate industry, in Brunswick County. (The Society of Industrial and Office Realtors (SIOR) is the other designation considered to be at the top as well; both the CCIM and SIOR are considered *top of industry* in the commercial real estate arena.)

For future reference, you may see me refer to commercial real estate as *CRE* (not to be confused with the Counselor of Real Estate designation, also referred to as *CRE*).

After several meetings with my team members and our accountant, it was painfully obvious that we needed to take action about our building due to the current severe real estate downturn. The issues at hand were an exceptionally large monthly payment, a very large interest rate, and a balloon payment coming due in 2017.

I equated the situation to flying a Cessna and seeing a giant mountain looming ahead that we couldn't avoid. We were going to run into that mountain unless we could come up with some evasive maneuvers. The Cessna/mountain concept became symbolic for us and a bit of a rallying cry. Our leadership team knew that the true value in any association is the people, not an asset. The Great Recession hit and all across our country things went into a massive tailspin, the likes of which none of us had ever seen before. It was all hands on deck.

It was time to act.

We made contact with Waccamaw Bank (since closed), who held the note on our building. We let their CEO (a decent guy facing the same problems many smaller banks would face) know that we needed help with our payment and interest rate, and the coming balloon payment. He did what any good banker would do, and reminded us of the terms of our loan.

We went back and forth quite a few times, working to negotiate mutually agreeable terms, acknowledging that things were dire for just about everyone. We finally had to remind all concerned that this was a volunteer association and there were *no personal guarantees on the loan,* thus the bank did not have a ton of leverage, other than the asset itself.

After several meetings, it became apparent that our bank execs were either not listening or were ignoring us. Presenting the fact that the bank had a large number of ambassadors in Southeastern North Carolina as a bargaining chip didn't matter to them. Pointing out that we were the highest and best use for the building and asking, "If not us, then who?" also did nothing in terms of advancing our negotiation. Neither the bank nor any of us wanted to see this new 14,000 square foot building in the heart of Brunswick County go dark. We appreciated the relationship with them, but we needed help and quickly. I watched their CEO age what seemed like 10 years in about three months.

Several times during the downturn, some folks asked for my advice about how to deal with their bank. Some would be incredulous that in their individual personal situations, the bank would not give them relief. I would always ask: do you share on the upside with the bank? In other words, when you receive the loan, do you give them a percentage of your profits; or if you experience major appreciation in your asset when you sell, do you share your profit with the bank? Their answer was typically a big fat "Heck no!"

I would then ask: *then why should the bank share in the downside?* The answer is they don't. And they typically have you as a guarantor on the note and your asset as collateral, and that is their leverage point.

This is why I said above that the bank did not hold a great deal of leverage. In our case, there were no guarantors and we knew there were not many candidates at that time who would want a 14,000 square foot office type building with an industrial-size kitchen, located in the middle of rural Brunswick County.

Check and mate.

On a tip from a friend and mentor of mine, who was one of my savvy and trusted real estate Jedi's, we finally called Trawick H. "Buzzy" Stubbs, Jr. of Stubbs Perdue Law Firm. Buzzy was a certified Bankruptcy Specialist and one of the best in our state.

Another mentor of mine, Ray Jones, who in 2003 had visited me in Brunswick to survey this "hot market." I had called him to discuss the market and he decided it was time to come down to Brunswick from Charlotte for a visit.

By the time we got through touring a sizable chunk of the 800+ square miles of the county (hitting the high spots only!) that day, Ray said, "Pete, this county and some of these developments have taken a page out of the Florida playbook from Florida 20 years ago." eluding to the overheated and speculative markets that had crashed back then.

I came back with something like: "Oh, come on Ray, it's not that bad is it?"

Standing in the middle of a field that was used to "pomp and circumstance" prospective clients of a large regional developer, Ray stared at the tiki torches and the helicopter landing pad sitting in the heart of Brunswick County and he leveled his eyes at me.

He then proceeded to explain that "your market is overheated. You have little to no industry, tourism is minimal. You have a second-home and retirement leg to stand on, but what happens if it dries up?"

Dries up!? Hah! This thing is going to go forever! Haven't you seen the news?

Cue the canoe going over the waterfall...

Ray was right, of course. Standing in the landing area of that development, the props of boat and shipped in sand and helicopter landing pad were all part of the "drama." The idea behind it all was to take prospective clients up in the air, show them the views, talk to them about the amenities that would one day be there, essentially give them the wow treatment, and then sell them a lot that they didn't have to make payments on for two years.

Two years seemed like an eternity at one point, didn't it?

For those of us who were in the middle of the storm, two years quickly became a blink of an eye. Those two years flew quickly by and – *boom* – lot values plummeted, and people were instantly way underwater on those lots as valuations in our region and across the country plunged.

In some cases, a $200,000 postage stamp-size lot in the middle of almost nowhere was now worth less than $60,000. It was financial carnage on a scale I had never seen. This was not just happening in southeastern North Carolina, but all over the state and across the fruited plain. It was just intensified in our market due to the influx of people pouring into the market from other locations or states.

We were fortunate to have a great volunteer leadership team with our Association, but there were two colleagues, Wilson Sherrill (Association-elected volunteer Board Member and Treasurer) and Steve Candler (Association Executive), who I leaned on heavily during my year as President. I couldn't have done any of it myself and lord knows the entire team pulled together to keep the ship floating, but in my humble opinion, those two guys especially, along with our leadership and staff team went over and above the call of duty. My experience is that the Treasurer position in any volunteer organization or company is usually the most thankless job on any exec team. There were many nights Wilson was at our Association office until the wee hours. We were all swimming in after current of the Tsunami called the Great Recession.

The CEO of now defunct Waccamaw Bank[2ii] got involved because we were a high visibility client with a sizable loan for the bank, even though it really wasn't that large of a deal in the overall scheme of things.

Buzzy knew all the judges and all the bankers knew Buzzy. If you have seen the classic movie *Star Wars*, I equated Buzzy to being a bit like the Darth Vader of the workout side of the banking business. (When I refer to "work outside", this essentially means "problem" or "trouble." Work out means to "work out the problem." When an asset is being "worked out" that typically means the asset is considered "non-performing" and the bank, the mortgagee, is now not receiving payments from whoever is supposed to be paying the monthly payment, known as the mortgagor. When an asset gets kicked into "troubled asset" status, it sets off a whole slew of activity. I touch on this in a bit more detail later in the book.) We had invited the CEO and his team in for what was going to be our last meeting. When the bank's team came through the door and saw Buzzy, the CEO looked at me and blurted, "Why is *he* here?!"

I said, "*Because you aren't listening.* We are prepared to give you back this building. We are your highest and best use for this property, and we're you're best user. We are it. What are you going to do with this building if we vacate? Look around this room, no one in here has a personal guarantee on this loan; as a matter fact, there are no personal guarantees at all. Now, we are asking you again: please push the balloon payment further out; we need you to cram the note down; and we need your help in adjusting the terms – or you can have this building back, and we will move on and call it a day." I slid the keys across the table to them.

So, they moved the balloon out, crammed the note down, adjusted the terms, which bought us about four years. At times in life, our goal is to live to see another day. Mission accomplished.

I can't tell you how many talented bankers I know (including my late father) who rightly despise it when folks go back on their word on deals they signed (or point a finger at the bank as if the bank forced them to sign) and I am with them on that; at the end of the day, we are only as good as our word and the deal we signed. With that, sometimes we have to do what we have to do for survival.

Sometimes negotiation is bluff, but not this time. None of us felt good about what we had to do, but we had to do it.

I'm grateful Waccamaw Bank worked with us when our backs were up against the wall in one of the most historic downturns our nation ever encountered.

Unfortunately, Waccamaw Bank went under not long after and a larger regional bank acquired most of their assets. This was known as the Loss Share agreement,[3iii] which were very prevalent during the downturn.

A little-known fact is that all three banks that failed during the downturn in the state of North Carolina were in southeastern North Carolina. And when you looked at why, it was because those banks were exceedingly long (i.e. heavily invested) on speculative land loans.

I am happy to say that Brunswick County is now one of the top growth counties in the country (again) and, along with our great state, have risen from the ashes. The Brunswick County Association has since relocated to a great spot and the membership is doing very well.

My point of this Association building story?

Do I think it's a coincidence that I was at the helm that year? I do not. I certainly did not do anything by myself. I had a great team that carried me. My colleagues and teammates were kind enough to give me the REALTOR of the Year award the following year, which is one of the greatest honors we can achieve as professionals in our industry, especially and most humbling since it is recognition from our peer group. I was beyond humbled.

So, my hypothesis?

WE ARE WHERE WE ARE SUPPOSED TO BE.

This is certainly not to say that we won't ever encounter valleys. The valleys will come, regardless of where we are in life or business. Sometimes, it may be that we are put in a certain place to help someone else endure a valley. It may be we are put in the valley to help strengthen us for a larger trial or test or battle down the road or even to make us a better, stronger person. The following is another example of this "concept" that is near and dear to me, admittedly an extreme example, but I think it is one that helps put a finer point on my hypothesis.

My son's great grandfather, Captain Isaac Sheldon French or Ike as he was affectionately known, fought in two critically important battles in World War II, The Battle of the Bulge and Normandy. Had he not survived either, my sons would not be here today, as their mother would not have been here! Those soldiers, in my mind, had two fundamental choices: 1) fold and lay down, or in the case of the Battle for Normandy, get pinned down on the beach or 2) advance and fight for themselves, their Brothers in Arms and their country. I'm grateful that as a group, they chose the latter. No doubt in my readings and in my discussions with WWII Veterans, including my son's amazing great grandfather over the years, that they viewed those two historic battles as "valleys" or an abyss. They did not choose to be in those valleys. But destiny called and that is where they were - nothing they could do it about it. Wow, did they ever rise to the occasion!

What this means to me is this: *we should make the most of wherever we are and do the best we can while we are there.* Sometimes, we go through what we go through and we look back and realize it may not have been for us, but for others to benefit from. That is the essence of my hypothesis:

we are where we are supposed to be and at times, when we are running the gauntlet, we don't see or understand why we are here...

I wouldn't have wished my experience during that time negotiating with the bank on anyone, but I got to see the character and the work ethic and the fortitude of my colleagues. And the caring. I used to joke about our "high-falutin' volunteer no-pay roles."

My Faith and my friends have often carried me. There have been times in my life, especially in the valleys, that I thought to myself "put your running shoes on and go, if you don't accomplish anything today, at least you got that done, you crossed that finish line and you showed yourself you had the strength to get up and get moving..."

We are where we are supposed to be, and while we are here, we should make the most of it and do the best we can, even if we're just passing through, hopefully helping others along the way.

Frandano is named 2012 Realtor of the Year by Brunswick County Association of Realtors

Story

Share Print Font Size

Posted: Tuesday, January 1, 2013 9:44 am |
Updated: 9:40 am, Thu Jan 3, 2013.

By Lee Hinnant, Staff Writer

When he's not selling property, consulting with investors or spending time with his children, Southport's Pete Frandano enjoys running marathons and triathlons. Those sports, he said, are a fitting metaphor for the sometimes-turbulent real estate market.

"Ten or 15 years from now, we can look back and remember how quickly things can go south," said Frandano, who was named Realtor of the Year for 2012 by the Brunswick County Association of Realtors (BCAR). "I told folks (back in the crash of 2008) that they have to weather the storm and look at it like an endurance race or a marathon.

"Now is not the time to throw in the towel. ... Gosh, if we can survive this, we can survive anything."

Frandano, a principal at Southport Realty, got into the business almost a decade ago after working for several years as global operations manager for paper and packaging giant Avery Dennison. Excessive travel helped persuade him to get into real estate, he said.

Read more about Frandano's thoughts on the local real estate business in this week's edition of The State Port Pilot.

Frandano

Pete Frandano (left) is congratulated by Ben Styers, whom he succeeded at Brunswick County Association of Realtors' Realtor of the Year. Both are with Southport Realty.

Waccamaw Bank has a new name. Actually, two new names.

CHAPTER 2

THE GIFTS OF CLARITY & PERSPECTIVE

"THE FUTURE AIN'T WHAT IT USED TO BE..."

-YOGI BERRA

Like many in the real estate industry, long before I arrived at the land of real estate, I had another successful career which in my case was in the world of Operations and Supply Chain Management. My experiences in that former career prepared me somewhat for some aspects of what was to come in my real estate career.

Those experiences certainly helped me gain perspective on the wide disparity around the globe between poverty and non-poverty; plus, they gave me a huge dose of *Hey Pete, don't take things for granted in life.*

I was grateful for my time in the Fortune 500 world, the training, the experiences and the relationships...I thought I knew poverty before I left our country. However, seeing it in other countries was crushing to me. Here in the United States, we have homeless shelters and soup kitchens. In some of the countries I traveled to on business, those two "luxuries" did not exist. In many of those countries, if you were hungry, you stayed hungry. If you were homeless, you remained homeless. Forget going into a shelter for the evening. These facts never fail to fall hard on me whenever I hear of a hurricane descending on places like the Dominican Republic or Jamaica or wherever.

It is something I have always taken with me...

THE JOURNEY FROM FORTUNE 500 LAND
TO THE WORLD OF REAL ESTATE

I was fortunate and I knew it.

Right out of the University of North Carolina at Chapel Hill, (Carolina), I had three job offers.

One from then North Carolina National Bank (NCNB), which was the predecessor of NationsBank, which later became the current day Bank of America (the "house" that CEO Hugh McColl built). One from Sara Lee Knit Products (SLKP), aka Hanes Underwear). One from Burlington Industries (textile manufacturer).

The NCNB gig was in Greensboro, NC. The SLKP job was in mountains of Galax, VA, which was in the far southwestern corner of Virginia, beautiful country for sure. Within SLKP, it was known as the "mountain cluster" and was where all Hanes Menswear T-shirts in the world were made at the time, pre-NAFTA.

NCNB offered me a $23,500 annual salary. SLKP offered me $28,500.

I took both offers to my Dad...

"Dad, which one do you think?"

"Son, I didn't send you to school to make stupid decisions...don't go into banking," said the lifetime banker.

I know this was a father's way of telling his son not to feel pressure to follow in his footsteps and to 'chart his own course'; not to stay away from a great industry that afforded us a wonderful life, which it was for him and did for us. Though I am grateful for the path I chose, my experience from both corporate America and the real estate industry has shown me the banking industry has some super talented people and should be a great and important career option to explore for anyone deciding on their future career!

So, Greensboro, NC, an hour down the road from my awesome alma mater in Chapel Hill and civilization or somewhere out in the hinterlands of southwest Virginia?

About my Burlington Industries experience; in my junior year in college I had applied, interviewed and landed an internship there between my Junior and Senior year at University of North Carolina - Chapel Hill.

The internship was going to be at the J.C. Cowan Plant in Forest City, NC (just west of Charlotte). I thought this internship was as good as going to class, so asked my graduate student instructor for my operations class about getting academic credit for it. She introduced me to Dr. Ronald T. Pannesi, who taught in the MBA program at Chapel Hill. He agreed to allow me, under his purview, to do an independent study that summer, which would allow me to get academic credit for the class and get paid.

Dr. Pannesi was an amazing man who had a major impact on me. We still trade Christmas cards to this day.

So, there I was, making $1,500 per month in an awesome job, getting amazing experience, and getting academic credit to boot. Yee Haw! It was an amazing summer. I landed a room with one of the plant engineers, Jeff Ball, who was a Clemson graduate and my rent was minimal.

In this internship, I worked in Quality Control and was shuttled through the various operations within the plant. My experience there formed a base for me, and I truly grew to love operations management. I loved being in the plants. I loved being out there with the folks who, in my mind, were getting it done, making things, making a difference, making it happen. This, to me, felt like and was America.

I loved the manufacturing industry. It would be my springboard into logistics and my first dive into the world of supply chain management.

That internship turned out to be instrumental in me receiving two job offers coming into my senior year in college.

Dr. Pannesi got me the interview with SLKP, which typically hired undergrads who were Textile Management majors from NC State University. Jerry Rowland, Vice President for SLKP and NC State's "Textile Man of the Year" for several years, was the hiring manager.

I interviewed with Jerry's team; fortunately, they all approved of me and I got the letter from Jerry. I can still see it now: $28,500 a year.

Jerry razzed me mercilessly about being one of those *University of North Carolina business majors* coming into his beloved Management Training Program, not one of his Textile Management majors from our vaunted rival, N.C. State University. I was the only one of six from UNC, my five colleagues all being NC State graduates.

The look on Dr. Pannesi's face, when I told him I had three offers on the table, one from a bank, one from Burlington Industries, and one from SLKP was one of sadness...

He seemed almost hurt that I would even be considering a "bank job" after my operations experience, summer internship, my loud and vocal enthusiasm for working in manufacturing and "making a difference", leading people. He had nothing against the banking industry, but Dr. Pannesi was an operations person at heart and loved factories and the people who worked in them.

Prior to making my final decision, I went to tour SKLP in Galax. I met with Willard Bullins, then Director of Manufacturing for the Mountain Cluster, and Bill Huffman, the Human Resources Manager. We met for breakfast at the Wagon Wheel restaurant at 7am, and I wondered who the heck eats breakfast this early? Although, the previous summer, during my internship at Burlington, I was into the plant every morning at 6am and out at 2:30pm.

During our breakfast, Willard didn't speak *as if* I would be coming to join them in the Mountain Cluster, but rather *when*. Willard was my first encounter with someone who had a natural gift for sales and leadership. I didn't know it at the time, but I was experiencing my first encounter with what is known as "assumptive close."

There was no choice but to join them.

Willard's conversation was full of enthusiasm: "When Peter gets here..." and "Peter, we're going to have you go through all of the operations. We need more talent. We have a seasoned group and you will add to our bench strength. The opportunities for you here are going to be limitless..."

SOLD! Between Willard, my Dad, and Dr. Pannesi – SLKP was it.

Decision made, SLKP moved me from Chapel Hill, NC to Galax, VA. I actually had a company apartment and was making more money than I knew what to do with in this tiny town, just minutes from the beautiful Blue Ridge Parkway.

I told my buddy Nat Shaw, a business fraternity brother of mine from New York, and was surprised that he knew about Galax as he blurted out, "Man, Galax?! That's where the Fiddler's convention is!"

Wow, I'm moving to a place that has an actual Fiddler's Convention? Oh, boy...

Nat was a string instrument aficionado, thus his "insider's knowledge." He and his father knew about the Fiddler's convention, one of the world's largest Blue Grass music gatherings in the world. People would pour in from all over the world.

I had an awesome company apartment right up the hill from where the Fiddler's convention would be held each year and my buddies would show up to people watch. RV's and campers and tents would roll in and pop up everywhere, and for a week, every type of string instrument imaginable could be seen and heard. Little Tiki lights were strewn all over and in the evenings you could stroll around and watch and listen to some amazing blue grass, country or you-name-it type of music. People pickin' and grinnin'. America at its finest, I thought.

The cost of living in Galax was incredibly low, not to mention the company was kind enough to carry me for a while on the company apartment. I played a lot of golf (played some during college but never like this). All of the managers played golf. It was a big social thing.

I joined the two clubs in town, Galax Country Club and Blue Ridge Country Club. I think for Galax CC, the fee was like $500. Blue Ridge CC at first had no room, but one of the managers I worked with talked Emmitt, the club manager, into "finding a share" for me. Blue Ridge CC was an equity membership, which means you bought a share of stock to become a member, and when you left, you could sell that share to someone else. That was the first and last time I actually earned money joining a "country club."

Looking back, it seems all I did during my time in Galax was work and play golf. When I left the plant in the evenings, during the summertime, I could easily get nine holes in. It was a simple life and was a blast.

The Galax plant was the flagship of the mountain cluster and we produced approximately 200,000 dozens (2.4 million units) of T-shirt cut parts (the body and sleeves of the T-shirt) per week, then shipped them to three apparel plants located in Hillsville, VA, Sparta, NC and West Jefferson, NC.

The Galax facility was a complete vertical operation for the manufacture of Hanes white (no dying or color added, only bleached white). We brought the cotton in as bales; processed it through the Yarn plant; shipped the produced yarn to the Knitting department; and then to the Bleaching and Finishing department. After that, the now-finished material moved on to the Cutting department.

The management team was awesome and taught me all there was to know about the textile manufacturing process. They also taught me about people and how to motivate and work as a team. They folded me into their family.

I always felt I was part of something larger in those plants. The only bigger rush to me in that world was watching the trucks pull off with our finished product, headed out on the roads of our great country, destination consumer!

TIME IN THE TEXTILE MILLS

Through my first year (actually a bit less than a year) on the job at Hanes, I worked my way through the processes, doing each job, spending time with the employees, and culminating in the final step of my management training process: managing a night shift in the Yarn plant.

We worked a 4-3, 3-4 schedule. This meant working four 12-hour days, then being off three days. Then, working three 12-hour days and being off four days. Our shifts ran on the 7's, which is to say, mine was 7pm to 7am. Those four months on night shift were tough. I experienced a bit of everything: employees sleeping on top of cotton bales, on one occasion, a couple having sex in the bathroom (um, not allowed), me dozing off in the front office (also not allowed, only happened once and from then on, I would get up and walk around), even placing black curtains in my apartment so I could sleep during the day.

All I had to do was show up and supervise, meaning provide leadership, help keep morale up and stay out of the way of those awesome hourly workers, each an expert in their respective jobs. I learned early on that it was a privilege to be out there with them and they would bust their butt for you if you treated them with respect. They all knew that the "college guy" wasn't going to be there long. He was just passing through. They joked, razzed and had fun with me.

Safety and health were paramount and SLKP took them both very seriously. We had a safety manager, David Swicegood, and our safety record in the mountain cluster was impeccable. We cared about everyone who worked there and wanted everyone to come in healthy every day and leave healthy.

Working through the Yarn plant my first couple of months, one of our card technicians lost a finger while performing maintenance on one of the "cards" (the carding operation was massive, shredding the cotton prior to moving it to the "roving" operation).

I felt sick for R.J., the employee who was hurt. I had gotten to know him and now he was minus a finger. That experience has stayed with me since. I had volunteered to go "clean the machine" and got a steel brush and warm soapy water in a bucket. I was doing all I could do to earn respect out there. The respect level jumped a bit for me with the employees when they saw me do that.

These operations were very well run but were dangerous and you could get hurt or worse if you didn't pay attention or lost focus. Safety and healthy first, along with the importance of focus, were my take-aways from this experience. And it stuck with me throughout my career.

We had approximately 2000 or so workers throughout the mountain T-shirt cluster. The people who ran the machines were my heroes, the backbone of what makes this country great.

It was a 24/7 operation and I loved that no matter time of day or night, the plant was always alive and humming! The only exception to this level of activity were two weeks a year for maintenance. We typically shut down a week during 4th of July and a week at Christmas and New Year.

Another plus to being in Galax was that it was literally two hours straight up I-77 from Charlotte, so was very easy for me to get home to see Mom, Dad, Sis and family.

In that Yarn plant, and in the Galax Plant in general, I learned some key management principles that I have carried with me to this day:

- Delegate
- Knock walls down for the experts
- I wasn't the expert
- If you rule with an iron fist and treat people poorly, they will always "get you back"
- Your team will make you or break you.

Carol Lineberry, a farmer, and known to be one of the best "Yarn Men" in the company was who I first reported to and was responsible for my initial training. Rumor was that Carol could come into the plant and "hear" if a machine was 'out of kilter'. Our Yarn plant was made up predominantly of machines produced by the German manufacturer, Trutzschler, expensive and amazing.

Carol always came in early to make his rounds. One morning, he saw me sweeping up and actually working on one of the machines. His eyes got wide and he came over to me and asked, *"What are you doing?"*

"I'm helping..." I replied.

"Come with me," he said.

I thought, "Uh oh, what's happened? What have I done?"

He walked straight out the front door and I was hot on his heels. By now, I'm thinking I'm about to get fired. We walked all the way to the far corner of the employees parking lot, which was a long distance from the plant (this was a huge operation). It was still dark outside. The plant was humming.

Carol stopped, and then said, "You hear that?"

"What?" I said.

"That!" And he pointed at the plant.

I said, "Yes, of course..."

And he asked, "What is it you hear?" Carol had an awesome southwestern Virginia twang of an accent.

"The plant running."

"Riiiiiight ... the plant ... it's running. And where are you?"

What a stupid question. "I'm out here..."

"Riiiight, you are out here. And the plant's running, isn't it?"

"Um, yes..." *Man, Carol was full of really silly questions this morning.*

"You're out here and the plant is running. Well, who do you think is running that plant? How is it running?"

Another dumb question. "They are, the employees are, of course."

"That's right, *they are.* They will get the job done, they will do the work. Your job is to lead and make sure those folks have the tools to do their jobs. They will let you do their jobs, if you want, but they would much rather see you leading. Keep that in mind. They appreciate your work ethic and you've shown them you'll bust your ass -- now lead. We pay you to lead, not to sweep..."

Lesson learned; message received, Sir! (I respected Carol, a lot).

One morning, toward the end of my shift, I heard Willard's familiar voice come over the intercom system: "Pete Frandano, come to the front office, Pete Frandano, come to the front office..." I gulped. *Why the heck was Willard calling me up front?*

I checked on a couple of things in my department, let my shift lead know I was heading up front, then turned and walked with purpose. When I reached the front, most of the lights were still off, but Willard's office light was on. I walked in and saw Gary Sumner, the Plant Assistant Human Resources Manager.

Uh oh, what have I done? (get the feeling I was paranoid?)

"Pete, you've done a good job in your management training program *(here it comes, they're letting me go, again)*. Have you ever heard of CBI? The Caribbean Basin Initiative? How about NAFTA, the North American Free Trade agreement?"

"Yes, but I don't know much about it..."

"Well, we are getting ready to embark on a journey and we would like to get your help. We're gonna begin shipping some of our cut parts to a place called Sandy Bay in the country of Jamaica. There's an apparel plant down there and we are going to roll them into our family. This is very confidential, so anything we discuss can't go outside of these walls. This may eventually impact jobs here and we don't want to scare anyone unnecessarily."

"I understand, you can trust me on that, for sure."

"I know ... currently there's a plant in Winston-Salem on Kimwell Drive shipping some product to this plant. Well, given our performance, which as you know is outstanding, they want us to take over this operation.

"I'd like to make you an offer. We'd like to pull you off night shift, have you go down to Kimwell Drive in Winston for a month or so and train with the team there. We'll obviously put you up in a hotel and take care of all your expenses. Then you would come back up here and train our group.

"Beyond that, we're creating a new position and would like to promote you. The job will be called Jamaica Logistics Supervisor and you would oversee and manage our logistics effort from here to Jamaica, and then help facilitate the return of completed goods back into the U.S. through U.S. Customs and on to our Distribution centers. This is going to require you to travel some. You will probably have to go to Jamaica about once a month or so, for maybe a year or eighteen months. We have a company town home there and you can use. We'll also bump your salary up to $36,000 per year. What do you think? Are you okay with that? You wanna go back to your apartment tonight and give me an answer tomorrow?"

My thought process went something like this: "Oh darn, you're pulling me off night shift? I'm 23 years old and getting a promotion and am gonna have to travel to Montego Bay for a year? On the company dime??? Uh-h-h, where the heck do I sign!?"

But what I said was more like: "Well, it sounds like a great opportunity and I'd love to be involved in any way I can and will do my best for all. I will have some questions, but I know you or others will have answers. Can you let me know time frame?"

"Next week, we need you in Winston-Salem next week..."

So, there it was: my first promotion and my entry into the world of global logistics.

Technically, this was part of what was known as the Caribbean Basin Initiative (CBI), which would evolve into NAFTA. This program was to promote economic development through private sector initiatives in Central American and Caribbean countries.

A major goal of the CBI was to expand foreign and domestic investment in nontraditional sectors; thereby, diversifying CBI-country's economics and expanding their exports. Two key 'receivables' for companies participating in these initiatives were 1) Low cost labor, and 2) duty free re-entry into the U.S.

Essentially, SLKP had no choice, as our competitors, like Fruit of the Loom and others, were doing it and if we didn't, our entire ship would have gone down. I watched SLKP close forty-six stateside apparel plants in the next three years. Fifteen dollar per hour jobs went down to about a dollar per hour – and offshore the apparel assembly process went. My heart broke for the life-timers in the U.S. that would now be unemployed, people who had a high school education at most and would have a tough time finding employment.

It was the evolution of manufacturing and the textile world here in our country and I was fortunate to have a front row seat to it. I was grateful for the opportunity to participate and play a small role. I quickly learned that 'low cost manufacturing' and 'great quality' were paramount.

Walmart was helping to drive the supply chain and was taking companies like ours to places we had never been before. Concepts like Vendor Managed Inventory (VMI) were being introduced to us. Over the course of my career I had the opportunity to visit Bentonville, Arkansas (I always jokingly referred to it as "AR Kansas"), HQ for Walmart. It was amazing and very humbling. While companies like Kmart and Sears were making their financial numbers by charging back vendors like Hanes for shipping errors. Kmart had an entire division devoted to coming up with 'chargebacks' – it was pathetic, Walmart was forcing us to manage our own inventory on shelf space they allocated for us.

As an example, if Walmart ran a circular in the Sunday paper that read: *Hanes underwear will be on sale for these dates and these products,* then we dang well better have our product on those shelves for their customers. Pushing the "managing of inventory" back to the vendors supplying that inventory was simple yet brilliant and Walmart was brutally efficient in supply chain management: which is to say, they knew how to squeeze cost and efficiency out of the supply chain, at the time better than almost anyone, and they expected us to partner with them in doing the same.

I look back with fascination and amazement that Walmart made up approximately 33% of our business at Sara Lee Knit Products and about 33% of our business at Avery Dennison Corp. What a coincidence!

I recall being in a conference in Winston-Salem with a futurist economist as keynote speaker. He rhetorically asked the audience that day: *Who would be the one to take Walmart down? Who would eventually give Walmart a run for their money?*

His answer: *The Internet, of course.* We were all baffled... How? (And today, we see Amazon giving Walmart a run for their money).

From Jamaica Logistics Supervisor, I was promoted to the first Process Improvement Advisor position created in our company. We had recruited some key managers from the Milliken Companies, a prominent and well respected Textile company, and they brought the world of PI, or Process Improvement with them. Process Improvement's role was to act as in-house consultants to the manufacturing managers and teams, and use Statistical process control (SPC) to help reduce variation throughout the operation.

This meant rolling up my sleeves and spending a ton of time back out on the plant floor with the employees (the experts) and their supervisors; flow charting the processes; and looking for ways to improve the process – thus the name: Process Improvement. I loved it.

From there, I eventually went to Department Manager at our flagship plant in Winston-Salem and to Process Improvement Manager for the entire facility.

By then, I had come to the realization that logistics or supply chain management was not going away. Manufacturing in our country had taken a beating and some of it had left for lower cost labor markets, but the logistics world would remain. So, I started angling in that direction.

Job security was a focus for sure, but given my background and having been there done that in manufacturing, I wanted to see the entire supply chain from the other side. An opportunity came up to do just that: managing the West Point Distribution Center in Winston-Salem, NC, one of our flagship distribution centers. This was the *Hanes Her Way* facility that received and shipped out all Hanes Her Way products for the entire globe.

It was an awesome experience.

Managing a 24/7, one thousand-person distribution center while going to business school at night created probably the toughest, but most rewarding, years of my life.

THE STORY OF PIT FANTANA

There are several defining moments in life that helped move me toward the understanding that I have it good. Where I realize I should not take that which has been given to me, the circumstances, livelihood and those around me, for granted.

My travels throughout the Caribbean Basins and Central America were growth periods for me, both professionally and personally. When I traveled to Jamaica on business and visited our plant in Sandy Bay the first time, I was stunned at the level of poverty of our workers. I had seen poverty in the U.S. and Lord knows, I know we have people here in the U.S. who need help. But I had never seen the scale of poverty that awaited me in the areas I would travel to on business in Jamaica and Central America. Crushing poverty.

I know many have criticized Big Evil Corporations for offshoring or for shutting factories down in the U.S. and moving them to other countries. However, the way I always looked at it is: if the playing field is tilted a certain direction, if the rules of the game are as well, then you better make sure you understand how the field is slanted and understand the rules of the game or you will lose.

Losing in this case, means the entire ship, not just a part of it, goes down.

As much as I despised seeing some of my colleagues and our hourly-paid team workers in the U.S. lose their jobs, I understood conceptually and business-wise that tough decisions have to be made at times to sustain the entire organization.

Put another way in a blunt conceptual example: if Fruit of the Loom (a key rival for us at Hanes) could move all their apparel assembly operations to the Caribbean Basin and cut their labor costs by forty percent, and my company did not do the same, and our customers viewed us as interchangeable, price would be the final and determining purchase factor. Labor costs would become critical to operating competitively and serious adjustments would be necessary to survive.

A LESSON IN BLESSINGS VERSUS ENTITLEMENT

So, when I say I saw poverty, that is probably an understatement. Some of our workers would walk down the mountain in Jamaica and come to work barefoot. Missing production goals due to rainstorms was a new phenomenon to me, but if it rained, some of our workers would not come in due to mudslides. We would, at times, provide shoes and clothing.

You would think, given the low wage these folks were earning and the long bus rides some had to take to come to work or walking down the mountainside with no shoes to work, would have made some workers angry or disgruntled, right? I was prepared for a group of folks that were not happy to see me or anyone else from the U.S.

But it was the opposite.

They were actually ... happy. Most seemed grateful. At times, I would hear them singing on their jobs. I remember being completely stunned my first morning there when Patrick (our production manager, a native Jamaican) called me over for the morning prayer. The entire team, 350+ some people, circled up and held hands and gave thanks, and in those thanks included the blessing of employment and the surrounding company teammates that were now family.

I went back to my room that night with tears in my eyes, mostly for being humbled at what I had witnessed; the joy they kept, no matter the circumstance – but also for all I took for granted.

I thought about myself and my colleagues back in the U.S. and I remembered a planning manager at our HQ in Winston-Salem who had bellowed at Willard during one of the Monday War Room meetings[4iv]. An explanation about a production miss due to people not being able to make into the factory because of a rainstorm was met coldly with: "can't you give those people an umbrella?."

The a-hole... I wanted to punch him and he's lucky Willard didn't actually do it, because it wasn't beyond that city of Galax Boy, who was famous for once wrestling a bear at the Grayson County fair, to do just that.

Entitled versus humbly grateful. It became a lifelong bucket of cold water in my face.

And so it was throughout the Caribbean, worse in other places like the Dominican Republic. And eventually, even worse in Asia, where many of these were contract facilities and they did not treat their people as well as we did in our self-owned facilities.

I remember one time I was hanging out in the side yard of our plant in Sandy Bay and saw some chickens roaming about. For a few minutes, for fun, I slowly walked after one until it took off running, then walked behind another and it would do the same...

Suddenly, from behind me, I hear a thick Jamaican accent saying, "Don't mess wit' me chickens, MON!"

I turned and saw an older man standing there, old worn clothes, torn flip flops, dirty hat.

"Excuse me?"

He repeated, "Don't mess wit' me chickens, Mon, dey are me chickens..."

It turns out that our yard maintenance guy would bring his pet chickens with him to work. How, I had no idea, but they were there more often than not. I didn't ask any more questions of him but did ask some of my colleagues in the plant. They explained that "Yes, those are Daryl's chickens..."

They laughed at me when they saw the shocked look on my face. I think he honestly thought I was going to steal and eat his chickens. I apologized and never messed with his chickens again.

———

"COOOOLLD RED STRIPE!!!"

Archie Rush, a Clemson alum and our plant engineer back in Galax was deployed to help with the engineering initiatives in our new offshore operations. One day, Archie and I had to take a plane from Montego Bay to Kingston to check in with the Jamaican port authority team. We learned about how drug smugglers could contaminate our shipments and use our shipments to smuggle drugs to the U.S.. For me, it was both scary and eye opening.

When we returned later that day and touched down on the tarmac of MoBay airport in our little Cessna, I heard: *"COOOOOOOOLD RRRRED STRIIIIIIPE!"* with the R's really rolling. Archie and I look to our left and this young guy is walking over to us with a grocery store-type plastic bag dripping with water. It's a seriously steamy tropical day.

I'm looking around and thinking *how is this guy even out here?*

Airport security was out the window (hey, this was Montego Bay and it was pre-9/11!). He walks over to us and asks, "Would you like some cold Red Stripe, Mon?"

Archie responds, "I'll take two!" holding up two fingers with a big eat you-know-what grin on his face.

With a returned big grin on his face, the beer savior says, "You saved me life, Mon, you saved me life!"

Archie said "No, you saved *my* life!"

———

Two years later, I was promoted to department manager of a large manufacturing operation at our flagship plant, the Stratford Road Plant (now long since demolished) in Winston-Salem, NC. Then up the pole to Cutting Department manager, and eventually, Process Improvement Manager for the entire 1500+ employee, 24/7 manufacturing operation.

As Cutting Department manager, my "internal customers" were the 36+ plants we shipped cut parts to, located throughout the Caribbean Basin, Central America and Mexico.

My first trip to San Salvador, the capital of El Salvador, was eye opening for me. El Salvador is bordered to the south by the Pacific Ocean, the north and east by Honduras, and to the west lies Guatemala. Ironically, El Salvador was the first place I had ever laid eyes on the Pacific Ocean.

I recall driving in downtown San Salvador and seeing a beautiful, green-glass, high-rise reflecting the gleaming sunlight back at me. Reaching the other side of the building, I looked back and saw a huge, blown-out, gaping-wide hole in it. I was stunned. There, right before me, was the evidence of the El Salvadoran Civil War, where the FMLN (Fababundo Marti National Liberation Front) attempted to turn El Salvador into a Marxist-Leninist state and oust any presence of the United States.

Several times during my stay there, I would see U.S. military personal in teams moving quickly through the city. In the early 90s, this war was not too far behind them and the U.S. and El Salvador obviously had concerns about the country back sliding. The tension in the air toward we *gringos* was always palpable and the poverty was devastating.

One night, arriving to the local Pizza Hut in San Salvador, I remember looking up from our car when a young man hurried up to the car.

Here we go, I'm going to die, he's going to shoot all of us.

But instead, he spit a BIG honkin' loogie right on our windshield! My eyes wide. My compadre, Jose, a local El Salvadoran looked at me and laughed.

The 'hawker' proceeded to take a big, now semi-white, towel and wipe the windows with his loogie. He was cleaning our windows. I gave him a dollar and you would have thought he hit the lottery.

I was sick again for these folks. My heart broke for him.

Looking beyond him, reality hit hard – I was in another world. I locked onto the man standing guard outside the Pizza Hut at full attention. He appeared to be a solider in pure green military attire, fresh with sawed-off shotgun slung over his left shoulder.

Pizza Hut, guarded by a guy in military garb, with sawed-off shotgun. Yes, I'm in another world.

I was in San Salvador for a few days, and then we took a plane to Honduras.

My first trip to Honduras was a good one. I had taken all my SLKP recommended and mandated hepatitis shots a couple of weeks prior to departure to Central America. If you have never flown into the airport, Tegucigalpa, it is a treat – but it's not for the nervous flier or faint of heart.

Tegucigalpa is located in San Pedro Sula, in the northwest corner of the country, in the Sula Valley. As you descend down through the clouds to the airport, you literally cut between rows of multi-family projects and you feel like you can reach out and touch the clothes drying on the lines. You feel like you are flying military style, nap of the earth.

I had heard about it but nothing really prepared me for the experience and I purposely sat in a window seat so I could experience it. A nervous flier I am not, having given that up a long time ago, realizing *Que Sera Sera*.

We touched down and my driver was sitting out front with his sign held up. It was obvious from the moment I saw him he was there for me.

The sign read: *PIT FANTANA*

He looked so proud and winked at me like – *yep, there you are, I see you and you see me.*

We jumped in his car and departed Tegucigalpa airport. On our way out, not much talk ensued between my driver and me, but he continued to have a proud grin on his face.

We were a few miles into our trip and I'm looking out over the countryside and noting how different Honduras seemed to El Salvador. Nowhere near as dense and crowded, it almost reminded me of a South Carolina countryside – serene, with foothills (that seemed like mountains) off in the distance.

Rounding a long curve on the highway, we crested a hill and I noticed my driver started to speed up. I looked over at him and his proud grin had turned into a serious, 3000-yard stare. He looked angry. The car was speeding up markedly. I could feel a sweat bead forming.

I looked up ahead and see what appears to be a toll booth in the distance.

...a toll booth, here?

But no ... no toll booth. It was a checkpoint manned by military personnel. Way off in the distance I see armored personnel, trucks, guards, etc. Now my driver has his foot all the way to the floor. I'm looking at him, and then back at the checkpoint now fast approaching. I'm in a full sweat and he appears to be, too.

Why is he doing this? "Senior! Por Favor!" (Sir, Please!) I say, the only Spanish words I could muster.

He yells out in decent but angry English: "TODAY I NO PAY!!!"

I'm thinking... *Man, I don't care what beef you got with these people but My God not now and not me POR FAVOR!!*

I yelled something inaudible. He yelled: "TODAY I NOOOO PAAAAAAY!!!!"

At this point, I'm wetting myself and am down in the floorboard of the car. It felt as if we were traveling 80 mph (truth be told, on those highways, in that car, it was probably more like 50 mph), and I see the guards leveling their guns at us.

I'm going to die in Honduras today.

We blow through the checkpoint and I'm waiting for the crack of automatic gun fire, but nothing...not a sound. *Am I dead? That was quick, and it wasn't even painful!*

I hear a low chuckle. God is laughing at me. I hear it again. It's not God, it's my driver.

I look up from the floorboard, eyes wide, and see my driver. He's okay and is cutting his eyes down at me and laughing.

As it turned out, the driver's brother is the military Checkpoint Captain at the checkpoint we blew through and this is the practical joke they sometimes played on first timers to make us *feel welcome.* I almost cried but managed a laugh.

I get to the plant and our plant manager, Arnoldo, wheels around in his chair behind his desk, jumps up, and bellows: "Welcome to Honduras, Pit! How was your trip?"

I give him a '*you fill-in-the-blank*' look and a big hug.

...yes, welcome to Honduras, Pit...

Several years later, I moved on from managing plants to managing distribution centers, as I had seen the writing on the wall regarding the continued trend in offshoring manufacturing.

Then, while managing West Point Distribution center for Hanes and wrapping up my 3.5- year tour at Wake Forest's Evening MBA program, Avery Dennison came calling, looking for someone with an ops/logistics background that could help run a startup global supply chain division.

While Sara Lee Knit Products watched their manufacturing base erode away, Avery Dennison Corporation, because of their relationship through the bar-code/UPC business with companies like Walmart, Target and Nike, was following those companies offshore and helping them connect with their factory base of suppliers around the globe. And they needed help exporting the data and importing product.

It was brilliant and I was all over it!

My first trip to China with Avery Dennison, was with my friend and colleague, Aubrey Prescod. I remember getting out of the cab on the drive to our hotel one late afternoon. I tipped cabdriver five dollars. He started hopping back and forth, then doing some Texas two-step-looking dance but seemed to be trying to keep a lid on it, like he was trying to keep his cool. I was confused. He then did a bow like gesture toward me, did the dance again, then hopped in his car.

I gave Aubrey a quizzical look and he said, "Dude, you know you just paid him a month's salary with that tip..." I was stunned and my heart dropped into my stomach.

The wealth disparity there was astounding, the population density at times overwhelming and the poverty breath taking. And this was Hong Kong, not mainland China, where poverty reached deeper levels, depending on where you were and your social status.

Looking back, with my globe-trotting and career, I realize I've been blessed and fortunate. Through my experiences and many wonderful people, I have received a large dose of clarity and perspective over the years. I've tried to never take one role or experience for granted and I've always been grateful. My folks had given me a gift by taking my sister (Kathleen)and I to visit other places. My Dad, the Jersey boy that had grown up on the other side of the tracks always wanted to make sure that we had 'stuff' and experiences he never had.

Sara Lee Knit Products and Avery Dennison, two outstanding companies, took those experiences further and took me to places I never would have seen on my own otherwise. As much as I enjoyed spending time in faraway lands and making new friends, I reflect back over the course of my career and realize I am a product of this great state of North Carolina and am grateful for that. Not many I know have had the good fortune to live in the Piedmont region (grew up in Charlotte), the Triad (Winston and Greensboro, where my two sons, John and Joe were born), the Triangle (my time at UNC-Chapel Hill), the mountains (Boone - my time at Appalachian State University), and the Coast (Southport/Wilmington area, where we eventually landed to raise our boys.).

The gifts of clarity and perspective. Lucky and blessed for sure.

I've always been proud to call North Carolina home.

Yacht Basin - Southport, NC

CHAPTER 3

MY RIGHT TURNS

"ONE DAY ALICE CAME TO A FORK IN THE ROAD AND
SAW A CHESHIRE CAT IN A TREE. 'WHICH ROAD DO I
TAKE?' SHE ASKED. 'WHERE DO YOU WANT TO GO?'
WAS HIS RESPONSE. 'I DON'T KNOW,' ALICE ANSWERED.
'THEN,' SAID THE CAT, 'IT DOESN'T MATTER.'"
-- LEWIS CARROLL, ALICE IN WONDERLAND

As I'm sure you will agree, and have most likely encountered for your-self, in life we sometimes have defining moments that push us in a cer-tain direction. The following stories are of two events, my 'right turns' that helped change the direction in my life, motivating me to depart the Fortune 500 world on a new course to pursue my entrepreneurial dreams and more time with my family.

JACKSON, WY - SEPTEMBER 2000 (GRAND TETONS)
September of 2000, my family and I hit the tarmac in Jackson, WY. This was our first trip out to this beautiful part of the country. My cousin

Jeff Pool was getting married to his love, Lee Killian. Lee had worked at Grand Teton National Park from '95 to '97 as park dispatcher.

As we walked through the doors of the tiny airport concourse doors, I heard a loud "WHOOOP!' and I looked up. There was Jeff – all smiles and running toward us. He was thrilled to finally have all of us on his home turf and we were thrilled to be there. He grabbed me by the shoulders and looked me right in the eye and said, "Cuz, I feel like I've hit the lottery..."

Jeff had traveled a long winding road to get to where he was that day.

Early in Jeff's career he had worked for a company called Shiplett Wilkens. He and I were chatting on the phone, which we did quite a bit, and when he told me what he was doing, I said, "You're where?"

Jeff was performing this mystical activity called 'commercial appraisal work' and he and a buddy, Paisley Gordon, were in West "By God" Virginia working on an assignment for the summer. Paisley later told me that "we only worried about good coffee and decent beer" and they spent quite a few evenings that summer at the local baseball team's ballpark. Life was good.

Fast forward several years and here we were at the week of Jeff's wedding. An avid outdoorsman, skier, cyclist and real estate guy, Jeff shipped out west and was a Park Ranger for a while before meeting Rob Cheek of Cheek Commercial Real Estate. Jeff had explained to me that they were doing all of the "big box" development and brokerage business and that the commercial real estate world had 'finally found them' in Jackson. They were essentially the only game in town.

It was a great day and a very happy and non-traditional, laid back, beautiful *Jeff and Lee style* wedding. We even got to see a little snow in the Grand Teton region that fall. I commented to Jeff that I could see myself living out there and he told me to hold the phones on that thought and to visit him in the winter. This gave me pause and I quickly came to my senses!

Our son John was only two, and this was his first plane flight. Spending time in that beautiful region with the moose and the bison and everything else was a true blessing and a memory I have cherished my entire life.

Jeff and Lee were on the way and as we boarded the plane to head back east, I was incredibly happy for them both.

APRIL 15, 2001 (EASTER SUNDAY)

Jeff, an avid cyclist, slipped out that Easter Sunday afternoon to go sneak a ride in Grand Teton National Park. It was a beautiful morning.

Wyatt Bodray Ditterline and Clinton Duane Hammers were working on an oil rig, had gotten off of work, and had decided to overindulge. They rounded the corner on Highway 89 in their white 1996 Dodge pickup (which matched a witness's description) near Jackson Hole Airport that morning and apparently never saw Jeff.

Park Rangers pulled them over somewhere way up the highway near Moran and they peacefully surrendered. Teton County Sheriff Captain, Jim Whalen, said his dispatch received four phone calls, likely all from cell phones, reporting the incident.

Jeff was struck from behind and still wearing his helmet.

From a quote in a local newspaper article (Jackson Hole News), Brian Schilling, another avid cyclist, saw Jeff's crumpled body lying by the road as he and friends, Brian Smith and Pam Dun, were driving north to ride the Jenny Lake Loop Road.

Brian was quoted in the article: "The thing that really blew me away, besides the initial shock of seeing a body on the side of the road, was that somebody had killed this guy and just took off. That was the most disturbing part of the whole scenario to me."

Jeff passed around 1:45pm, not long after he was found.

At Grand Teton, acting superintendent Joan Anzelmo said her staff was focused on the investigation and on remembering Jeff, who was an entrance station fee collector in 1996, where he met his bride, Lee.

"The Park community has been especially hard hit by this tragic fatality of one who they claimed as their own," Anzelmo said. Rob

Cheek, Jeff's boss, had basically adopted Jeff and was preparing at some point down the road to pass the company over to him.

When I spoke with Rob later, he confirmed this, telling me that "Jeff was a like a son to me." Rob was in Salt Lake City when the event went down and immediately headed back to Jackson, where he told the Jackson Hole News: "We're all upset. We were like family up there. He was just a sweetheart of a guy. He was just so considerate of everybody else and methodical in his work. He was like a son to me. It's one of those great stories of one of those guys who came to Jackson and made it, bought a house, got married last fall."

Jeff wanted to make a positive impact on the community and was part of a Jackson Hole Chamber of Commerce leadership course that was scheduled to have a class that following Friday on transportation issues, ironically, including bike paths. The class was postponed until May. All agreed that bike paths most likely would have saved Jeff.

So, how did my Uncle Joe and Aunt Sandra find out about their son?

Well, Lee was, for good reason, beside herself and simply not in the frame of mind to make the call. So, the Jackson Hole police called the Charlotte Mecklenburg Police department and two officers had the excruciating task of knocking on my Uncle and Aunt's door around midnight, Easter Sunday. I will leave the detail to your imagination.

Uncle Joe, who has done so much good for so many in our community, later expressed concern (in a church video about blessings and being grateful) that he was concerned for those officers who had to knock on their door that evening. That was my Uncle Joe. Always worrying about others.

To give you an idea, growing up, I used to think my uncle really liked soup because he spent a lot of time at these places he called 'soup kitchens'. It wasn't until later, when he took Jeff and me with him, that I learned he was giving soup to others, not eating the soup.

Jeff was a bright shining light to all of us. He was more of a brother to me, we had grown up together, born six months apart. He, my sister

Kathleen, and my cousin Natalie (more like my second sister), were all together every holiday and everything in between. Cousins, yes, but brothers and sisters for sure.

I had pulled up the Pro Golf Discount store about a mile or so from my house in Greensboro late that Monday morning, grateful to be home for a few days and not in an airport on a Monday. My cell phone rang. I answered it and heard a familiar warm voice, "Hey, Son..."

"Hey, Dad..." I could tell something was wrong. "What's up Pop?"

Dad didn't waste any time. "Son, I don't know how to tell you this any other way than to just say it: your cousin Jeff was in a cycling accident and he didn't make it..."

I don't remember much after that, or my ride home.

When talking or thinking about destiny, I can't tell you how many times over the next decade or so, and even to this day, I ask myself, "Why?" And then the "if only's..." If only Jeff had fumbled with his shoes another minute or two, maybe even a flat tire? Just that one morning? If only he had the sudden urge to go to the bathroom one more time before heading out the door. If only Lee had yelled to him before he went out the door because she needed help moving something. If only he had tripped going down the stairs and hurt his leg a bit that morning.

If only...

We play those scenarios in our heads. We don't know *the Why* ... 33-years-old ... ripped out of our lives... It's not fair, is it?

The first time I ever saw my Uncle cry was when we met him at the gate at the Charlotte airport on his return from Jackson. This was pre-9/11 – remember those days? You could actually walk all the way down to the gate to greet family and friends. He and my Aunt Sandra came out of the gate, Lee with them, and Uncle Joe fell into my Mom's arms, crying. I would say he was crying like a baby, but he wasn't. He was crying like the *father who had just lost his son*. It ripped my guts out, seared into my soul forever.

I was flying across country not long after we lost Jeff. Seated to my left was a guy that was older than me by, I would guess, twenty years or so. We connected and chatted most of the way. It was dark, a red-eye flight coming back from the west coast. We started talking about our personal stories and life and death, and the discussion veered toward how short life can be. I brought Jeff up and let my new friend know how much he meant to me and that I had just lost the equivalent of a brother. I went on about how much we would all miss him and how a huge part of my regret was the stuff Jeff would miss out on, seeing my son grow up, having his own kids, what a great father I knew he would have been, being with us at holiday gatherings, parties or Carolina tailgates.

And on I went.

I was sinking into despair, feeling sorry for myself. My new friend said, "Pete, your cousin is with you now and will be with you always. He's watching and smiling." I thought it was a strange thing to say but it brought me comfort and he said it with such conviction.

We exited the plane together and I thanked him for the conversation. As he walked off down the concourse and into the distance, I remember saying to myself, "I think he was an Angel..."

———

SEPTEMBER 11, 2001
"Something Wicked This Way Comes", Ray Bradbury (1962)

The clock radio chimed on at 5am to the sound of Jimmy Buffett's "Margaritaville." I rolled over and slapped the snooze button and rolled back over for ten more glorious minutes. I thought about the day ahead. Ahhhhhhh...

Dick's Sporting Goods, Pittsburgh, PA, here I come. There and back the same day to meet with their VP of Logistics and team to discuss what our firm could do for them and their supply chain. Logan Airport down to Pittsburgh and back. Slam dunk. Dick's was a good customer of ours and I was looking forward to the meeting.

I popped up, turned the clock radio off, did my normal routine, tossed on my running shorts, shirt and shoes, went down to the lobby of the Crown Plaza hotel and out into the cool air.

It was a beautiful fall morning in Natick, Mass. I got my quick 5K in to get my heart pumping, hopped the elevator up to the Concierge level, had a quick breakfast and was off and running.

I had an 8:45am flight to Pittsburgh to catch...

Traffic was normal as I took the Logan Express. Got to the airport in my usual one hour before departure time, and skipped right through the noticeably light security. No bags to check, easy peasie. We started boarding around 8:15am and took off a few minutes later. There were only about twenty of us on that USAir flight that morning – a Boeing 737 – plenty of room. We all had our own row to ourselves, so everyone just spread out.

As we took off, I watched Boston from above as we circled the city and headed toward New York, and then what would be a final zig then zag down into Pittsburgh. I was looking out over the wing, caught up on a few white papers and downloaded emails on my laptop.

About 25 minutes into the flight, the plane intercom crackled and the Captain came on.

"Ladies and Gentlemen, good morning. Well, this is a strange one and I don't want to concern you, but Ground Control has issued a security alert and have asked us to re-route to Rochester, so that is what we are going to do. I don't have any more information than that. This is a new one on us...We're very sorry for the inconvenience but we'll get back with an update just as soon as we know more."

When your pilot says, "I don't want to concern you...", you get concerned.

Security Alert? As much as I was flying, and it was almost every week, I had heard every excuse in the book, from mechanical to animal (yes, animal) to you name it...

Avery Dennison Corporation, my new employer, had recruited me away from Sara Lee Corp on the premise of 25% travel. Business ended up dictating almost 100% travel for close to 5 years, which was tough but we did what we had to do. Think about most first days on just about any job. Most folks are taken around by the human resources manager, shown the break room or company cafeteria, workout facilities (if they exist) introduced to teammates and colleagues, provided with lots of documents, policy manuals to review, process manuals possibly and a ton of other mostly completely useless crap to read, shown their office or their "cube" or their work space. Cue the sound of robots marching into battle...

Life at Avery Dennison was unorthodox and very entrepreneurial in terms of the environment, which I loved. When I first joined Avery Dennison in the grand year of 1999, my first day on the job was anything but ordinary: instead of having me show up at the office, *they handed me a plane ticket to Hong Kong and pointed toward the airport.* Some folks may have freaked out over this non-conventional day 1 start and intro, but *I loved it!* It strayed heavily from the normal and was different, out of the box and creative. This was a by-product of how my boss, Kim Macaulay managed and lead. She forced herself and others on her team to think creatively, break norms to get better and push the limits within legal bounds. I got to see this my very first second on the job. Walking through the Greensboro airport to catch my connecting flight to Los Angeles, with final inbound into Hong Kong, I thought "well, this is a different kind of first day on the job!." The "keys to the Kingdom" Avery gave me were as close to running a new start up business under the protection of a Fortune 500 company as one could get. I think that's why I got along so well with my new team right off the bat. From the first day, my boss and my colleagues saw I could *roll with it.*

Day 1 for me with Avery Dennison was June 15, 1999 (according to my passport), and was the day before I was originally scheduled to start and it was spent on a plane to Hong Kong sitting between two men the size of Sumo wrestlers (who both happened to fall asleep not long into our flight, leaning into me) so I could attend a meeting with Nike's Logistics team. Nike was a huge client of ours at Avery Dennison and from that point on, I was flying almost every week. Once on the ground, I let our corporate travel agent have it for sitting me in the middle on my first trip to Hong Kong. "Michelle, if you ever do that to me again..." She thought it was funny...I actually did too, once we landed and I was off the plane!

––––––

TWO LIFELONG FRIENDS

In addition to Kim and a few others, I am grateful of my time at Avery Dennison Corporation for several reasons, two of them being my dear friends, Trevor Kong and Steve Hills. Trevor was our managing director in Asia and Steve was a logistics client with Nike.

One day on a client visit to Cole Haan, located in Yarmouth, ME, Trevor and I and a few others had to travel from Framingham, MA to Yarmouth. For some reason, we had multiple cars and Trevor and I were "racing" (not to worry, MA State Troopers) up I-95. I'm on the outside lane, Trevor is on the inside lane. I can feel him coming up on my left.

I turn, look, and I see Trevor's profile. He then turns slowly, grins at me with a big, toothy, devilish smile and blows by me. I saw him throw his head back and laugh. I then see his license tag, a New Hampshire tag, and of course, it reads: 'Live Free or Die.'

I think how appropriate that my dear friend, a native Hong Kong-er would be blowing by me with that inscription on his tag. That moment, the joy on his face and the 'message' delivered to me is frozen in my mind forever. Many of us want to live free or die, don't we?

One trip prior to our Yarmouth, ME excursion, Trevor and I flew into the Dallas/Fort Worth airport around midnight one night for a meeting the next day with JCPenney, who were based in Plano, TX. For those of you who have not flown into this airport, it feels like the size of some mid-sized U.S. city and sits between Dallas and Fort Worth, thus the name Dallas/Fort Worth or DFW.

Trevor and I got lost on the airport grounds that night for about 30 minutes. Driving around, we couldn't figure out how to exit the airport property. If you've seen the movie *European Vacation*, starring Chevy Chase, it was the "Look kids, Big Ben…" scene when he's stuck in the traffic circle. By the 4th time around, Trevor shouted while laughing, "I cannot believe we cannot get out of here!"

It was a sad day indeed for me when Trevor announced after 25 years he was departing and was going to pursue his dreams for his family. He joined United Metals as their COO to help take them go public. Selfishly sad for me, but happy for him. Lifelong friends… He and his awesome daughter, Alison, and his son, Matthew, would later visit us in Southport. It was a very happy day for me indeed when I saw my dear friend again.

Steve Hills and I met and became very good friends early on in my tenure with Avery Dennison. Steve, the 12th employee that founder Phil Knight brought on at Nike, and Trevor and I bounced all over the globe together. Steve's company (Nike) was the reason I had to start a few days early for Avery Dennison on that plane to Hong Kong. My first MLB game ever was with Steve in Seattle.

Just a few of the relationships for which I am grateful I still maintain today from my corporate days.

––––––––

I had never heard the term 'security alert' when flying before. It shook me a bit. I could feel myself flush as I glanced out the window at the wing. Still intact. I had read way too many Tom Clancy novels, so my mind started racing. I looked up at the flight attendant and mouthed '*security alert?*' with brows arched. She looked back, eyes wide open, shaking her head, shrugging and mouthed back '*I don't know*'.

A few minutes later, I heard the pilot click on the intercom.

Okay, good, here comes the explanation, all a simple mistake no doubt, so let's get on down to Pittsburgh folks.

But his voice now had a since of urgency, almost a sweat-like quality to it. I could feel his palms perspiring and now mine were too.

"Okay, ladies and gentlemen, ground control has come back to us and they want us on the ground *now*, so we are diverting to Syracuse. Again, no explanation other than a security alert. I can assure you that our plane is just fine. We just don't have a clue what's going on down below; so, Syracuse here we come. Flight attendants, please prepare the cabin for arrival. We are going to be going down a bit quicker than normal."

A bit quicker than normal...

At this point, I'm wetting my pants, pulling my seat belt tighter, closing my laptop, and loading my bag back up. If you look at the map, Syracuse is, in fact, closer to Boston than Rochester, but not by much. I looked at the map later and thought, *wow, they really did want us down.*

The twenty of us on the plane are chatting a bit nervously, trying to keep it light, all trying to speculate as to what could be going on. Nuclear bomb go off somewhere? Wings on our plane are intact so that's good. Who the heck knows?

I look out and see the ground of upstate New York gaining on us quickly, and then – touchdown. At that point, cell phones start to flip on. We quickly taxi to the gate, the "ding" goes off, and we all jump up from our seats to begin collecting our stuff.

I was scurrying down the aisle when our office assistant, Norma, calls me.

In her sweet southern drawl she says, "Good Lord, Pete, I'm so glad you are okay! Kim wanted me to check in on you, are you okay?"

"Yes Norma, I'm fine, but what the heck is going on?"

"We're not sure but the news said all planes in the continental U.S. are being grounded due to a small plane, I think they called it a "Cessna", hitting one of the World Trade Center towers and they are taking precautions all over the country..."

My colleagues all knew I was flying out of Boston that morning. I had no idea they were concerned I was '*toast*', but they were.

The airport staff shuttled us quickly off the plane and herded us like cattle down to the main concourse.

USAir Club here I come is my thought, I'll rebook and catch another plane and get down to Pittsburgh, late for my meeting but making the effort. But when I get there, it was closed. Airport and USAir staff are all waving us ahead like parking lot attendants – shaking their heads anticipating our questions. They didn't know. None of us did.

By this time, a second plane had hit the towers and there was speculation that the planes had originated from Boston. We later learned that we had gotten an "early divert" or security alert message to divert and that all U.S. airspace was officially cleared by 9:45 a.m.

My phone rang again, this time it was Pamela; she got through to me as I was being herded through the airport and I told her briefly what had happened. By then, I'm almost down to the main concourse level of the Syracuse airport, now realizing getting to Pittsburgh is not in my immediate future.

She asked what I was going to do and I said I didn't know, maybe get a room there. I wasn't thinking clearly and was a bit dazed. She countered suggesting to I try and get a rental car and drive back to Boston. So, try I did.

I angled quickly for the rental car area but when I rounded the corner, I saw what looked like a two-mile-long line of people waiting to rent cars. Others were obviously in the same boat I was. Feeling my blood pressure start to elevate, I hear an angel cry out: "Is anyone going to Worcester?" It was belted out in a very thick New England accent and sounded more like "WUSTA!" but I got it. I knew there was a Worcester, MA, but not if there was a Worcester, NY.

So, like I'm in a game show, and last to throw a hand up or bang on the buzzer *loses*, I shot my hand up immediately with a panicked smile on my face, giving my "I'm in!" look.

The New England angel was Linda, a GSA employee who was in the same boat I was. She was taking off out of Logan also that morning and was on a different plane heading to Washington DC. David was also in a similar boat on the same flight as Linda, and finally Peter (yes, another Peter) was heading to Texas. Linda had procured a four-seater and knowing others would need help, yelled out her kind words. We all took her up on it. Four complete strangers getting ready to drive across upstate New York, who by the end of that awfully long and lonesome day, would no longer be strangers.

———

American Flight 11, a Boeing 767 bound for Los Angeles had taken off from Logan 14 minutes late that morning, around 7:59 a.m. on September 11 and was tragically hijacked. Our division H.Q. was based in Framingham Mass. Avery Dennison's Corporate HQ was in Pasadena and this was a flight many of my teammates took quite regularly, and I had taken a few times. From what I remember hearing from our team, our Senior Vice President, Simon Coulson, was scheduled to be on Flight 11. Simon was a talented corporate climber and a wide-eyed, crazed British soccer fanatic. He was fun and ran very hard, which is to say he could instantly be a pro with customers or his underlings, even coming off of a long night. From what I recall, Simon had a personal situation with one of his children come up and he canceled his trip. Lucky us, for sure.

TAKE OFF, NOT LANDING SOUNDS

By then, we had gotten the news that all planes were supposed to be grounded. But as we are walking toward the main doors to exit and track Linda's car down, we heard four distinct take-off sounds...more like focused or controlled explosions.

As much as I was flying those days, I knew the difference between a *take-off sound* and a *landing sound*, and these were definitely takeoff sounds.

I'm a fan of the military and a military history buff, so I know my fighter jets. I look up, and see four F-15s taking off and heading west in formation toward New York City. At about the same time, we heard an announcement come, almost in a loud, movie like, surround sound stereo effect, from the various cabs lined up, who all seemed to have their radios tuned into ABC radio, and we could hear Peter Jennings say, "We have breaking news coming in: we have word that the Pentagon has been hit..."

A chill ran straight down my spine. I remember feeling a bit faint and I don't get faint.

Linda yelled out in her New England accent, "Oh my GAWD!! Weyah at WAW!"

"*We must be*," I thought, wondering who would be stupid enough to attack us here on our own soil? This mystery enemy seemed to effectively be bringing our great country to its knees that morning.

We hopped in the car and took off. Highway 90, which runs from Seattle, WA to New York, is the New York Thruway, which turns into the Massachusetts Turnpike when it hits the NY/MA border. From where we were, it's about a 4 hour 30-minute drive to the Boston metro area.

The drive across upstate New York that morning was absolutely beautiful. I was in the back, left passengers' seat. Linda was driving, Peter was riding shotgun and David was to my right. I was gazing off into the distance, still in a complete daze, trying to reconcile what was happening and wondering *What the heck is going on out there?*

I started thinking about the Dicks Sporting Goods folks on the other end of the line of my trip that was not to be and wondered if they thought I was just a no show, but then quickly realized they would understand and knew my office team would contact them.

This was happening everywhere, whatever ***this*** was, so I knew they weren't concerned about me not showing up.

We arrived around 11am at our first rest stop. We entered and saw people gathered around TVs mounted up high in the corners. CNN was on. The cameras were focused on the World Trade Center, both towers smoking and on fire.

About that time, one of the towers started to come down. I couldn't believe it. It was like I was watching some strange horror movie. Surreal and seemed to be in slow motion. I realized I was watching it being played back, that it had just happened, and they were analyzing it. Everyone in the rest stop started screaming or gasping. It was one of the most horrible sounds I've ever heard in my life, and one of the most horrible things I have ever seen in my life.

My God, there are people in those buildings...

We all watched in perfect, dazed and sickened numbness.

We got back into the car and started driving. Complete silence. We were all in shock and drying up tears. Fifteen minutes or so after leaving the rest stop, my cell phone rings. It's a 336 area code, Greensboro/Winston Salem, NC, but a number I don't recognize.

"This is Pete..."

"Pete, hey, this is Don Patterson, reporter from the Greensboro News and Record, Tony Martinette gave me your number. I was looking for people from our region up in the New England region and Tony had a hunch you might be up there and traveling and was kind enough to pass on your phone number, do you have a minute?"

Boy, did I have a minute. Tony Martinette was my good friend and neighbor across the street from us at my permanent home in Greensboro (emphasis on permanent, as Boston was my other "home").

Tony is my #2 son's (Joe) Godfather. (Joe was born in 2002, our "Life is short, 9/11 baby) Tony was the Director of Marketing for the Greensboro News and Record. We were lucky that he, Mary Rose, and their two children moved in on Redfield Drive a few years earlier. Tony gave my phone number to Don, who, with two other reporters, was putting a story together with a local focus. Like everyone else, he was trying to figure out what the heck was going on.

Don: Can you tell me what you were doing this morning, where you were going?

Me: Well, I was flying to Pittsburgh out of Logan and a few minutes into the flight the pilot came on and told us we had a security alert and they wanted us to divert to Rochester. A few minutes later, he came on and told us that they wanted us on the ground now and we were diverting to Syracuse, then all hell breaks loose. After shuttling down to the main concourse, I was lucky to find this great person, Linda, who is now driving me and two other nice guys across upstate New York heading back to Massachusetts.

Don: You know all airspace in the U.S. has been shut down, right?

Me: No, I didn't know that. Do you know what's happening?

Don: No word yet, but its sounding like a coordinated terrorist attack on multiple targets across the country. The Twin towers were hit, the Pentagon...we think the White House and Capitol buildings were also hit. There is word coming in from Los Angeles that something is happening out there, but nothing confirmed. We understand that some of the planes originated from Logan (I flushed again). Can you tell me how you are doing?

Me: I'm fine. But wow, that is horrible...I'm sick for all of those folks.

Don: Why were you heading to Pittsburgh this morning?

Me: I was going to visit Dick's Sporting Goods Logistics team. Guess they won't be happy with me no showing on them...

Don: I have a hunch they'll understand. Do you have any message for our readers? Is this going to scare you away from air travel?

Me: (putting on my stiff upper lip hat): Well, no, I mean, if it is actually terrorists who did this, that is exactly what they would want – for us all to cower and stay hunkered down and not live our lives. My message would be that we all have to keep on keeping on and live our lives. That is the ultimate counter to anything cowards like that would do – live our lives and not live in terror.

Don: Well, I appreciate Tony putting me in touch with you and appreciate your taking my call today. Have a safe rest of your trip. Crazy day for all of us, for sure.

Me: No problem at all. I actually appreciate your call – can't believe you found me. I'm glad I answered. Please, give my best to Tony and all. I'm not sure when I'll be home. I guess they will have to sort this mess out. But yes, crazy day to say the least. I know that we're all the lucky ones...

Don: Yes, we are lucky. Take care, Pete.

Me: You too, Don, thanks.

What actually went to print was brief, I'm sure they talked to 100 people that day and they had to get it to print so they clipped our conversation and the following is an excerpt of what hit:

AIR TRAFFIC BAN STRANDS TRAVELERS AT PTI\ PASSENGERS DIVERTED UNEXPECTEDLY TO GREENSBORO ARE LEFT TO FIND ANOTHER WAY HOME.

BY DONALD W. PATTERSON, ALICIA RUTLAND, AND TAFT WIREBACK Sep 11, 2001

Many say they won't be flying. A morning of hijackings Tuesday turned airports around the country, including Piedmont Triad International, into cavens of chaos, confusion and concern.

Shortly after terrorists crashed two planes into the World Trade Center on Tuesday

Pete Frandano of Greensboro had been flying from Boston to Pittsburgh on Tuesday when his flight was diverted to Syracuse, N.Y.

He managed to catch a ride with three other people in a rental car bound for Worcester, Mass. From there, he hoped to get to Boston and then back to Greensboro. He said he would fly if he could.

``What we all have to do is keep on getting on with life,' Frandano said. ``You have to move on.'\ Staff writer Amy Joyner contributed to this report.

By "move on" I meant not stop doing what we would normally do, because that is what all terrorists want: to make us scared, live in fear and divert us from our normal activity. I get that is how they "win" by terrorizing and making us divert from our normal lives, our normal behavior.

I've never forgotten that day, and every 9/11 since I say a prayer for those victims and their families, and have always realized that, yes, we truly are the lucky ones.

Linda, in all her kindness, decided to not just stop at Worcester. She kept driving all the way into Natick and took me to my hotel. We all jumped out of the car, gave big hugs and promised to stay in touch, which we all did for several years, but time and life tend to sweep us away. We were all changed forever.

When I was watching President George W. Bush that evening in the hotel restaurant I frequented (a little Irish pub near the local hotel I frequented that ironically had one of the best pasta dishes ever). I was still in shock as the President confirmed the events of the day, and they were the actual nightmare they were rumored to be.

———

Planes took off with terrorists out of Boston (American Flights 11 and 175 both bound for Los Angeles), Newark (United Flight 93 bound for San Francisco) and Washington Dulles (American Flight 77 bound for Los Angeles). The first two hit the Twin Towers. Flight 77 hit the Pentagon. The fourth plane had targeted either the Capitol Building or the White House, but there were heroes on that plane (Flight 93) that had gotten wind of the attacks on the Twin Towers and the Pentagon, and were going to have nothing of it. These brave people had rushed the cockpit and took the plane back over, crashing it 80 miles southeast of Pittsburgh in Somerset County.

I also learned soon thereafter that Mohammad Atta, the maniacal, lunatic, hijacker leader from American Airlines Flight 11 was by my estimate approximately 5 gates down from me in Boston's Logan airport that morning.

Five gates away from getting roasted. No idea why, but for some reason I was one of the lucky ones spared that day.

Atta had connected into Boston on Colgan Air that morning from Portland Maine. He's the one who piloted American Airlines Flight 11 into the North Tower of the World Trade Center that morning. His fanatical cell was launched from Hamburg Germany.

I remember a few months later being in Hamburg for the first time, looking around, and getting a sick feeling.

Wow, this is where it started.

Atta had met Osama Bin Laden and Bin Laden had convinced him to be involved in the plane's operations. Atta had researched it, came to Venice, Florida, and went through an accelerated training program, obtaining his instrument ratings in November of 2000. Apparently, in August of 2001, Atta traveled as a passenger on several "surveillance" flights to establish how Bin Laden's horrific plan could be carried out.

Yes, I admit I do obsess a bit over this man, but I do so only because I feel he was instrumental in my life's detour...

———

I remember looking at myself in the mirror that night in my hotel room, recalling the surreal, horrific events of the day. That quiet, peaceful, beautiful hotel room. My belly full of food. My king size bed waiting on me. I felt guilt. Like I should have been on American Airlines Flight 11. I thought about my family and office mates, them thinking I was toast, ashes on those planes, because somehow word had gotten out that those planes had departed from Logan and they all knew I was departing out of Logan.

It's such a small world. I don't believe in coincidences.

And then, the voice in my head: "Man, what are you doing? You just had an angel on your shoulder, and you got lucky! You're missing your son grow up..."

That night was the beginning of the end of my Fortune 500 career.

Having lost Jeff a few months ago and now, combining it with the day's horror -- that night the concepts *of life is short* and *being grateful* took on new meaning for me. I was determined to make a change. Not out of fear, more out of *want to*. I enjoyed my job, loved the company I worked with and for, and loved the people I worked with, including our clients.

But the wheels had been set in motion.

A few days later, with airports still shut down and after much consulting with my Avery Dennison buddies at lunch, we decided it was best that I avoid NYC on my pending drive back to Greensboro.

So, I took the Mass Pike west and somehow found my way down to Hwy 81, which took me down through beautiful West "By God" Virginia. I eventually picked up Hwy 220 into Greensboro.

I stopped overnight near Winchester, West VA at a Hampton Inn. It was a surreal drive and gave me plenty of time to reflect.

When I pulled into my house on Redfield Drive in Greensboro, early on the afternoon of September 13th, my then 2-year-old, John, came running out onto our back deck flanked by Pamela and my mother-in-law, Jean. I remember scooping John up and about squeezing the life out of him. It was good to be home.

About a month or so later, I got my "flight legs" back under me and made my first trip back to Boston. If my schedule allowed, I always caught the 6am flight out of Greensboro on Monday mornings, and always sat on the left side of the 50+ seater jet. I called them "fighter jets" as they were nice and small.

Back then, I traveled so much for Avery on USAir, Delta and United that I was priority status with all three and typically got bumped up front if I asked for an upgrade. Back then, they did so at no charge. And we even got a pack of peanuts or pretzels. Remember those days?

A HOLE IN THE GROUND...AND IN OUR HEARTS.

The flight from Greensboro to Boston was direct and took around two hours. I always knew we were getting close when we would start to bank off of New York City and slowly descend down toward Logan airport.

To give you an idea of how much I was flying, when the good folks at Legal Seafood in the USAir concourse in Boston saw me coming, by the time I got to my seat at the quick serve bar, there was a Sam Adams on the counter and a bowl of chowder (aka "Chowda") not long behind it. No questions asked, only smiles and hellos, my own personal version of the previous long running TV show, *Cheers* based in the same great city.

This clear October morning, when we started to bank off of New York City, a familiar sight was missing. One my Mom and Dad took my sis and me to see when we were kids. I remember getting close to the window one time up on the 110th floor of the World Trade Center and my Dad called out for me to get back. He was afraid of heights and somehow thought I was going to fall through the glass. We joked about it years later.

I looked out my window on the left side of the plane, another beautiful fall morning, and looked up ahead. Lower Manhattan was scarred, there was a huge void. Nausea washed over me. The Towers were gone. This was the first time I had actually seen it with my own two eyes, no TV filter, all real and all gone. All that was left was what appeared to be, from way up here, a big, gaping crater or hole. Although I'm sure I couldn't see it that well, my mind filled in the blanks. Tears streamed down my face. I could always count on the sunlight glistening off those two beautiful American icons in the early morning on our final approach into Boston.

We went and saw Bruce Springsteen, November 16, 2002, in Greensboro on *The Rising* tour – an album completely dedicated to the days' events and the families of the victims of 9/11. Bruce and the E Street Band released this album July 30, 2002. I did not know this at the time, but it was his first album in seven years, and the first with the E. Street Band in 18 years. Apparently, the Boss got the inspiration for the album a few days after the 9/11 attacks, when a stranger in a car stopped next to him, rolled down his window and said, "We need you now."

Again, probably an angel.

FROM HONG KONG TO SOUTHPORT (NORTH CAROLINA)

A couple of weeks after that fateful attack (October 16, 2001), I was back flying International and began a hop through Europe, starting with London. During that trip, I hit several places in Europe, including the Netherlands (Amsterdam), and then Hamburg. The place that Mohammad Atta called home. I felt like I was chasing him and didn't feel all that safe there, even though I knew I was being paranoid.

In June of 2002, I found myself back in Hong Kong. If you haven't been to Hong Kong and you have the opportunity to go, you should. It's a marvel. Think 'New York City with a mountain backdrop'. It's amazing; although, the crush of people can make you feel claustrophobic.

The entire South China region is quite amazing. The factory cities that were created and their size and magnitude were remarkable. Shenzhen (located in the Guangdong Province, just across a tiny river and Shenzhen Bay from Hong Kong) in particular was fascinating to me.

Until 2010, Shenzhen had Special Economic Zones. People left their families to come to these Economic Zones to work.

In 1980, Shenzhen became a Special Economic Zone with a population of 310,000 residents and about 30,000 workers. By the end of 2000, the peak of when I was traveling there, the population had grown to about 4.3 million with a labor force of over 3 million.

My colleagues told me about the fields and grass now adorned with skyscrapers. Exponential growth was an understatement.

These good people who came in to find work for their families, lived in dormitories and sent money back home. I remember seeing some of the workers at their machines sleeping on their breaks. A very hard life for sure, and one of the many things that would hit me during my travels, slamming me in the face and reminding me, like my father used to gently remind me, to never take what I had for granted. Nothing, not even running water.

I have always tried to keep that in mind. Gary Sumner, an HR manager at Sara Lee once said while our country was engaged in the first Gulf War in our meeting room in the Yarn Plant: "God has a funny sense of humor, we could have been born in Iran or Iraq." Not that there is anything in the world wrong with those two places in terms of their people (I have friends in both places); he was referring to the tyranny and oppression many of the good citizens in those countries had to endure. I know we have it lucky here in the United States.

One page of many from my Passport: First Trip to Hong Kong/China

I also will never forget being in South China trying to come back to Hong Kong on a Saturday, aka Shipping Day. Saturday is the big shipping day when all of the large shipping companies push off and send their goods around the world, particularly to the United States.

I was in a hurry, trying to make a business dinner. Bad idea. In a hurry, highway coming into Hong Kong on Saturday, shipping day. I remember looking back as we crawled along. It seemed like a military movement there were so many trucks carrying containers. As far as the eye could see it was container truck after container truck, lined up to try and get into the port of Hong Kong.

This is where it has gone. This is why we shut forty-six factories down at Hanes Underwear in three years. It's all over here now, I thought.

To see it was both amazing and heartbreaking. I was grateful to be there, because I knew I was working and had a great job.

But... I was half a world away... and I was never home. The travel had begun to wear on me. "Life is short" replayed in my head. A gentle but steady pulling, the need for a different direction.

Why??

I had the best job situation anyone could have. I had a great salary, great package, great bosses, great teammates, great clients. It was an awesome situation. But I was also missing my son grow up.

Our team was a very mobile group and we hopped on conference calls when we could, but there are times in business when you simply have to be face to face. I was a professional commuter for sure. I could work just as easily at 35,000 feet or in an airport kiosk or in Framingham Mass at my temporary work desk or in Greensboro at my temporary work desk or wherever I needed to be. It was a grab travel docs and go life...

Mine was a precursor to the millennial workforce today and how many prefer to work. I worked 80- to 100-hour work weeks at times. I've had people ask me over the course of my career "are you mobile?" or "do you work remotely?" Heck, I've been "mobile" since my first day on the job with Avery Dennison in 1999.

As anyone who travels for a living knows, the company basically owns you. I was doing "hoteling" before co-working or WeWork came into existence. If I waited until I was at my comfy desk to write a report, instead of doing it at 35,000 feet, I would have ground my team to a halt. If my team and I waited until we were gathered at any one spot on the globe to "get stuff done", we would not have accomplished much.

As it turned out while in Hong Kong one evening, I was speaking with my then brother in law, Blake on the phone and I was lamenting the travel. I had voiced my desire to leave the corporate world and find a different path. I wanted to go out on my own and I thought this was the time to do it. It was time to exit.

9/11 had spooked me. Losing Jeff was a major wake up call for me. I felt God was nudging me, gently trying to tell me something. I guess you could say that fate caught me at the right time and the right circumstance.

We had done a lot of research trying to decide where to move and what to do.

Our father-in-law had a place at Oriental, North Carolina a tiny sailboat town. Blake new that I loved that town and the water.

When I told him about our plans and not knowing where we wanted to land, he said, "What about Southport?" (Blake had a friend who had retired and moved to Southport).

The conversation went like this:

"Where is Southport?"

"Below Wilmington..."

"Wilmington where?"

"Wilmington, North Carolina, you idiot!" Laughter on his end... heck, I didn't know. I knew there was a Southport, Maine but had no idea, even growing up in North Carolina, that there was a Southport there as well!

Avery Dennison had long since kindly made the offer to get me to relocate to Boston, but we wanted to remain in North Carolina, and I was fine with commuting. I loved Boston but it broke me of cold weather. I promised myself once I got back to warm weather full time, I would never complain about it again. I used to joke that Boston had two seasons, summer in July and August, and then winter. An exaggeration of course, the falls there are also amazing (and the food and sports, unreal!), but the winters can be quite brutal.

Avery Dennison Corp and Sara Lee Corp had both been beyond good to me, but I wanted more.

I had several great bosses while at Sara Lee Corp and Avery Dennison, but Kim Macaulay was my best and favorite. Though I loved my time in operations and logistics, managing manufacturing operations and distribution centers at Sara Lee Knit Products, I always felt fortunate that Kim had recruited me away and even though what we thought was going to be approximately 25% travel as we started up the business turned out to be almost 100% on a global basis for nearly 5 years, I didn't regret one moment of it: the people, the company, the clients, the experience were amazing and I knew I was very fortunate.

Below is a personal email from Kim referencing the 18th anniversary of 9/11 in 2019. She was responding to my email, which I send to her each year.

———

From: Kim
Sent: Thursday, September 12, 2019 7:25 PM
To: Peter Frandano <peter.frandano@cbcmeca.com>
Subject: Re: Thinking about you as always!

Hi Pete,

I am very grateful for your note and kind words. I am in Lisbon with friends. We are leaving Saturday for Porto and a river cruise on the Douro. Tonight at dinner of course we all reflected on that day in 2001. I talked about you, where you were, how you got home and the impact that day made on choices you made regarding your career. Then we got back to the room and I saw your note.

I'm still awed by how lucky I was to not have been in the air that day, how lucky I have been to work with so many talented and genuine people over the years.

Thanks for staying in touch. I know that you are like me, no matter how many years pass we will never forget .....And we will always be grateful for our many blessings in life.

Best,
Kim

My youngest son, Joe was born March 2, 2002. As I mentioned previously, we called him our 9/11 baby. I had pushed client and business travel off for weeks pending his arrival, but once we got him home, about 10 days later, I was literally gone for weeks. Off to London, then I returned after 7 days, touched down in Atlanta for literally about four hours and was off to Brazil for 7 days. Though Pamela knew I had to do it, she didn't appreciate it. I had missed the first few years of being there with John (now 3) and I was determined not to do the same with Joe, and felt I had some making up to do with John. As with John, Joe's birth was positive in so many ways and certainly was a positive motivator for me.

Over the next year, in the spring of 2003, after much thought, and much discussion with family and friends, I had decided to leave the corporate world...we were stepping out. I was leaving my safe and cushy corporate "cocoon."..

More research ensued, much of it trying to decide what business to either enter or buy.

I spoke with several real estate professionals about the area, and spoke with people in the industry, both commercial practitioners and residential experts I knew, did a ton of reconnaissance and information gathering and then an acquaintance of mine introduced me to Mary Anne Russ, owner of Southport Realty.

When I was introduced to Mary Anne Russ, founder of Southport Realty, I learned she was well established and well respected in the town of historic Southport. She instantly reminded me of both my mom and my grandmother. She let me know that she was seeking someone to start up the commercial side of her firm and voiced concerns about me leaving the corporate world without a stream of business already in hand. She explained that "John (her husband) and I had his income, his salary with Progress Energy, to stave off the highs and the lows of the real estate business while I muddled through and got my start. Even though you'll be focusing on commercial, I highly recommend you also sell some homes, that will help put food on your table and help you learn the business."

The rest, as they say, is history.

I decided I was going into Real Estate.

The following is Simon Coulson's (Kim's boss) letter to me when I decided to depart Avery. We lost Simon way to early.

God's speed, Simon.

———

From: Simon on 08/15/2003 10:08 AM
To: Pete Frandano/NA/AveryDennison@AveryDennison
Subject: Re: Thank you (Document link: Pete Frandano)

Pete,

Thanks for your note. It has been a pleasure to work with you and I have always admired your positive attitude , dedication , flexibility and the hard work that you have given to RIS.

I wish you and your family the very best and success in your new venture. As I mentioned to you , if for whatever reason you want to to return to "corporate" life at some point in the future the door will be always be open.

Good Luck !
Simon.

———

Let me say unequivocally that some of the smartest people in the world are in the real estate industry. Brilliant finance people. Brilliant business people. People that can pencil whip me doing an NOI/cap rate calculation on the back of a napkin in 30 seconds.

T. Cooper James, a neighbor of mine and a long-time friend now, who happened to be a very seasoned commercial developer, was one of those people. Cooper took me on a tour of his properties early on after my leaving the corporate world in the summer of 2003. One was a Food-Lion-anchored development.

Afterwards, over BBQ sandwiches in Mocksville, NC, he casually said, "Pete, if I can't figure the deal out on one piece of paper, I'm not doing it." He then pulled out a napkin and drew out an IRR calculation on a seven million-dollar deal. When he was done, he looked at me, smiling like the Cheshire cat, and said, "Pete, there it is... I'm plus or minus a few hundred thousand dollars and I'm still good..."

When I first pulled into Southport, I loved it from the start and reminded me of Maine without the winters. It's a tranquil fishing village in the far southeastern corner of our great state, North Carolina, right at the mouth of the Cape Fear River, coming off the Atlantic Ocean. Its "sister" town, Oak Island is the beach area.

To me, they are linked at the hip: if you live in the Village, you have the blessing of the beach right around the corner. If you live on Oak Island, you have the Village of Southport right over the bridge. Truly, the best of both worlds.

Southport was a town of about 2,500, at the time. To put that in perspective, the high school I attended in Charlotte, Myers Park High School, was larger than the entire town of Southport. I got a kick out of that. Later, when we discussed it, we knew that later in life, if our boys ever did anything wrong in school, we would know about it before they got home!

When my lifelong banker Father found out what I was doing, he thought I had lost my mind. He set up a meeting with a friend of his, Ray (Jones) who he knew through a tennis club they belonged to, in addition to both being members of St. Gabriel Catholic Church.

I think Dad was thinking Ray was going to talk me out of it, but my lunch and conversation with Ray only reinforced my decision. As mentioned previously, I've been fortunate to have Ray as a mentor. I've told him many times that had he not been on my proverbial shoulder saying "don't do it, Pete" on several deals, I would have gone under. He is always very modest and humble, but it's true, there are some people we can never pay back for the time, experience and wisdom they have shared with you. For me, Ray is one of those people.

Once in Southport, I knew that I was in the place I was supposed to be, on the path I was supposed to be on. I would be a part of my sons' lives, part of the growing up, the learning experiences, the sharing that was extremely important to me. I would get to be there for them, coaching their teams and just plain ol' being daddy.

The night before the movers were to arrive in Greensboro to take us to Southport was upon us. I remember staring at the ceiling fan ... womp, womp, womp... The cold sweat of leaving my safe, corporate cocoon started setting in on me.

What in the heck have you done? I thought...

Here I was, not even having passed the state real estate licensing course yet. What if I were to fail that? How was I going to support my family? (my boys were then 4 and 1 years old). "

Pete, you idiot! a tiny voice said.

But I loved it. I felt free. Home every night, I got to be "Coach Pete" and Dad again. I was in Heaven...

And, as it turns out, I would need every bit of the savings, nest egg, war chest I had built up to survive the looming valley ahead.

———

Some of my right turns I realize I will never have an answer for while I'm here on earth. Why did my cousin have to go? Why was I lucky enough to be on the *right plane* that infamous September morning? I've also come to realize that we all have these types of questions, don't we?

These types of stories or events in our lives often ping us in different and unexpected directions. But *we are where we are supposed to be.*

Our "right turns" or curve balls or whatever you choose to call them are what they are and can be a positive for us, as long as we choose to make the most of where we are...

CHAPTER 4

THE ROAD TO ENDURANCE REAL ESTATE

"NEITHER A WISE NOR A BRAVE MAN LIES DOWN
ON THE TRACKS OF HISTORY TO WAIT FOR THE
TRAIN OF THE FUTURE TO RUN OVER HIM."
-DWIGHT EISENHOWER

I harken back to 2005 and Jean Brown in Brunswick County asking me if I would be interested in "getting into leadership." I had no idea what I was getting into, but I thought the least I could do was get involved and help some in an industry that was giving so much to me.

In that meeting, Allan Holden, the incoming President of our Brunswick County Association, stood up after our "interview" for my Board of Director position, and jokingly said, "Fresh meat…"

Yes, he nailed it. But it's been worth it. As a soon to be new Board of Director team member, I recall Allan saying at his outgoing speech the year he was passing the gavel: "Give back, get involved. I promise, this business will give back to you ten times what you put in…"

And he was right. The same has been true with my CCIM affiliation, involvement with the Wilmington Commercial Board (RCASENC), the North Carolina CCIM Chapter, the North Carolina Association of REALTORS® and the Charlotte Regional Commercial Board of REALTORS®.

I recall what my cousin Jeff's boss, Rob Cheek, said to me when I was departing the corporate world about the CCIM designation: "There is this thing called the CCIM designation and even if you don't get the designation, the learning and the network will be worth their weight in gold to you..."

Good friend of mine Rob Pressley, CCIM, also told me when I was getting into the real estate business to get involved and give back.

Since then, I have had the opportunity to serve our award winning state CCIM Chapter, and as Past President of our awesome chapter and now a proud and humbled member of our North Carolina CCIM Chapter Hall of Fame, *I sure hope Rob and Rob feel I listened to them!*

As mentioned previously, I didn't come up with *Endurance Real Estate* idea overnight. At my installation as President of the Brunswick County Association of REALTORS in 2011, I told everyone in the room that day that "If you are here and you're standing, you've made it. The light at the end of the tunnel is no longer a train." I mentioned to everyone that real estate is an endurance event and we are all endurance athletes. I meant it then, I have seen it firsthand, and it's still true today.

If you were in real estate at that time and had made it without being washed out by the Great Recession, *the long war,* you had made it through one of the most grueling economic periods in our nation's history. You had endured one of the Endurance tests of a lifetime. History and the facts thereafter have proven it. Many experts believe the financial crisis earthquake that kicked off the tsunami called the Great Recession was worse than the Great Depression.

Research has since proven that a generation of wealth simply vanished during that time.

After purchasing Southport Realty in 2007 (yes, great timing!), one silver lining I kept in front of me through it all, and something I realize some others unfortunately could not say:

We were young enough to recover.

I knew I had enough *runway to achieve liftoff again.*

At some point along the way, I made a promise to myself that no matter how arrogant, over-confident or cocky I got after getting back on my feet again, I would always remember how quickly the switch could be flipped, and would always do my best to make wise decisions and help others to do the same. "Humbling" is the word that came to mind quite often then and it still does today.

I've been on a mission since to help others learn how to protect themselves and their families. How to run from peak to peak and through the valleys that inevitably will come.

Has it all been peaks for me? Far from it. I've had plenty of valleys in my life, the Great Recession being one, and now staring into the valley we currently call the Pandemic of 2020. I'm prepared to do my best to run through any valley that comes my way.

From the Great Recession, I unfortunately knew some who got wiped out in the fourth quarter of their lives. Some of us had time to recover, some did not and ran out of time.

So, in 2003, this seasoned, somewhat oblivious Fortune 500, B-school, post- 9/11 guy jumps off the corporate treadmill, and out of the safety and security that came along with it, into the world of real estate to pursue his entrepreneurial ambitions, more time with his family and the American dream.

All the while thinking he's in a *'normal market'*...

In 2003-2004, real estate was like picking gold up off the streets. Nurses left nursing to get their real estate license. Attorneys left law practices to become home builders. I remember at one point during what I have come to call "the silly season" (that period from 2003 to 2006 where the industry was on a rocket ship to the moon) a successful chiropractor at a dinner party telling me about the development deal he was doing.

Uh oh...

I made more money my second year in the real estate industry than I did at almost any one year in my first decade in the Fortune 500 world.

Wow, this is easy...

Now, picture a roller coaster on its ascent up the first hill. CLICK...CLICK...CLICK....

During this upward trip, I waded into leadership positions within the real estate industry: our local Brunswick County Association of REALTORS, the North Carolina Association of REALTORS® Exec team and Board of Directors, the Wilmington, NC Commercial Board of REALTORS® (REALTORS® Commercial Alliance of Southeastern North Carolina (RCASENC), and the North Carolina CCIM Chapter (NC-CCIM).

In 2007, my two partners and I purchased Mary Anne's firm, Southport Realty, which was a full-service real estate company. CLICK...CLICK... WHOOOSH!!! Down the slope...

Over the top, wind in my hair (when I had hair!), I find myself at the epicenter of one of the financially hardest hit areas in North Carolina and ground zero for the land gold rush in our state.

"Welcome to the real estate industry, Mr. Frandano, we're glad you're here...Right this way..."

Now, picture swimming in a shark-infested tsunami and you have the picture of my life's ultimate endurance test. My fight for survival was on...

I believe we can become better people because of our experiences. I have learned that sometimes it's the tough times that strengthen us and where we learn the most.

I had a front row seat to some people, much brighter than me, who got heartbreakingly crushed. Some who succumbed ... and their families suffering from the loss.

There have been many books written about the financial crisis and the ensuing Great Recession. I list a few of these books in the "Rubber

Meets the Road" Chapter and they primarily do a particularly good job of telling the story about the 2% on Wall Street, not the other 98% of us.

A great deal has been written about the impact the downturn had on Wall Street. In the pages ahead, I touch on what happened to some of us who were out in the field, in the trenches, in the arena on main street. More importantly, I talk about how to deal with the next financial downturn, when it comes again, and a few tips of how to swim in the tsunami if and when you must.

Over my 30+ years in industry, I have learned quite a bit of what works and what doesn't. I've also had the good fortune to have a front row seat to some of the best practitioners in the world and to witness what has worked (and not worked) for them.

I harken back to an industry event in Charlotte in 2018. Van, a friend and CCIM colleague, and I were sharing a cup of coffee in the annex area prior to the event starting.

While standing there, I asked Van a simple question: *"How's business going?"*

Most folks would have given a flippant answer like, "GREAT!" Not Van. He said, "Pete, it's going well. I've finally gotten my feet back under me and things are tracking in the right direction. But if we head into a recession, I just don't know if I'm ready for that yet..."

Was this in 2009 or 2010? Um, no. This was almost ten years after the Great Recession officially ended. And keep in mind this was in booming Charlotte, which had experienced an extraordinary turn around, essentially reinventing itself since the Great Recession, still maintaining a great banking core but not completely reliant on it now.

So, I would ask you to ask yourself this pointed question:

Are you ready for the next downturn?

Will you be able to not just survive it, but continue to be successful in whatever way you define "success"? To push through the valley to the next peak and onto to your next finish line?

If not, why not? What do you need to do to advance your ball today to make sure you are ready? What do you need to do to keep it simple, cut through the distractions and focus on what enriches your and your family's life?

Take a look at the cover of this book, as it pretty much sums it up: Business, the economy and life ... cycles ...

They always cycle. Are you prepared to run from peak to peak and survive and thrive in the valleys?

CHAPTER 5

TO ENDURE: WE'RE ALL ENDURANCE ATHLETES

"RUN WHEN YOU CAN, WALK IF YOU HAVE TO,

CRAWL IF YOU MUST, JUST NEVER GIVE UP..."

--DEAN KARNAZES [ENDURANCE ATHLETE AND AUTHOR OF

ULTRAMARATHON MAN: CONFESSIONS OF AN ALL-NIGHT RUNNER]

To Endure (definition):

Merriam-Webster Dictionary:

1. to continue in the same state; to remain firm under suffering or misfortune without yielding
2. to undergo, especially without giving in

I think both the above definitions are real and relevant.

My favorite of the two is the second one: *to undergo, especially without giving in.*

If you think about it, you can see from the definitions alone why I say whether you run marathons, triathlons, 5K's, 10K's, half marathons or if you are in the real estate business or another business or the business of "life", *we are all endurance athletes...*

Front Page News

Frandano heads Realtor group
By Morgan Harper
Features Editor
Published: Wednesday, January 19, 2011 11:11 AM EST

The gavel was passed from one Southport Realty desk to another on Saturday as the Brunswick County Association of Realtors (BCAR) held its change-of-presidency luncheon.

Pete Frandano succeeds Mary Ann McCarthy in the leadership role. McCarthy, in turn, was named Realtor of the Year for the approximately 750-member association.

As outgoing president, McCarthy thanked committee chairpersons for "helping return the association to its grassroots level," and recognized 2010 BCAR board members for "representing the association in the finest, most professional manner. I just can't say enough about this team."

McCarthy said she will wear the award pin in honor of her board of directors.

Jane Anderson was named Committee Chairperson of the Year for her "tireless work to improve the services brought to Brunswick County Association of Realtors members," said McCarthy.

Margaret Bishop of Margaret Rudd & Associates was recognized for her induction into the North Carolina Association of Realtors Hall of Fame during the year.

Past president of the North Carolina Association of Realtors, Cindy Chandler of Charlotte, was present to introduce Frandano as 2011 BCAR president.

Frandano said he was humbled and motivated by being named to the position, and could not think of a better theme than this year's — "Today's Challenges, Tomorrow's Opportunities."

"We have endured the greatest economic downfall of our lifetime," he said, and compared the real estate business to an endurance sport, with the athletes (Realtors) showing great commitment, endurance and hard work.

"We may have been knocked down, but not knocked out," Frandano stated, adding, "There is a light at the end of the tunnel, and all indications show that the trend is going to continue."

"We're in a great position in a wonderful location," he told Saturday's audience at BCAE headquarters. "It couldn't be any more appealing, with the quality and value of life" that Brunswick County has to offer.

Frandano said he is looking forward to serving. "You're stuck with me this year," he said, "and I'm going to give you my best."

The 2011 Installation and Presidential Awards luncheon honoring 2011 BCAR officers and directors was sponsored by Century 21 Brock and Associates.

HOW LONG CAN YOU HOLD YOUR BREATH?
Think about the last business cycle (the Great Recession)...

This is how I often describe the economic environment to someone who was not in the real estate business during the worst downturn in our nation's history. Just about everyone could have survived that steep, cliff-dive-like drop off. But it was that long run along the bottom, the length of the valley, that wiped so many out.

Not to be morbid, but some of my hunter/outdoor/nature loving friends have explained to me that if you are in the everglades and have an unfortunate encounter with a crocodile, the croc won't eat its prey immediately. Nope. It takes dinner down to the bottom and shoves it under a log or rolls with it and drowns it, then begins to eat it in chunks.

In similar fashion, this past downturn was a croc that took many down to the bottom and drowned them. I was one who almost drowned. I knew people in the 4th quarter of their life that got wiped out. *I knew some who took their lives.* Heartbreaking, gut wrenching. So, when I say *I'm on a mission to save lives and livelihoods*, whether it's yours or someone else's, it is true.

Those who survived were able to hold their breath the longest and escape the crocodile.

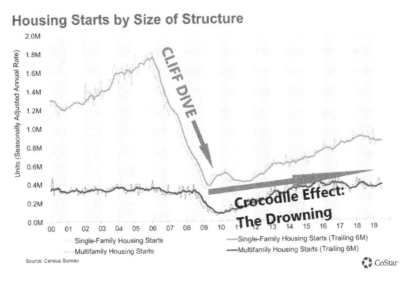

Housing Starts by Size of Structure

Source: Census Bureau

Single-Family Housing Starts
Multifamily Housing Starts
Single-Family Housing Starts (Trailing 6M)
Multifamily Housing Starts (Trailing 6M)

CoStar

As of this writing, time will tell what the cycle actually turns out to look like from the "Great Shutdown" of 2020. Some have argued a V-shape recovery, while others say more like a Nike Swoosh, and many suggest the shape of a W.

Like a friend of mine, who had survived the Great Recession, said of our COVID-19 world: "Nobody knows nothin' and I don't trust any of the information..."

Probably not a bad way to look at things. His message: Keep your own counsel and plod your own path forward, taking in information that validates your decisions, but also offers up a trusted, but dissenting, view. At that point, after you have gathered enough as the CEO of You, Inc, it's time to make decisions and go!

There is no such thing as perfect information and, in my experience, you can enter "information overload land" really quickly, if you're not careful. Paralysis by analysis is real and it's a dangerous thing.

As mentioned, I've been fortunate to have participated in a few actual endurance events in my life.

Endurance sports have given me the gift of realizing I can push myself beyond where I think I can go, forcing me to reach deeper than I ever thought I could and at times. I'm convinced on certain occasions having endurance sports to fall back on saved my sanity, if not my life.

I've always considered myself a runner first, with cycling and swimming my weaker sports, but I love them as well.

In my early foray into the triathlon world, at my first triathlon, I was determined not to wear goggles during the swim leg. If you swim, you know that goggles can fog up. At the time, I was a newbie and that potential seemed unpredictable (which, looking back, is hilarious).

I showed up to the opening leg with my buddies, DeWitt and Kevin Brown, and went in the water with no goggles. I looked around. *Wow, everyone has goggles except me...*

A guy beside me turns and says, "No goggles dude?"

And I proudly retorted, "Nope." And he said, "You da' man..."

I knew right then I was in trouble. Let's just say never again did I participate in a triathlon without goggles. It made for a miserable experience during the swim leg of the triathlon, having to take my head out of the water, water in my eyes to spot my position and the next swim marker (buoy) ahead. Take it from me, during the swim leg in any triathlon, no matter the distance, goggles are highly recommended! The phrase 'Idiots R Us' comes to mind... that was me, but hey, I was a rookie, I got through it and loved it. I can and often do laugh at myself.

For those who don't know, there are different levels of triathlons, but they all have a swim, cycle and run component. My favorite distance is the Olympic or International distance, which consists of a mile or so swim, depending on who sponsors it, what body of water it's in, etc. and a 26 mile +/- bike ride and finishes with a 10K run (6.2 miles).

There are longer iron events I have participated in, but I found that during the course of my career the International distance struck that fine balance of being able to get a darn good workout, and being able to maintain your career without going broke training. If you are independently wealthy and have all the time in the world to train, iron events are awesome! For the record, many of us are not independently wealthy and don't have all the time in the world to train, but we still manage to figure out a way to participate in these great events! An iron event is either an iron half or full iron and they are both considered "ultra" categories, which are those categories that you reach just above the marathon (26.2 miles). The half iron event is the first entry into the ultra-category and is a triathlon consisting of a 1.2 mile swim, 56 mile cycle followed by a 13.1 mile run (a half marathon).

There are only a handful of people in every event who actually compete for a living. The rest of us are doing it for ourselves and hopefully, doing some good for others along the way by raising money for charities or to inspire someone or both.

When you do marathons, and then get into the iron triathlon event distances, the training really ramps up. The time drain can be a challenge if you are trying to raise kids, coach, work, make a living. However, they are also a blast and the relationships formed and the camaraderie are worth their weight in gold.

In the tri world, I used to joke with my friends that they don't call me 'The Rock' for nothin' -- hit the water and right to the bottom I go. I would quip that part of my training for the water leg of the triathlon involved practicing the roll over and yelling *Kayak!*, which is what they tell you to do if you cramp or run out of steam during the swim leg of the triathlon.

Over the years, running, even a short run, has been a bit of a personal calling card for me. Whenever I visit a city, I always tried to at least get a 5K run in so I could say I had "crossed that finish line" wherever I had been.

I've been fortunate to do this in quite a few cities around our awesome globe, including Hong Kong, South China, Macao, Taipei, Monterrey (Mexico), along the Isar river in Munich, London and Wooburn Green (UK), Amsterdam (Netherlands), Rotterdam and Eindhoven (Netherlands), Dusseldorf, Hamburg, and Frankfurt (Germany), Brussels, Lille (France), Overloon (Austria), Luxembourg, Copenhagen (Denmark), Stockholm (Sweden), San Salvador (El Salvador), Honduras, and the Dominican Republic.

And in the States, San Francisco, San Diego, Port St. Luce, St. Augustin, Boone, Blowing Rock, Chapel Hill, Raleigh, Winston-Salem, Greensboro, Asheville, Hendersonville, Myrtle Beach, Miami, Dallas, Plano, Bentonville, Houston, Austin, Los Angeles, Pasadena, New Port Beach, Yarmouth, Freeport (Maine and Bahamas), Nassau, Framingham, Natick, Boston, Washington DC, NYC, Chicago, Detroit, Toronto, Elizabeth City, San Diego, Orlando, Miami, Jacksonville, Tampa, Montgomery, Birmingham, Atlanta, Philadelphia, Oriental, Charleston, Portland, Seattle, Beaverton and Edenton.

I've tried not to ever take any one run, workout or endurance event I participated in for granted. I always knew that each could be my last and that I might not make it to the finish line ... always thankful to cross the finish line. I try to keep in mind the paradigm that "no day is a given, every day above ground is a great day..."

According to Marathon Training Schedule Blog from 2015: There are about 570 marathons held in the US every year. About 0.5% of the US Population has run a marathon. From a July 14, 2017 Washington Post Article by Amby Burfoot, a new report, the largest-yet analysis of US road race results, titled *American runners have never been Slower.*

My take on that: whether you have run a marathon in 2 hours or 6 hours, you are still a marathoner. Put another way, what does the person who ran 26.2 miles in 2 hours have in common with the person who ran 26.2 miles in 6 hours? They both ran a marathon!

There is another saying that the golfing world likes to employ: "It's not how you drive, but how you arrive."

In MBA school, we used to joke that "B equals MBA."...

Or how about, Q: what do you call a medical student who passed Medical school with all C's? A: *Doctor*

Or how about if you passed your real estate licensing exam, I may call you a Real Estate Agent, Real Estate Broker, and if you are affiliated with your local Board, which is under the National Association of REALTOR'S umbrella, you have earned the distinction of being referred to as a REALTOR®.

What do you call a CCIM Candidate who barely passed the 6-hour CCIM Exam en route to attempting to earn the CCIM designation? A "*CCIM*"!

My point is, all exceptional. You did it, you crossed that finish line.

Why do we choose to push ourselves?

I've had many people ask me "why in the world would you want to run, much less run 26.2 miles?" My barber used to say, "The only time I'm running, is when someone is chasin' me!" A family member once sent this to me:

From a USA Today article, titled "*9 reasons to run a Marathon*" by Victoria E. Freile, published September 10, 2015, the author mentions that the 1% of us who push ourselves to run a marathon are interested in achieving a goal, overcoming obstacles, pushing ourselves to levels we never thought we could, and changing.

The marathon is just one example of "pushing yourself." You may push yourself with a 10K, a half marathon, a full marathon, or maybe you are pushing yourself in other ways? Pursuing a new designation or certification? A higher degree? Publishing your own book. The list is endless, but they have a common bond.

They are all an investment in: *You, Inc.*

I get that some of the endurance "stuff" is over the top. There were some days when the rain was coming down sideways on a dark cold morning or the thunder was crashing and lightening was popping all around, and I'm still going out for my 15-mile training run. My youngest son, several years ago, flippantly said to a friend of his when describing what his dad did, endurance sport-wise, blurted out: "My Dad is a freak..."

I wonder where he got that from?

There was a time when I set the indoor record of 15 miles around a 1/12th -mile track because I didn't want to deal with the weather – tropical storm level winds that day (I have my limits). Or 20 miles on a different indoor 1/12th-mile track for your last training run; boy, that made the outdoor runs (always my preference!) a pure joy...I had to force myself into an out of body experience, become kind of robot-like for those. The list could go on.

I mention these only to highlight the fact we sometimes push ourselves in ways we never thought we could.

Willard Bullins, the Director of Manufacturing at Hanes I mentioned earlier, once told me he had run three miles. I said, "All at once? Who does *that*?"

Next thing you know, I'm out the door and one mile leads to two, and off I go. He had planted a seed and had helped, knowingly or unknowingly, remove an artificial ceiling I had inside my brain.

I've learned something about myself over the years, during these runs, cycles, swims and all. Those hard moments where I wanted to stop, I wanted to throw in the towel, and I had to reach deep. And when I finished, it opened up a new world to me. I realized I could actually keep going. I might get knocked down or be out on my feet, but I could keep going and cross the finish line.

My experience in the real estate world also falls into the endurance event category.

I'm sure many of you who were swimming in the tsunami of the Great Recession had similar experiences. I learned more about people, character, knuckling down, falling flat on my face, getting back up again, running the gauntlet, and trying to survive and run from peak to peak during that downturn than all my other experiences combined. Put another way, nothing in my time spent in management in Fortune 500 arena and nothing in the classroom in business school could have prepared me for what I would go through. Provided me with some skills, for sure, but prepare me? No way.

What humbles me even more at times is to see first-hand what others endure.

The Marine with a prosthetic leg. The mother pushing her child in a stroller 26.2 miles while she jogs behind it. The person pushing himself in a wheelchair.

Seeing those folks pushing through and overcoming their obstacles; seeing them sweat and hurt and keep moving forward; seeing them endure was more inspirational to me than 1000 inspirational speeches or books. If I was feeling sorry for myself, all I had to do was look around and I would hear an instant *get-over-yourself* inside my head. If I was sweating my business or a closing or whatever, all I had to do was think about the strength of the person who had no legs, pushing himself the 46 miles the rest of us were cycling that day in the Wounded Warriors ride, and he would give me strength to keep going, to endure.

When you get to the plateau, where some think you are a bit nutty or compulsive or obsessive or addicted – that means you've done quite a bit. Yes, I've been fortunate enough to be there. Lots of early morning runs, cycling, swimming ... and late morning, early afternoon, late afternoon and nights, too.

At the YMCA in Greensboro, there was an older gentleman who was always at the front desk. And when I was departing around 6am he would shout out: "YOU GOT THE HARDEST PART OF YOUR DAY DONE!"

Well, I would laugh, but later I realized -- *he was right*.

I had, before 6am, already accomplished something that day. And once completed, it could not be taken away from me. It was done and in the books.

If nothing else had happened that day, I had at least crossed that finish line.

At one of my oldest son's middle school awards programs, Colonel Calisto came and gave the kids a great talk. He left a calling card titled *Colonel Calisto's Words of Wisdom* with them. On the card were these five things:

- Hard work always pays off.
- Attitude is everything.
- Always believe in yourself.
- Like what you see in the mirror.
- Never quit!!!

Colonel Calisto & John

As you know by now, I'm a big fan of the military and the discipline they exact in their own lives, not to mention the inspiration they provide to those of us who admire and observe them. I once sent a YouTube video, a brief snippet of NAVY SEAL Admiral Williams H. McRaven to my sons. This decorated SEAL was giving a commencement address to new graduates from the University of Texas Austin. In his talk, he discussed the ten lessons he learned from his "basic" SEAL training, what he called a lifetime of challenges, crammed into six months[5v]. The first lesson, was the reason to make your bed every day:

"Every morning in SEAL Training, my instructors, who at the time were all Vietnam veterans, would show up in my barracks room and the first thing they would do was inspect my bed. If you did it right, the corners would be square, covers pulled tight, pillow centered just under the headboard and the extra blanket folded neatly at the foot of the rack. It seemed mundane, almost ridiculous; they were aspiring to be battle-hardened SEALS. But the wisdom of this simple act has been proven to me many times over. If you make your bed in the morning, you will have accomplished the first task of the day. It will give you a small sense of pride and it will encourage you to do another task, and then another, and another. And by the end of that day, that one task completed will have turned into many tasks completed. Making your bed will also reinforce the fact that the little things in life matter. If you can't do the little things right, you'll never be able to do the big things right. And if by chance you have a miserable day, you will come home to a bed that is made, that you made, and a made bed gives you encouragement that tomorrow will be better. So, if you want to change the world, start off by making your bed."

That stuck with me.

Dr. George Sheehan said in his book *Running and Being: The Total Experience*: "He runs because he has to. Because in being a runner, in moving through pain and fatigue and suffering, in imposing stress upon stress, in eliminating all but the necessities of life, he is fulfilling himself and becoming the person he is."

The Endurance seed for me was planted on many hot August summer days off Colony Road in Charlotte, North Carolina, at football practice at Myers Park High School with Coach Glenn Sasser working our behinds off.

If at times during an event I wanted to have a letdown or give up, I could hear Coach Sasser in the back of my mind barking at us, running us at the *end* of practice, telling us to envision the 4th quarter and yelling and cajoling us along.

"You're feeling sorry for yourself! You want to quit, don't you?! Well, *QUIT*! Do us all a favor and quit! If you can't take this, you won't be able to reach deep on game day and you'll let us all down!"

I think athletics, exercise of any size, shape or form, and sports in general can teach us all a lot about teamwork, ourselves and reaching deep. I think any movement is good, any activity is good. On a personal note, if you exercise on any level, walking, running, cycling, swimming, lifting weights, working in the garden, whatever, that is awesome, keep it up. If not, I hope you'll consider starting for yourself and for those who love you. They need you here for a long time.

A high school friend of mine, an experienced commercial broker and developer, Rob Pressley, CCIM, told me when I was getting ready to take the dive into the real estate industry: "Pete, there will be times between closings, and that time can be a very long time, that you will want to throw the towel in...and right before you do, another deals hits and you muster up the strength to keep going."

He was right for sure...

So, real estate and business and life are all endurance events, but sometimes they are also sprints. You have to train to your event. Some of my 5K runs were more brutal than my "easiest" marathon – if there is such a thing. They are all different. The art is in recognizing the event you are competing in, the deal dynamics, and adjusting and training and performing accordingly. They can all be rewarding, and they can all be humbling.

Carolyne Chen wrote an article, *10 Ways Marathon Training Humbles Me*, published *May 7, 2015 in the publication: Women's*

Running[6vi]. See if you can see how this article applies not only to running a marathon, but to life, real estate, business. Patience, working hard and strategically, recognizing not everything is in your control, sacrifice, balance, making mistakes, the reminder to stop comparing yourself to others. In my HUMBLE opinion, I think the parallels are obvious.

I took Carolyne's list (below in bold) and drew what I feel is a parallel to each as it applies to real estate, life or business.

1. **It calls for Patience.** Working with clients, vendors, city or county staff, appraisers, walking a project through rezoning - no closing happens overnight, some take much longer than others. You have to breathe deep and often. Meditate if it helps –and yes, for someone who didn't believe in meditation, I do now and I've seen the difference it can actually make.

2. **You have to work really hard and very strategically.** Brilliant people, a few not so brilliant that in some cases will pick your pocket. Where are the disruptors along your path? Think: SWOT Analysis or apply Michael Porter's 5 Forces. (I touch on this in the "What are the 3 Things" section toward the end of the book)

3. **Not everything is in your control.** See the Training Chapter later in the book where I outline just a few items during the due diligence phase - financing, appraisal, title, environmental, governmental, legal - so many things outside your control that can blow your deal up. You have to focus on your circle of control and drive those things to the wall which will invariably drive your probability to close up, but certainly won't guarantee it will cross the finish line!

4. **You have to make some sacrifices.** Expenditures of time and your dollars: education, time away from family on weekends, investment in your business, marketing, educating yourself, staying on top of your performance and industry. All investments in *You, Inc.*

5. **That said, it is also about balance.** You have to be able to "walk away" from your business temporarily. This will keep you fresh, helps you recover, stay mentally on top of your game. The real estate industry will "allow" you to work 24/7 if you wish, you have to be disciplined enough to strike a balance. It's also a great industry to be able to strike that balance if you are disciplined -- attend your daughter or granddaughter's game, play or dance recital, attend your son or grandson's game or performance. You have to block time for your personal interests as well. Balance that investment in the Physical, Mental, Social/Emotional and Spiritual side of *You, Inc.*

6. **Running fitness does not always translate into everything fitness** - Cross training is key. What do you do to push yourself outside of your current level of knowledge base? Having said that: where is your expertise? Where is your area of focus? Be careful not to go outside of your area of competency or you may encounter an "overuse" injury, which in this business could translate into a disservice to your client or, at worst, a licensing issue. Put another way, yes, I have brokered and represented buyer's in new home purchases. But now, since I have been focused on the commercial side of our business since 2007, I would refer just about all residential deals to a residential expert, unless someone, like a family member (Uncle Paul and Aunt Denise!), insisted on me representing them. But even then, I would still lean on a residential colleague or two!

7. **There will be some days you don't want to run** - Somewhat tied into #5 above, this is the time you need to take a break, recognize you are tired, run down, not fresh. When your eyes start to cross you know it's time to briefly walk away. I call it "burnout prevention." The great thing about our business is if you work Saturday and Sunday, most of us are independent Contractors, the CEO of *You, Inc.*, and if you want to take Monday off or half of Wednesday and half of Friday, you do it! You're in a meeting...

with yourself! And aren't you important enough to meet with you? Let me answer that for you: Yes, you are! Your clients, husband, wife, significant others, children, friends will all appreciate it, I promise.

8. **You are going to make some mistakes.** That's why we have what is called Errors and Omissions Insurance in our business. My boy's grandfather was a talented attorney and when I was leaving Corporate America to get into real estate, he said "Pete, you will get sued. It's not a matter of "if" but "when." Someone will sue you because that is what some people do and most likely it won't be something you brought on." But yes, we all make mistakes, learn from them, pick yourself up, dust yourself off and keep moving with the intent of not making the same mistake again. (note: so far, after many years now in the industry, I have not been sued. *Can you hear me knocking on wood?*).

9. **It makes you stop comparing yourself to others.** *Run your own race. You have a story to tell and only you can tell it.* Have your own system, roll within your own style. If cold calling is not your thing, don't do it, but come up with another method/system/process to help create leads. Can you "hire" someone that doesn't mind cold calling and train them on what you want said? Don't get worked up about that "multi-million-dollar producer" that keeps advertising over and over again. Or invite them to coffee and learn about what they are doing. You have your loyal circle and so do they. You're not trying to steal their clients, you are working to better yourself, raise your bar. Measure your own curve.

10. **You are training for a marathon!** Yes, the real estate industry is certainly an endurance event. *Life is an endurance event.* They both can be very humbling indeed. That deal that falls apart. The time you put in, only to come up short at times. Business always cycles. Valleys will hit, what do you do to get to the next peak and help others along your journey? How do you stay positive? (later in the book, I will introduce you to one of my main men, Fred,

my PEM, positive endurance man; he helps me and I hope he can help you too!). Stay loyal to your system, your work ethic, your plan and who you are and you will cross more finish lines in this business than you ever imagined.

"THE MARATHON CAN HUMBLE YOU."
-- BILL RODGERS, VETERAN MARATHONER

Dean Karnazes in his book, *50/50*, where he chronicled running 50 marathons in 50 days, said, "William James said that 'War is, in short, a permanent human obligation.' The runner (aka, the endurance athlete) fights this war against the most savage of enemies: Himself."

This can be said about endurance sports but also about most anything we do. We have to get out of our own way, believe in ourselves and keep going. That small space between our ears is often our biggest, most daunting hurdle.

Don't let anyone tell you "you can't." If they do, use it for motivation, because you can.

You didn't get that deal? Do you want to throw the towel in? Or do you reach deep and keep going? Believe me, I know we all get tired, worn down at times.

Endure...persevere...you can do it...

I'm always blown away by those I would encounter on my journeys and some of their stories, what they were going through or having to overcome, and often just to be able to get out there and participate. It's the same in the real estate industry. What about your business? My bet is it applies for your business, too.

We don't know what the person sitting across from you on the light rail into town has gone through the night before, do we? I've realized that there is almost always someone who has a harder obstacle or higher bar to clear, who has had to come further from the depths below, than I did. During the downturn, as bad as I got socked, endurance sports were always a humbling reminder that someone had it worse than I did. It would help me remember to help others whenever I could, in whatever little way I could. Far from perfect, I'm one of the fallen also.

These experiences I've encountered have been the proverbial stars of the 'play' and I have been for the most part a humbled character actor playing a role and doing the best I could do in that role.

As Roy T. Bennett once said: "Your hardest times often lead to the greatest moments of your life. Keep going. Tough situations build strong people in the end."

———

On one final note in this chapter on Endurance. Let me share another story about a young man that has had to endure the endurance event of a lifetime. I've had the pleasure of witnessing and having a front row seat to his amazing endurance and he's an inspiration for everyone in his world.

Seth's mother, Becky, was a rock star to him and vice versa. Becky was beautiful, healthy and had just had a baby, Ethan, Seth's brother. Becky contracted non-Hodgkin's lymphoma. What we later learned about this insidious disease, Diffuse Large B Cell Lymphoma (DLBCL), is that it is the most common type of non-Hodgkin Lymphoma. It is an aggressive cancer. However, 3 out of 4 are disease free after treatment and about half are cured, according to WebMD[7vii].

We thought Becky had beat it. Unfortunately, it came roaring back. By the time we got her to the hospital in Chesapeake, the tumor was almost choking her to death. We learned that the diagnosis is both complex and critically important and can prove difficult. It is important because the diagnosis steers you to the treatment plan. We felt we had lost time with Becky but also thought we had it under control. We learned that this disease has amazingly superhuman endurance. Mary, my significant other (Becky's mother and Seth's grandmother) and I often wondered, with the army of doctors and family fighting this disease, where it got its energy from. We finally realized that the disease's ultimate goal was to kill its host in heartbreaking fashion.

This is the shortened version of this story. The disease ultimately 'won' and took Becky from us, leaving Seth, Ethan, Mary and family behind to attempt to pick up the pieces. In my opinion though, cancer may win a battle, but God always wins the war. I know Becky is now a cheerleader for Mary and Seth and Ethan and the family from her beautiful seat up in Heaven.

Seth was ten years old and Ethan was two when they lost their beautiful mother. To add to this devastating tragedy, Seth had been diagnosed when he was two years old with Cystic Fibrosis, a genetic disease, meaning it is caused by a person's genes. It affects the glands that produce mucus and sweat, causing mucus to become thick and sticky. As the mucus builds up, it can block airways in the lungs. This makes it increasingly difficult to breathe. Mucus buildup also makes it easier for bacteria to grow. This can cause frequent infections in the lungs.

While major strides have been made in fighting this insidious disease, the average life span is only thirty-seven years.

So, two major strikes against this young man. Most adults I know would have folded. But if you meet Seth, he always has a smile on his face, he's always finding the rainbow, the bright spot, the silver lining. I've made the comment before that if 20% of the adults in my world had the same kind of attitude Seth has, with what he has to face daily, the treatment regime (now as a teenager) and having lost his Mom, well, the world would be a much better place, and that's putting it mildly.

Yes, Endurance Athletes come in all shapes and sizes and have all kinds of differing obstacles. All humbling to me and the least I can do is lend a helping hand when I'm able and to give every day my absolute best, to endure in life and help others endure and hopefully even better, to overcome.

WHEN THESE GUYS SHOW UP

There are people in this industry that have an innate ability to root out a deal, an intuitive sense that the market is shifting.

Some people call these folks *flippers*, but for me it is more than that. A flip is essentially purchasing a property with the idea of turning it (selling it again) in a short amount of time for a profit.

Coming into the subprime market in the 2003 through 2007 period, I had a front row seat to a few such people. This was my first exposure to it, so I had no idea about the ride in which I was about to embark.

I'll give you two examples of flippers that I worked with during the long war here. I have changed the names to protect the innocent. Both of these gentlemen were eminently honest with me (and for all I could tell, with others), never did anything other than follow through on their word and put a lot of money in my and my family's pockets because of their skill.

One of the two got hurt because he did not get out in time. One of them did very well. We shall refer to them as Jack Cargile and Frank Camden.

When the Jacks and Franks show up, look out! The market is turning!

These are opportunistic buyers that seem to have a sixth sense about where things are going. The rest of us sit there and watch in awe or horror at their success or the ensuing train wreck. A few make money, many get crushed. I tried my hand at it, got lucky a few times on some small deals and, fortunately, had a few in my "inner circle" who waved me off of some that would have bankrupted me (us).

The long war, 2006 to 2012 crushed many would-be flippers, otherwise known as speculators. Let me say this as my strong opinion:

If you buy real estate for anything other than income stream, i.e. an income-producing property (for commercial real estate) or to live in or enjoy (for residential real estate), and you are simply betting on future price appreciation so you can sell it and make a profit at some future date, you are *speculating.*

Speculation in any industry, whether real estate, the stock and bond markets, futures markets, etc. is a very risky game and not for the faint of heart. If you are out there doing that, you are running with the *big girls and boys.* You are swimming with the whales and you'd better hope one doesn't roll over on you, if even by accident, and crush you.

MY FIRST RESIDENTIAL SALE - 140 STUART AVENUE, SOUTHPORT, NC

When I joined Southport Realty, the founder, Mary Anne Russ, told me due to the typical shorter sale cycle (as compared to the typical longer sales cycle of commercial real estate), I would need to do some residential work to feed the family, so she initially had me working the duty desk.

My first listing and sale was right in the heart of Southport: 140 Stuart Ave. *What a rush!* I got both sides of the transaction (meaning I represented both buyer and seller, in North Carolina, we call that 'dual agency') and put a little over $6000 in my pocket.

This is pretty cool. I sure wouldn't mind doing this over and over again.

Some people outside our industry do not get how hard real estate agents work for their fee. They also don't understand that there is typically a split, where the agent shares a significant portion of their fee with "the house", the firm where they hang their real estate license. I can tell you from experience: most agents earn every penny of their income. Deals can fall apart for any or no reason and most real estate agents only get paid if the deal closes.

Working in the residential world helped me later when I moved full time to the commercial side of our business. I then had a solid feel for what folks are looking for and the dynamic between rooftop growth (residential real estate) and the commercial real estate sector.

It also helped me when I began brokering larger land transactions for residential developments; specifically, what many residential buyers were seeking. I look back fondly on many of the relationships I formed on the residential side of the business, both with clients and with other brokers.

WHEN DUTY CALLS

The phone rang in the Southport Realty office late Sunday afternoon when I was *on duty*, meaning it was my time to cover the office which is how many firms operate: its a *win/win*. It helps the firm keep their staff overhead low and it gives the brokers a chance to get sales leads for people seeking to purchase or list their property. I gave the phone my "hairy eyebrow look." I was whipped from a long weekend of working and was ready to go home for the evening and have Sunday dinner with my family. When you work for yourself, you quickly see that Saturdays and Sundays are more often than not workdays also.

The calm, quiet voice on the other end of the phone explained that he was Jack Cargile and wanted to see the Yaupon Pier, located on Oak Island, that my colleague Kim Anne Russ (friend and future business partner) had for sale.

I was now in the business of "eating what I killed", which means I was only getting paid when a deal closes, so I packed up my car and headed from Southport, over the bridge to Oak Island.

I met Jack at the corner of 58th St. and Oak Island Drive. He was driving an old older gray Buick that was in decent shape and had two little yappy dogs with him that jumped out of the car to come greet me.

I love dogs. I remember one little guy was named Pierre, but cannot recall the other one's name. I recall thinking, "Oh brother, what have I done, this is going to be a major waste of time."

This true story emphasized for me the old axiom of 'never judging a book by its cover' that my parents used to (gently) beat me over the head with. Over the next several years, Jack and I did quite a bit of business together, and it was never a waste of time. On the contrary, it was actually very lucrative for my family and me.

As it turns out, Jack was a major apartment developer out of the Raleigh market, and he also owned a logistics company (Jack is featured as Exhibit A when I talk later on about the importance of diversification and alternate income streams as a hedge against the cyclical and often fickle real estate market). Jack never let me down, never did anything dishonest, was always a man of his word, had a nose for a deal and a feel for upward price appreciation.

I'm not a surfer but having the privilege of proudly living for a long period of time in what I consider to be the best coastal region in the world, I've been around enough surfers to know the good ones have a feel, a sixth sense, for when the big wave is coming and when to get ready for it. That was Jack. But his sixth sense was related to real estate waves.

A FORESHADOWING

We put the pier under contract and Jack tried to make it work, spending a significant amount of money on due diligence. This is the initial part of a contract period where the buyer moves forward to determine whether or not she or he can do what they want to do with the property. This often means spending money on surveys, environmental assessment and impact, what the building envelope would be, since he wanted to convert the site to a small multi-unit residential complex. We look at the subject of due diligence in more detail in the chapter titled "Training."

Unfortunately, by the time we figured out the setback requirements and available footprint to build, after adhering to CAMA (Coastal Area Management Act)[8viii] requirements, and the building pad that would remain after taking those into account, the project was simply not financially feasible for him, so we pulled the plug, to the dismay of the seller. Easy come, easy go in this business.

Having passed on the Yaupon pier, we moved on to other projects.

The following is a good example of a foreshadowing of things to come, a great example of an instance where I actually thought this period of time was *normal* and everybody was doing it, but later realized it was *definitely not normal.*

WHEN STANDING ON THE BEACH, IF YOU LOOK OUT AND SEE A TSUNAMI ON THE HORIZON, THE TIME TO RUN HAS LONG SINCE PASSED... YOU BETTER BE A STRONG SWIMMER.

WEST BEACH DRIVE

Nice address, nice plot of dirt...

I closed quite a few deals for Jack, chasing several what I call "elephants" (large pieces of real estate that can really hurt the buyer if not turned over successfully, based on their goals) but most of them were smaller deals.

The following deal stuck out to me as a foreshadowing of things to come...

We had spotted the lot on West Beach Drive on Oak Island that my colleague Tricia had for sale. It was 50 feet wide by 150 feet deep or 0.17 acres. In another words, a typical tiny beach-community size lot, where one would build a home on pilings, just in case a large storm came around. Tricia represented a gentleman by the name of Milton, who had purchased the lot in October 2003 for $150,000.

The lot was one street back from what is considered oceanfront. You could see the ocean from this lot. I love it out there. I used to joke that the second row was eventually going to become oceanfront, which I guess, in the overall scheme of things and given the direction of climate change, may or may not come true at some point – depending on which expert is talking.

Having lived at the coast full time for 12 years and part time now, my respect for Momma Nature has gone up exponentially. And having owned oceanfront property, I am now well satisfied to be a few rows back with easy access to the ocean, and truly have no interest in owning an oceanfront property.

We experienced two Category 1 hurricanes our first two years living at the coast. I wish you could have seen my two son's eyes, they were golf ball wide when it seemed like a giant was trying to rip the roof off our home. Our rule of thumb quickly became "Cat

2 or higher we go inland!" I have friends and know of others who would not own anything other than oceanfront property — not me. Not good or bad, to me it's simply a function of two factors: 1-risk tolerance and 2- preference.

The lot on West Beach Drive was for sale because Milton, Tricia's client, was a flipper. We closed on that lot in May 2004 for $350,000.

Not a bad pay day in a short amount of time for Milton.

Jack had building plans put together for a nice home to go on the lot, but immediately had me put it back on the market for $550,000. I wondered why he would do this, but I followed orders. A year later, we closed at his asking price.

Not a bad pay day in a short amount of time for Jack, and now me.

So, from 2003 at $150,000 that lot magically appreciated to $550,000 in 2005.

To help you get the full picture of what happened with this piece of property over several years, the following table from the Brunswick County appraisal card (all public record) highlights the sales history of this particular piece of land (Brunswick County Register of deeds).

SALES DATA*							
OFF. RECORD BOOK PAGE	DATE MO	YR	DEED TYPE	Q/U	V/I	INDICATE SALES PRICE	
	3	2018	GW*	Q	I	675000	
	1	2008	FC*	U	V	378000	Lot foreclosed
	5	2005	WD	U	V	550000	Jack sells
	5	2004	WD	Q	V	350000	Jack purchases
	10	2003	WD	Q	V	150000	Milton purchases

*Brunswick Co. Register of Deeds

If you start from the bottom of the table and work your way up, you can see:

- October 2003: Milton purchases the lot for $150,000
- May 2004: Milton sells to my client Jack for $350,000 (Note: this is only 7 months after Milton purchased)
- May 2005: Jack sells the lot for $550,000
- January 2008: Lot is foreclosed for $378,000

My client was incredulous when he found out what Milton had purchased the lot seven months prior to his purchasing it. Some things just aren't right, and in Jack's mind that wasn't right. But he wouldn't let that get in the way of what was in front of him for a relatively easy days' work.

Take this one example and multiply it across the real estate landscape in southeastern North Carolina and you can see why I called southeastern NC *the land of the modern day land gold rush*, and why I say *I had no idea what was coming.* The tsunami was out there, and we were all soon to be swimming in it. Some surfed it successfully.

This is why, when back in 2015, I first heard the term 'flip' again after not hearing it for a very long time, it made me shutter.

The other client of mine I mentioned, Frank, would often joke:

Q: How do you become a millionaire?

A: Buy two lots in the wooded section of Oak Island for $50,000 and wait a few years.

His prediction was headed in the right direction, but unfortunately for Frank and many others who got caught holding the bag, in this market, these lots would eventually peak at around $200,000, and then the *defecation would truly hit the oscillator.*

Fortunately and then unfortunately, I brokered for a good client and friend, who actually built my home in Southport, his purchase of two lots in the wooded section for right around $200,000. His name was Jim. Jim got caught up in the frenzy of a submarket directly across the Cape Fear River from Southport, Carolina, and Kure beaches. He purchased some lots there (I did not broker for him), built a few spec homes that never sold, and then things went sideways and downhill sharply. You can probably guess the rest of the story, and it was not good. He ended up moving back to the greater Raleigh market. "Helping" him buy those two lots in the wooded section at the peak was not one of my finer moments.

Jim had a Wake Forest law degree and was an exceptionally talented builder.

This is why I say quite a few people much smarter than me got caught up in what a mortgage broker friend of mine and client coined "the silly season." It is a term I use from time to time as well when referring to it. Although admittedly, people going bust or bankrupt was not "silly", it is and was sad to me.

Thankfully, this market has since stabilized and recovered nicely since the "silly season" and Brunswick County, due to its amazing quality of life, is consistently one of the top growth counties in the country. During the "silly season", the long war, it was a brutal and often harrowing roller coaster ride for many.

When the spigot of people pouring in from the northeast dried up, when they could no longer sell their homes and relocate south because the market had turned there, too, the merry go round stopped and a lot of people were caught in difficult situations. North Carolina in general benefits significantly from its low cost of living and its quality of life. It is a major net "importer" of people from all over the country, a function of shifting demographic patterns.

You may have heard about the "sunbelt" – well, southeastern North Carolina is right in the heart of it. With close proximity to the town of Wilmington, an awesome coastal city that is home to the University of North Carolina Wilmington and a great airport that can get you just about anywhere you want to go are two of many other attributes. When visiting there, you quickly come to understand why there is such growth. Brunswick County is bordered by New Hanover County (Wilmington, North Carolina) to the north and Horry County, South Carolina (Myrtle Beach aka "the Grand Strand") to the south. Brunswick County is sometimes referred to as "Grand Strand North" and has a ton of truly diverse water features, awesome rivers, the Atlantic Ocean, and lots of golf courses.

The above is key to understanding why the area experienced such overheated and exaggerated upward price pressure in the run up to the Great Recession. New Hanover and Horry Counties pushed toward one another, creating the upward "squeeze" on demand for Brunswick County. The long war exacerbated it and it went nuclear.

The West Beach Drive flip was small potatoes for me, compared to what was coming. The chasing of land deals, the breathtaking run up – I got to be almost numb on the "doubling" that seemed to be occurring in the crazy run up of land prices. At times, banks were making 100% and 120% land loans. (exceedingly rare, and in hindsight, not wise.).

I had a friend, a seasoned real estate veteran, once tell me: "Pete, it was crazy, at one point, when I went in to ask for a loan, the banks would ask me for my financial statements, my income for the previous three years, and just about every other detail under the sun – and would want collateral, my first-born child, my left arm, etc. Overnight, that all went way away, and they would say, "Nah, forget about all that, we don't need any of that anymore. How much do you want your loan to be?"

My friend was joking about the first-born child and his left arm to make a point with me. Like a light switch, it seemed overnight, the handling of real estate loans had just flipped.

Later, when I started appraising land tracts in that post-2012 time period, some of those same land tracts that in 2006 to 2008 had sold for four, five or six million dollars, we were placing liquidation values on for $500,000 or $600,000. Ouch.

For me it redefined the terms easy come, easy go, pigs get fat - hogs get slaughtered, what goes up must come down and a whole host of others... I coined my own term, and I'm sure I'm not the first, but I started calling it "flipping the elephants." It got to be where we were flipping small properties, and then I started hearing about much larger properties being flipped. Those properties are the "elephants" and boy, when they landed, they landed hard and people would often get hurt (financially).

The following is a visual since some of us are visual learners. Again, in this case, the elephant represents real estate. Please note that in my concept, the real estate elephant never gets hurt... but if not "flipped successfully" the people involved can, and often do, get hurt financially...

Don't be this Guy

Moral of this story? Be careful when "flipping elephants."

I hope this image sticks with you the next time you hear the word "flip" or are considering do so yourself.

Some, like Frank C, let greed take them over. At times, I thought it drove him mad. I had some relatively inexpensive vacant land lots on the market in a development called River Run Plantation. Frank once belted out, "I want to buy it all, GD it!" I saw crazy in his eyes...

When I look back, I realize it was more greed than crazy. There were times he would be laughing almost like a mad scientist when he was signing an earnest money check, because he knew he would be flipping that $11,000 lot into a $30,000 lot.

Unfortunately, Frank turned out to be our smiling stick figure and got crushed.

Later in the book, in the chapter titled "Training", I discuss the Cypress Tract. The story of an unsuccessful "elephant flip" that actually later turns into an opportunity for one of my clients.

WHEN THE JACKS AND FRANKS SHOW UP, IT'S TIME
TO LOOK OUT FROM THE BEACH TO SEE IF YOU
SEE THE TSUNAMI CRESTING THE HORIZON...

CHAPTER 6

THE ABYSS AND RUNNING THROUGH VALLEYS

"SEPTEMBER AND OCTOBER 2008 WAS THE WORST FINANCIAL CRISIS IN GLOBAL HISTORY, INCLUDING THE GREAT DEPRESSION..."

--BEN BERNANKE, CHAIR OF THE FEDERAL RESERVE, 2006-2014

2008 was a paradox: a crappy year, yet a good year for me.

If my father, who was also one of my best friends, hadn't passed away unexpectedly on his birthday, March 17, 2008, an Italian American who came in to this world on St. Patty's Day and went out on St. Patty's Day, I think the financial crash of September 29, 2008 might have done him in.

His net worth was more than cut in half. Being the former banker, he was heavily tied into local bank stocks. Fortunately, our investment adviser and family friend, Paul Mayeux, had waved us out of some of those stocks and moved us into 'flex funds' for my Mom and Dad's estate.

We woke up that morning and called Dad to sing him a happy birthday. I was in Southport and heading to Charlotte later that day for the International Council of Shopping Centers (ICSC) Ideas Regional conference, and to take him to birthday dinner.

Looking back, I'm grateful we called. As I was pulling out of my driveway late that morning, I got the call from my sister Kathleen, she had gotten word that "something wasn't right with Dad." Twenty minutes into my trip, my mobile phone rang. This time it was my Mom: *"Son, Dad didn't make it..."* She was stunned. I could hear the confusion and disbelief in her tone.

April 15, 2001 was my first major wake up call, losing Jeff -- now this. *Nothing, No Day, No One ever taken for granted.*

———

Being the boy from Harrison NJ, Dad had a great banking career and he was a quick study in the world of finance and asset-based lending.

While at Avery Dennison, I was in New York City in the spring of 2000 for some meetings and to visit a contractor manufacturing operation outside of Newark. I also wanted to pop in to see where Dad had been raised in Harrison, prior to moving to Woodbridge, NJ. I had visited the latter location often as a child to see my grandparents and my Aunt Debbie (Dad's younger sister).

This is the note I wrote to my Mom and Dad after first visiting my Dad's hometown of Harrison, NJ:

Subj:	**Harrison**
Date:	2/13/01 9:43:25 PM Eastern Standard Time
From:	Pawfran
To:	Popfran, Pfrandano

Mom and Dad,

I think my experience this week was God was letting me know that I was taking things for granted (as he likes to do from time to time - which by the way I appreciate).

I think - as I was half heartedly joking about the place I was visiting with my colleague, I knew there was a certain "strangeness" to the whole experience - like I was actually closer to "this place" than I could ever possibly imagine. I bet God was smiling down on me yesterday and today (as were my grandparents) as I was laying into *this place* and thinking "boy - you have no idea how close you are to *this place*". And boy - were they right!

Really a neat and strange experience. One that I will never forget. The big guy was spinning a tale - and he knew I was going to find out (or be reminded) about my roots. As I was walking around Harrison yesterday - with this strange sense of familiarity, I was making fun of a place I was a bit afraid of - probably fairly close to the feeling dad gets sometimes (especially when he returns north) - almost a type of defense mechanism that pops up - we make fun of it because we don't want to end up back there - and even though I was never "there" - if my family was there - I was there. Grandpa made the move in the right direction, and Dad took it and ran with it. However, it's good to know about part of our origin. No - I wouldn't want to live there - but I appreciate Harrison tonight more than I ever thought I could!

I love you guys very much - we sure are blessed.

HAPPY VALENTINES DAY!
Love your son,
Pete

Dad and the former Chairman of NCNB[9ix], Mr. Hugh McColl, used to play racquetball together at the Dowd YMCA in Charlotte way back in the day. The word was, Dad was very good at the sport, really any sport involving a racquet. Mr. McColl was apparently not as good and the humorous rumor my Dad liked to spread was that if Mr. McColl got down or behind, he would start aiming for your backside, laughing wickedly while doing so. Dad would come home with welts on his backside. No doubt, in Mr. McColl's defense, this was Dad's side of the story and, most likely, grew over the years via the tool of embellishment. Akin to the fisherman who catches the catfish and, ten years later, that catfish has morphed into a record setting tuna. It was legend and lore around our family, so we went with it.

Ironically, Mr. McColl was our commencement speaker at UNC Chapel Hill for our graduation in May, 1990. Dad left NCNB in the mid-70's because of a boss, a guy named Dan Crowle as he and Mr. Crowle did not see eye to eye management philosophy-wise.

It was a first of many lessons in life for me.

Not long after Dad left to open up Bank of New England's southeastern operation (Charlotte to the southern tip of Florida), Mr. Crowle was fired from NCNB.

Dad would always tell me later: "Son, never leave a job because of one person. That person may get promoted, moved laterally or fired."

Although he had a great career in banking, I think Dad regretted leaving NCNB. He definitely had to run the gauntlet of the banking industry consolidation. Dad took a lot of people from NCNB with him to Bank of New England, so much so that Mr. McColl called the CEO of Bank of New England and told him pointedly: "Tell Frandano to cease and desist..."

It pissed Dad off, but he did.

Later in life, according to Pop (what I called my dad on occasion), he and Mr. McColl made amends. Below is a letter Mr. McColl wrote to my dad in reply to a note Dad had sent him informing him of the National Bank of Canada's acquisition of Bank of New England, and also highlighting his commencement speech to us that day in May, 1990 in Chapel Hill:

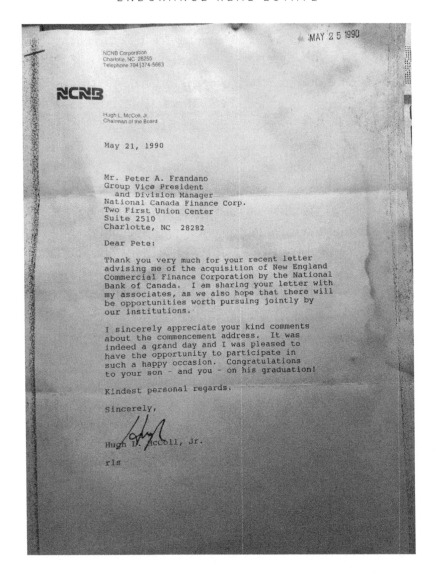

During my tenure at Wake Forest's business school, I wrote a white paper about how the war between NationsBank and First Union (later Wachovia, then Wells Fargo) had helped grow my hometown, Charlotte. And grow it did!

March 17, 2008: Just like that, Dad was gone. 64 years old.

Nothing, No Day, No One ever taken for granted.

I don't remember much of my trip to Charlotte that day, other than Father Barry calling me from Southport while I was en route. His call was like a bucket of cold water in my face, for sure. He had gotten word of what happened, found out I was on the road to Charlotte and was calling me to wake me up. Looking back, I believe God had him call me.

He may have saved my life that day as I was in a major fog during my drive and his call woke me up and snapped me out of it.

The day of my dad's passing, after we had called him and sung him happy birthday, he headed out to a golf course called Birkdale, one of the courses he loved to play. Truth be told, any golf course was where Dad wanted to be, although he would be quick to complain about conditions if they were not up to "par" or what he thought should be "par", no pun intended.

Dad and I had made many wonderful memories on the golf course together.

One of the highlights of my 'golf career' with him was when he and Mom had to go to a wedding in Jacksonville, Florida. They invited me to fly in and stayed with them at the then Marriott at Ponte Vedra.

For you golfers in the world, you know that this is home to the Tournament Players Club, Sawgrass, and also the PGA's Headquarters. But more importantly to us, the home of the famous #17 Island hole! Dad and I both parred the Island hole that day, from the back tees. Dad from the front pot bunker, me putting it squarely on the green. You would have thought the two of us had scored 17 touchdowns! We were both on cloud Ten. It was an amazing day and was going to be the first of many of the Top 50 we had promised each other we were going to play together.

Oh no, Dad. Not now. So much left to do!

It's interesting how we try to rationalize how our loved ones go. Later, we would say, and still do, "How freakin' cool if you have to go, to go *that* way?"

I like to think Dad was saved from *the Abyss,* spared from having to ride out the next several years that were coming with the Great Recession. From time to time, I would give him a bit of a hard time, as in his retirement years he began watching CNBC a lot. I joked with him that he had become a "day trader" and his mood at the end of the day would rise and fall with the stock market that day. Of course, this was an exaggeration, but not too far off point. I selfishly wanted him here with us but looking back, I don't think the pain of the coming years, truly kicked off by the Lehman Brothers collapse and the overall market collapse soon after, would have suited him well.

And yes, if I had to pick a way to go, to leave this earth, that would be it: *doing something I love to do.*

The morning of, when things were "hitting the fan" right in front of us, my sister, Mom and I were all confused during the "fog of war" of the moment. We didn't know what was going on or who Dad was playing golf with that day...

I called my Dad's best buddy, Fred Dula, who is a dear family friend and has become over the years an uncle-like figure to Seth. Fred and I continue to organize breakfasts with the "Breakfast Club" and Fred calls it "Breakfast with Pete", which warms my heart. Getting together with these guys periodically is an absolute joy for me. I know Dad is smiling down on us every time (and telling us not to take all of the strawberry jelly, an inside joke - Dad loved to hoard the strawberry jelly).

One of my lessons learned from going through this with Dad and I hope it helps someone reading this book: You have to follow doctor's orders and adhere to your "walking program" immediately after any bypass surgery to keep plaque from building up which can cause clots.

Dad had double bypass surgery about two years prior to his massive heart attack. He went down on the courts one day playing tennis at his tennis club, Olde Providence Racquet Club where we were members for quite a few years.

The lesson learned resulting from our experience with my Dad's bypass surgery...

After a heart patient has bypass surgery, he/she needs to adhere to the walking program. That is, they walk some every day and this walking apparently helps prevent the plaque from building up in their legs and keeps the circulation up. We were not militant enough about this program and I was ignorant to it. Mom was not willing to be the bad guy with Dad, who could sometimes get a bit grumpy.

So, what we think happened is that plaque built up in Dad's calf areas or elsewhere and on his birthday, on the practice range at Birkdale golf course that day in Huntersville, NC, a piece of that plaque dislodged at that was it.

One of the saddest moments of my life was arriving at that hospital, then known as "Presby Huntersville", with Mom and Sis waiting out front, then going in and spending one last moment with Dad in a little waiting room.

Later, with the help of my awesome Uncle Joe (Pool), going back to Birkdale and thanking the Birkdale team and collecting Dad's car and golf clubs.

As Father Richard Bellow said at Dad's service, and I like to think it is true, "Pete took one last swing, dropped his club and walked into God's arms..." Yes, not a bad way to go indeed.

If you have loved ones who have gone through bypass surgery, please, get militant on them and make them follow doctor's orders and walk!

The club was kind enough to extend a one-year courtesy membership to Mom after Dad passed, and I used it for their gym when I would come into town. They also gave us his locker plaque which had his name on it: Pete A. Frandano, Locker #185. I was touched at how the entire community reacted around Dad's passing.

My Sister and I eulogized him at the service for him at St. Gabriel Catholic Church.

Dad's favorite ice cream was Butter Pecan. One time, not long after Dad had passed, my youngest son, Joe, then 6 years old, and I went to the little ice cream shop there in Southport. Joe ordered Butter Pecan, which he had never done before.

I said, "Joe, why did you order Butter Pecan ice cream?"

He looked at me with his blue eyes, a little twinkle in them, and said, "Ha Haaa, I stole Grandpa's favorite flavor!"

In my little talk at Dad's service, I ended by saying and *"You will always be the butter pecan ice cream of our lives..."*

During the family get together the night of his service, we gathered for a big Italian meal over on Morehead street at a restaurant that is no longer there. My boys and their Mom had left to go back south and east, but I stayed behind to help Mom.

As everyone was eating and being somewhat festive after a very long and emotional day, I remember sinking down into my loneliness, thinking about the best friend I had just lost. My phone rang. It was Pamela's number.

I answered the phone: "Hey..."

It was actually Joe on the phone, who had never called me before.

"Joe, where are you, buddy?"

He whispered, "I'm up in myyyyy room..."

"Where's Mommy?"

He whispered, "Downstairs..."

"Why are you calling me?"

"Because... I just wanted to ... and I wanted to say goodnight..."

"Joe, did you know that I needed you to call me right now, at this very minute?"

And he said, "Yes, Daddy..."

I told him how much I appreciated him calling me and we told each other goodnight and that we loved each other, and I told him to get some good sleep.

I don't believe in coincidences.

At the dinner that night, I had told my family that I was going to put off pursuing the completion of my CCIM Designation. My Uncle Anthony, leveling his eyes across the table, said, 'Finish it...your Father wouldn't want you to put it off. *Finish it.*"

And I made up my mind that night I would do so.

So that October, I was in Chicago and sitting for that Hellish exam. We would find out the results, whether we had passed or failed early that evening. I remember being told that a phone call after the six-hour exam was a bad thing: it meant "retake" the exam. I had spread the word, no phone calls. So, when my assistant called me as I was on the treadmill of the Chicago Hilton, I about went right off the back...

"Darn it, Marlette!"

She laughed. There was a client issue.

Turns out I passed the exam, somehow. As hard as any exam I had taken at the Graduate Business School at Wake Forest University. At 5 hours and 45 minutes, I stood up and, in that room of 350 people, about half the room was still sitting.

The picture here is one my Sis posted in a scrap book that year with a nice message from her and a family friend, That's her finger (a selfie of me somewhat in shock and still somewhat coherent.).

CCIM pin and hat! Pete's self-portrait taken hours after the ceremony. He calls it "cheesy," I say it's "relieved and exhausted!")

------ Original Message ------
From : Jim Perkins
To : pfrandano@southport-realty.com
Subject : Re: Pete, Jr

Pete:
Congratulations on passing the CCIM test!!! I am sure it is a big relief after all the time and effort put into accomplishing the task. Your Dad would be very proud as we all are of you.

Jim

Not long after that, we also celebrated my Uncle Paul's (Frandano) retirement celebration from 32 years of distinguished service with the Central Intelligence Agency. The entire family had the opportunity, through clearance, to go into CIA HQ in Langley HQ.

My uncle has been and is a hero to me. He served his country with great honor and distinction. So much so that he was recognized with the Distinguished Career Intelligence Metal, which is awarded by the Central Intelligence Agency for an individual's cumulative record of service, reflecting a pattern of increasing levels of responsibility or increasingly strategic impact and with *distinctly exceptional* achievements that constitute a major contribution to the mission of the Agency.

If that doesn't say it all I don't know what does?

My uncle also know how much I thought of the former DCI (Director of Central Intelligence) George Tenet, who served under both President's George W. Bush and Bill Clinton.

Standing in a circle with my uncle directly across from me, surrounded by some of his colleagues and family, a hand came up on my right shoulder. I looked, saw the hand there, looked back to my left, and there was Mr. Tenet, smiling at me.

My uncle said, "George, this is my nephew, Peter Frandano..." He cut his eyes at me, then back to Mr. Tenet with a smile on this face. I guess he could see my reaction.

Mr. Tenet handled it nicely and with a big smile said "Peter, they love your uncle inside these walls..." The implication being "outside of these walls, in countries far away, not so much..."

I admit I about passed out and never wanted to wash my right shoulder again. Learning that day, that the stars on the CIA Memorial Wall represented the CIA Agency members who died in the line of service is something I will never forget. It was a humbling day for me all the way around.

My Uncle Paul on receiving the Distinguished Career Intelligence Metal

The Family at CIA HQ on my Uncle's big day with Uncle in the Middle
(holding his granddaughter, Gabriella - boy time flies!)

My Uncle and I (when I had that pesky hair)
in front of the CIA Memorial Wall - on his big day

Uncle Paul knocked his speech out of the park. Driving down the George Washington Parkway, I was in the back seat with him. Aunt Denise was driving, one of my cousins was in the front passenger seat. I told him how proud we all were of him. I also told him how his older brother would be super proud of him.

Uncle Paul said, "Yes, yes, my big brother would have thoroughly enjoyed this..."

Indeed, he would have, and I have no doubt he did enjoy it from his awesome seat! It was truly a glorious day.

Those two events, my earning of the coveted CCIM designation and my awesome uncle's celebration and pinning ceremony turned an otherwise crap year into a great finish.

Prior to jumping into real estate, I had never really had a "career setback." I had never experienced a long period of falling down, stumbling or any type of financial hazard. The Corporate world and b-school never prepared me for the magnitude of the financial crash that came with the Great Recession.

I've looked into the abyss and it's a scary, lonely, humbling sight.

An "abyss" is defined by Merriam Webster as "an immeasurably deep gulf or great space."

How does it feel when your prayer is not selfishly about yourself: "Dear Lord, please don't let me go broke."...but more like "Dear Lord, please don't let me become a burden to others, I have so many people depending on me, please don't let me go down."?

How does it feel when at some point, you wake up and realize you are worth more dead than alive to those around you, at least in pure dollar terms?

A mentor of mine, T. Cooper James, who is a successful developer of grocery-anchored centers and other projects, gave me this bumper sticker as I was leaving the Corporate World and heading into the real estate world:

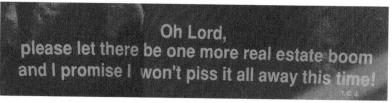

Oh Lord, please let there be one more real estate boom and I promise I won't piss it all away this time!

Amen, Cooper...

Mary Anne Russ came to me in the fall of 2006 and said, "Young man, I've been in this business almost as long as you have been alive. John (her husband) and I want to travel some and start winding things down. Do you want to purchase the company? You and Pamela will own half and Kim Anne (her daughter) will own the other half?"

We were in. The next few years, due to no one's fault, would be a fight for our financial survival. The music had stopped and there weren't enough seats at the table. Not enough lifejackets and lifeboats to go around.

We had no idea what hit us and thought we had gone stupid overnight.

We dove into expense control, working to sell the house we had built, consolidating, all the while growing our property management business. People could not sell their homes, so we helped rent them out, which kept some out of the financial abyss.

At one point, yes, I was staring directly into the financial abyss. I was asking myself repeatedly what I had done to both myself and my family.

Through this all, I found my faith again. I'm certainly not going to "preach" to you. And I'm no pastor or rabbi. What makes me different than your priest or your rabbi or your pastor? I am not one. I'm the one who has been preached to – I am the "fallen." The prodigal son.

I woke up one day and realized that the Ultimate Lender had canceled my debt. I had not earned it, I didn't 'deserve it' and there wasn't anything I could do about it.

A good friend and an early mentor of mine, Tony Rickard, CCIM was active in prison ministry. We lost Tony far too young due to pancreatic cancer. He was highly active in a group called "The Victory Junction Gang", a camp for kids who come from less than fortunate circumstances. He was also highly active in Prison Ministry. I understand that those prisoners would ask for Tony by name: "Where's Tony?" "When is Tony coming?" I believe it because I was asking for him, too, and I wasn't even in a physical prison. Tony was a bright shining light for everyone he touched, *and he lived it.*

At his service, a gentleman sang a beautiful rendition of a song I had never heard before: "I will Rise." I know that song was a gift from Tony to all of us that day.

I hear that things work out the way they are supposed to – I have faith that they do and am convinced that God does truly make "beauty from ashes."

I don't think He was finished with me yet. Again, I'm not preaching, just sharing.

So, how does it feel when you feel you may soon be among the hungry or homeless? Maybe you know. I was there at one point. Even though I realize I was lucky to have a safety net.

Those nights you wake in a cold sweat wondering where your next deal is going to come from? Or sit in a parking lot, numb, after you just found out the large deal you were counting on just fell through... And your sons are coming to the car all smiles and get close enough to see your face – and you can't hide it?

I've been in that lonely place. Filled with sleepless nights, gremlins that haunt and not much peace.

I realize someone reading this may be looking into the abyss, may be feeling that they are worthless because they have failed, may be you or someone in your world feels you've reached the bottom and are drowning and there's no way back up. Well, I am here to tell you from personal experience, there is a way back up and you will make it back up.

You're worth a great deal to a great many people and there are others that are willing to help. There are many counting on you to be around and that need you here...

That's not a burden, it's a blessing.

I know what it's like to be in *the Valley of the Shadow of Death*, and it's not a fun place to be. It's a horrible place and things can seem hopeless there. But I've found that there is truth in this phrase:

It's always darkest before the dawn.

If you happen to find yourself there, keep your faith, keep pushing, don't give up, keep fighting..

I believe your next finish line is up ahead.

———

TROUBLED ASSETS, TROUBLED WATERS - A BRIEF PRIMER

"YOU CANNOT FAIL, UNLESS YOU QUIT..."
--ABRAHAM LINCOLN

Given what many of us in the real estate industry went through during the Great Recession and what some are going through now during the COVID-19 Pandemic, I wanted to do something I wish others had done for me on the *front end of my real estate career*: provide an overview, (a primer if you will) of the *troubled assets* segment of our industry. Why? Well, if you are in this business long enough, you will come across a "troubled asset" and will need to either solve the problem for yourself, or help someone else solve their problem. You will find some basic tools, terms and concepts to arm yourself with as you work toward problem solving – for yourself or for someone else. The topic of troubled assets or bankruptcy in the real estate industry or any industry sometimes invokes feelings of fear for obviously reasons, some of which are due to simple lack of understanding; I have often found that a little knowledge with the goal of problem solving can go a long way to putting that fear to rest, so part of my goal in this section is to help lower or remove the "fear factor."

My father was a banker, so I say this with compassion and all due respect: most finance professionals or bankers are competent, honest people. But, as with any industry, there are a few finance professionals and bankers (aka lenders) who want you to think that what they do is really complex, almost magic. *It's not.*

Don't get me wrong, some of these folks have brilliant finance and math minds; however, with some quick research you will see that the terms and process are really not that complex.

If you can gain some understanding of financial processes, learn some of the tools that are available and are familiar with the basic rules of the legal game, if even just the vocabulary and some of what it means, you will be further along than 95% of the general population. And if you are staring into the financial abyss you can quickly learn about actions you can take to protect your situation or benefit your circumstances.

Having said this, I always advise folks who are running through that valley to reach out to experts; legal, financial or otherwise for help. Having the courage to utter the words "I don't know" is often a great first step in the right direction to cross any finish line.

I have found asking for informed help and educating myself to be empowering. Asking questions is not a sign of weakness, it's a sign of strength and of a person who wants all the tools they can get to start problem solving.

As the CEO of You, Inc, one of the best most prudent courses of action you can take is to know when you're back is up against the wall and need outside expertise, another set of eyes on your problem. If you aren't sure, ask the tough questions. You're still the CEO, but don't let your pride, fear, lack of understanding, denial of reality or anything else stand in the way of adding an expert to your team who can help you navigate your situation successfully.

If you think *I don't have the money to add someone to my team*, get creative and consider innovative way to engage with experts, perhaps finding someone who will work on contingency or barter your way into the information you need. Everyone needs something – look for how your expertise can be valuable to others whose help you need. There are, as my grandmother used to say, "all kinds of ways to skin the cat."

When faced with unknowns or situations that might be challenging, I always try to remember this quote from Proverbs 16:18:

"PRIDE GOETH BEFORE DESTRUCTION AND A
HAUGHTY SPIRIT BEFORE A FALL."

I had a friend of mine of mine (Jim S.), who managed a large flagship plant for Sara Lee Knit Products in Winston-Salem tell me that the primary reason he chose to go to business school was because he was "sick of the accountants who seemed to rule his world with their mystic accounting-speak."

Truth be told, we both respected our accounting colleagues, but we were frustrated with our lack of understanding of even the most basic vocabulary in that world. After all, we were operations people, not accountants.

Going to business school and achieving his Master of Business Administration was Jim's way to "learn the language", so that, in his words, he could at least be fluent enough to call "BS" if he felt he needed to.

In my corporate career, doing the b-school thing helped me in that way as well; although, I was fortunate in that most of my accounting teams were very good people, very competent and knew how to "do accounting using Crayola's" for us non-accountants.

I found that the best accountants are those who try to understand the business they were working with and not, as my father would say, "just count the beans." Dad would say that we need accountants because *somebody has to keep score, somebody has to count the beans*. Well, the best accountants are far more than just people who count beans, they are invaluable business partners.

The long war provided me with a crash course in "street finance", loan workout, and a front row seat to debt restructuring. I am by no means an expert on these topics. If this is all new to you, I highly recommend you research your situation thoroughly and consult legal or financial experts.

During the course of my 30+ year career, I have found that understanding the applicable terminology can go a long way toward helping solve a problem.

Below, I've listed some basic terms I think are important to know, based on my experience. They're not in any order, certainly not alphabetical, as this is not meant to be a glossary, but I have tried to place some logic in the sequence if terms are related.

- **Loan Workout** (also called loan modification or even asset resolution): a plan on how to restructure debt in the face of foreclosure
- **Foreclosure:** legal process, where the lender (creditor) attempts to recover the balance of a loan from a borrower, who has stopped making payments to the lender, by forcing the sale of the asset used as the collateral for the loan
- **Short sale:** in real estate, an asset sold for a price less than what is owed
- **Creditor (lender):** someone who is owed something, typically money (from a debtor)
- **Debtor (borrower):** someone who owes something, typically money (to a creditor)
- **Default**: failure to fulfill an obligation: when on a mortgage or loan or credit card payment, i.e. missing a payment.
- **Special Assets (also known as "Troubled Assets"):** in real estate, the word "special" means a payment or two or three have been missed and the person or entity who has missed the payments now has special attention placed on them; most likely a foreclosure sale is in the near future.
- **Bankruptcy - (from Investopedia):**[10x] legal proceeding involving a person or business that is unable to repay outstanding debts. Several types of bankruptcy classifications exist:
  - **Chapter 7** Liquidation Under the Bankruptcy Code (meaning that the company and its assets are sold off, shareholders are wiped out, proceeds go to the creditors)
  - **Chapter 9** Municipality Bankruptcy (e.g. a city or state)
  - **Chapter 11** Reorganization Under the Bankruptcy Code (usually for a corporation or partnership, the reorganization

allows the company to keep running, pay creditors over time, under specific rules and supervision)

- **Chapter 12** Family Farmer Bankruptcy or Family Fisherman Bankruptcy (for a family farmer or family fisherman as defined by bankruptcy code)
- **Chapter 13** Individual Debt Adjustment (also called a wage earner's plan and enables individuals with regular income to develop a plan to repay all or a part of their debt)
- **Chapter 15** Ancillary and Other Cross-Border Cases (added in 2005) to provide a mechanism for disputes involving more than one country

How assets are typically divided up if bankruptcy proceedings take place:

- **Collateral** - something pledged as security for repayment of a loan, to be forfeited in the event of a default (usually the real estate itself)
- **Secured Creditor** - a person or entity that has collateral; least risky loan because of this collateral is "handed over" or forfeited to the lender if foreclosure is executed. A secured creditor is usually the bank
- **Unsecured Creditor** - typically an individual or institution that lends money without obtaining specific assets as collateral; a higher risk loan, as there is no collateral to hand over or forfeit; interest on an unsecured loan is typically higher than on a secured loan
- **Shareholder/Stockholder/Business owner** - the owner; in many cases, these folks get wiped out or paid last if there are any assets left over; the benefits of business ownership = highest risk, highest reward, highest penalty if the defecation hits the oscillator
- **Deficiency judgment** -typically related to a short sale; this is a ruling made by a court against a debtor in default on a secured loan (e.g. a mortgage on a home) indicating that the sale of

the property to pay back the loan was not enough to cover the loan, thus a "deficiency judgment" is a lien levied for future money to be collected. Some folks were doing cartwheels when they were successfully awarded short sales, only to have a turd-in-the-punch-bowl moment when they realized they still had to pay the bank back all the money originally owed. During the downturn, some banks agreed to short sales, then booked deficiency judgments as future receivables. Ouch.

- **Debt restructuring:** process used by companies or individuals to avoid the risk of default on existing debt; could be in the form of lowering interest, an extension of the term of a loan to lower the monthly payment (e.g. moving from a 15 year term to 30 year) or any other negotiated items.

- **Forbearance:** in the real estate world, this means loan payments are postponed but interest typically continues to accrue (build, accumulate).

- **Mortgage**: a debt instrument (loan) secured by collateral, being a real estate asset, that the borrower (debtor) is obligated to pay back.

- **Second mortgage:** a lien taken out against a property that already has a loan on it, thus the term "second." The first mortgage (original mortgage, sometimes called a "senior" mortgage) has first place if the property is foreclosed on. The second mortgage holder gets whatever is left up to their balance. There are also third mortgages. Anything after the first mortgage is considered a junior lien.

- **Lien stripping:** the process of eliminating junior liens during Chapter 13 bankruptcy.

Understanding the basics of the legal tools available to you may prove invaluable. These tools, these "laws" were set up for a reason. A few harsh souls like to cast disparaging names on people who fall behind on payments, but if you are up against it, don't let that get you down. Take bankruptcy, as an example. Think of it as an eject button that you have available to you if your plane is going down.

Live to see another day. Live to cross another finish line.

There are plenty of success stories of people who went into bankruptcy, came out the other end, and ended up doing great things, living prosperous lives, crossing future finish lines. That's one of the many beautiful things about living in this great country, second chances abound.

My short and simple advice to folks is this: if in trouble, communicate early and often -- if possible, communicate before you miss a payment. If you are already kicked into a "special class", then missing a payment is no longer on the table during negotiations, because you have already missed a payment.

I'm not encouraging anyone to miss a payment. If you are communicating early, during negotiations, missing a payment can be a negotiating tool. Most banks are reasonable and want to work with you and do not want to own the asset. They are not in the asset management business (some of my colleagues may disagree with me on this).

Plenty of people smarter than me have, unfortunately, had to declare bankruptcy. While I'm certainly not recommending bankruptcy if you can avoid it, it may be the tool of last resort for you. That is where restructuring debt and negotiation come in to play.

An understanding of the basics may help you or someone else, whether in the field of real estate or in some other business. Understanding these tools and the terminology should be a part of any business *Endurance plan.*

Yes, there will always be the "Judgers", the haters, those who look down their nose at anyone else who may fall on their face, but to those I respectfully remind that a man much greater than all of us once said: *Let he who hath no sin, cast the first stone...*

If you get to the point, and I truly hope you don't, where you are looking into the financial Abyss, be aware that there are people out there that will prey on you. Many companies or people will give the indication they are "there for you", but the hard, cold, insidious truth in some cases is they are not. Instead, *some are there to eat you.*

They will tell you that they will help you wipe out your debt problem. Be aware of circling sharks in these treacherous waters. If you can negotiate early on by yourself, that's great. Do it. It will save time and money. If not and you are unsure, there are others who can help: hire a trusted source if you can, like an attorney or a CPA.

Someone who has one or more of the following sets of letters after their name, who can be a part of your team and help you navigate and steer you toward other competent and trusted experts and professionals:

CRE: The Counselors of Real Estate - https://www.cre.org/
CCIM: Certified Commercial Investment Member - https://www.ccim.com/
CFP: Certified Financial Planner - https://www.cfp.net/
CFA: Certified Financial Analyst - https://www.cfainstitute.org/
MAI: Designated Member of the Appraisal Institute - https://www.appraisalinstitute.org/our-designations/
CPA- Certified Public Accountant - https://www.aicpa.org/

Any competent person with one of the above designations should be able to help you begin the process of navigating your situation and helping you put a basic plan of action in place. They should also be able to recognize when something is outside of their area of expertise and will know how, when and who to reach out to (again, examples would be an attorney, or an accountant/tax adviser).

Getting somebody on your team early, who can run point for you, be a quarterback for you, should be of paramount importance if you get to that point of need (preferably before you get to that point).

All loss is relative and real. I know some who lost $10 million in the Great Recession. I know others who lost far more. I know some who lost far less. It's all relative and real.

"IF YOU'RE GOING THROUGH HELL, KEEP GOING..."
- WINSTON CHURCHILL

The old runner's axiom says:

"IF YOU'RE RUNNING AND YOU LOOK UP AND REALIZE YOU'RE
IN HELL, PUT YOUR HEAD BACK DOWN AND KEEP RUNNING..."

Oh, and please don't spread the word that Pete Frandano was encouraging anyone to declare bankruptcy ... or that I'm giving legal advice. I'm not. For legal advice, please consult your attorney. I'm simply hoping that a basic understanding of some terms, concepts, and fundamental rules of the game will help you or someone you care about put the guard rails up and avoid the abyss.

Reach out for help, it's there. And remember: *There is no shame in that game.* (A quick internet search on President Abraham Lincoln yields a great and breath taking example of failures, second chances and rising from the ashes.).

So: if you find yourself running, look up and realize you're in Hell, put your head back down and keep going ... next peak is up ahead.

My bet is it will be a glorious view for you from up there.

THE AUTHOR ON BIKE STAGE OF BEACH
TO BATTLESHIP TRIATHLON: WILMINGTON, NC

CHAPTER 7

KEEPING IT SIMPLE, STAYING FOCUSED – (CEO OF YOU, INC)

"BREVITY IS THE SOUL OF WIT..."

--WILLIAM SHAKESPEARE

Wow, we sure do make things complicated at times, don't we? Shakespeare had it right when he wrote the above in the play Hamlet.

My boss at Avery Dennison once said under her breath, when talking about a top-notch consulting firm we had hired, "*These guys must get paid by the pound on the written or spoken word...*"

Things, life, business, relationships can be complex, but how do you boil things down to their essence, keep it simple, and get up and get going? Do you overthink your road or run ahead? How do you just put your shoes on and go?

At times, we all suffer from *Paralysis by Analysis* syndrome. I find I am at my best, that I perform best in business, endurance sports or life when I keep things simple, focused and keep "things" uncluttered.

I've seen a common "theme" over the years in both observing and living this idea. Those who survive and thrive have some mechanism, business process or model that generally keeps things simple and focused but also helped them motor through the valleys and run through the business cycle gauntlet.

As a small example, at the height of the downturn, I had previously socked dollars away, had a property management business and an appraisal business to rely on, instead of relying solely on sales when it had essentially dried up. If I hadn't had these cushions in place, I would have been wiped out like so many I knew.

General Patton once said, "*A good plan, violently executed now, is better than a perfect plan next week...*"

Perfection is a good goal, but done is better than perfect. Some would argue "perfectly done" should always be the goal. I'm not so sure I agree with that.

During my time in business school, I remember reading Lee Iacocca's book *Iacocca*. Lee was the auto exec icon who helped save Chrysler, back in the day. At the time, I was feeling all warm and smug about the MBA degree I was working on at Wake Forest, and then I read this (paraphrasing):

"There's no such thing as perfect information ... Having a bunch of MBAs around a table collecting and analyzing data is all well and good, but at some point, someone has to say "enough, it's time to get up and go..."

To me, both Patton and Iacocca are saying much the same thing: *don't over think it, make a well-informed decision -- but act!* There is no such thing as perfect information.

What they both were telling me was: "Don't overthink that CRM system..." "Don't forget to network..." "Don't forget to make that phone call or send that text or email to a client or a friend." "Don't forget to advance the ball every day on your own business..." "Make that new App!" "Create that new business!" "Write your book or that article..." "Keep your eye on *your* ball!"

General Patton and Lee Iacocca are both saying the same thing Shakespeare told all of us when he wrote Hamlet those many years ago: "*Brevity is the Soul of Wit...*"

At times, we also get bogged down due to fear of making mistakes. The message to me also seems to say: It's okay to make mistakes, as long as we don't make the same ones over and over again. I had a boss at Sara Lee once tell me: "Pete, if you aren't making mistakes, you're not doing anything ... I don't mind the mistakes, just try not to repeat the same mistakes." If you are alive and moving forward, you are going to make mistakes. Make honest mistakes, learn from those mistakes, become better because of them and move onto higher ground, to your next finish line. Sometimes, we learn more from our failures than we do our successes.

Most know the famous definition of insanity: *Repeating something over and over again and expecting different results.* Well, how about doing something over and over again and pushing yourself to a higher level because of it? Because it worked and was repeatable and you were able to fine tune it and move to the next level?

We often give up on a routine before its benefits kick in. Have the courage and the guts to stick with *your* system, with your simple but well thought out plan. We all get caught up in chasing the next great idea, the next great system. Take CRM (Customer Relationship Management Software), for example.

When it comes to this topic I saw this following true sequence in what I call a "Dilbert" moment (the awesome cartoon primarily about business by Scott Adams), unfold before me one day while sitting with some of my colleagues:

Tom: So, what CRM software are you using?

Bill: Man, I've tried three in the past four years and the one I found that worked best was APTO. I spent the first three months entering my clients' data. Then, I had several training sessions. I'm pumped as I'm plugging in all of the milestones on a closing I have scheduled, and this thing is auto populating my project plan and making it really easy on me!

Tom: Wow, three months for the data enter?

Bill: They're all like that, they import the data automatically but then you have to go back and clean it, scrub it, make sure it's in the right format to suit the software.

Tom: So, how did you choose the one you are currently using? How is it better than the other two you've used?

Bill: Well, the jury is still out. All I know is that once I get up and rolling, I'm going to have to spend less time managing my process and more time focusing on bringing business through the door.

Tom: Why don't you just use Outlook and Excel? I hear some folks actually make that work and have figured out through some tutorials and YouTube videos how to create a fairly robust CRM process using the tools already available.

Bill: That would be way too easy ... *and easy scares me.*

Dilbert: in my opinion, the best business cartoon ever
Thank you Scott Adams!!

Sometimes we spend so much time getting caught up in the tool of the month, in the example above, the CRM process of the month, that *we forget to work on and in our business.* We are so bogged down getting this new "process" up and running that we've taken *our eye off the ball.*

Gary Keller wrote a book called *The Millionaire Real Estate Agent.* and in this book, he does a good job of outlining a system to help real estate agents create a system to manage their business. He gives you the bones, plus detailed suggestions and plans, and a proven system that works. Some might complain about its complexity, but my suggestion would be to take his system and tailor what will work for your business. You don't have to take all of what he presents and implement it as he outlines, exactly to the letter. If you implement a nugget or two, that's better than what you were doing yesterday.

Additionally, the real estate business can eat you up in overhead so you have to be very careful not to just watch the top line, but also all expenses as well.

Sometimes we get so focused on the top line that we tend to throw good dollars after bad on marketing "schemes" or systems or the latest and greatest gadgets. Be careful with that. It doesn't have to be complex to be good.

Maybe you've heard the saying that *good is the enemy of great?* Well, related to that: overly complex can often be the enemy of top performance.

Implementing a complex process or system can be impressive, but I'm here to say that in most cases, the simple, elegant routine more often than not will win the day.

This is not all-encompassing, of course, and I wouldn't dare try and outline every scenario here, but I will say to use your best judgment on this as you will know if you are heading down the proverbial unproductive rabbit hole. If you're getting *brain damaged (Why is this so complicated?)* over something or sense you are off in a ditch, *you probably are.*

Know enough about yourself to make your system work for you. If you know you are not a detail person and even slightly complex processes get you down or are overwhelming, you can still get the benefits of a more complex system for your business. How? Hire someone or partner to help you implement and maintain that system. Perhaps you can handle the end report compilations or working through the system checkpoints to assess accuracy. Even if it's a short term hire or a training session to help you advance your ball.

A focused hour with a trainer can be time well spent versus you spending six hours banging your head against the wall. The basics always apply, and if you get away from the basics you are asking for trouble or at the very least risk going down the rabbit hole...

Create a plan that works for you and don't over complicate it. Watch your expenses along the way, rely on data to be a guide and a means but not the end, and recognize when you fall into the *paralysis by analysis* hole, so you can pull yourself out!

It's great to be a life-long learner. There is nothing wrong with seeking that "magic bullet", that one extra nugget to propel you ahead. But we need to remind ourselves that there is also today, we already know a great deal and we shouldn't prolong the all-important *execution phase, taking action.* Continued learning shouldn't over complicate things, it should enhance – and should never keep us from moving forward.

IN GENERAL, WE KNOW WHAT NEEDS TO GET DONE AND HOW TO DO IT.

There are an infinite number of people selling or promoting or advocating an infinite number of systems, plans, prescriptions, but I'll let you in on a secret: when you boil them all down to their essence and cut out the noise and clutter, the basics, the bones, the core are all simple and all the same.

Basic business tenets:

1. Marketing (networking/prospecting),
2. Human Resources or investing in your number one asset, You, Inc!
3. Finance and Accounting (managing top line and bottom line and all in between)
4. Operations, Ops (execution: The *"Do"*: Zig Ziglar's > Be, Do, Have: "First you have to Be, then you have to *Do*, then you can have...")
5. Delivery to customer (Logistics)

The world bombards us with information overload. Those I have seen that are most successful cut through the noise and keep it simple and don't forget about the "doing."

There are many great systems, coaches, processes out there and at times we feel like we have to find the perfect one: the key is to keep it simple and focused and suitable to *You, Inc.*. I know that to run from peak to peak in the Endurance sport of real estate or any other business, we have to keep things *simple, repeatable and sustainable*. We can't get bogged down. We must recognize when we do, pull ourselves out of our rut, and keep moving.

My Dad used to say on the golf course "Wow, you look great, have sharp golf attire, your practice swing is awesome, but at some point, you have to hit the ball!" I would toss in a running analogy: *to cross the finish line, at some point we have to put our shoes on and go...*

Outstanding performers, the best performers, cut through the noise, keep it simple and keep moving. They come up with a training plan that suits them, and they don't get hung up in perfection.

In his book *You Already Know how to Be Great*, Alan Fine nails the essence of keeping it simple. He presents his idea as an equation:

Performance = Capacity + Knowledge

Alan then goes onto state that *"the biggest obstacle in performance isn't not knowing what to do: it's not doing what we know. In other words, the problem is not as much about knowledge acquisition as it is about knowledge execution."*

From a Stanford Graduate Business School article dated November 1, 1999 by Jeffrey Pfeffer, he discusses his widely regarded *Knowing-Doing Gap*[11xi] (they have a book of the same title) that he and Robert Sutton created together. Their basic conclusion was that 1000's of books are published each year with similar analysis and suggestions/ solutions, and they conclude that the translation of reading that book or attending that seminar into real action is very rare. This means the knowledge gained is never implemented by the reader or the attendee.

Know, then Do...

Focus.

A good coach or consultant, one who helps you deliver results, not just drops a 200 page deck on your lap that can't be executed and wishes you well, can help you advance your ball and get out of a rut for sure. Sometimes a good coach can help you achieve new levels.

Part of our annual business plan should include a healthy dose of annual (or bi-annual) self-reflection, with objective feedback from others, and possibly even getting the help of a competent coach or consultant. Sometimes, a competent, fresh set of eyes can spot things we don't because we are lost down in the forest...and overwhelmed by the trees. We've lost sight of the "big picture" due to getting buried under the details.

Recognizing the insanity cycle mentioned above is critical. If you're not getting the results you want or need from your 'system', it's time for a check-up to see if it's too complicated, not gathering the data you really need, or your parameters are inaccurate or skewed. Are you on a tread mill? Are you making progress or just making motion?

An example I like to use with my colleagues involves going to conferences or taking some new course to help you learn a topic. I go in hoping to find one, two or three things that I can implement immediately, the quick and easy return on my investment. Yes, the low hanging fruit. I work to implement the things that fit into my business and *go with it,* and I may also discuss anything else that piqued my interest with partners or experts.

Finally, a tool or process should always serve you and your business, not the other way around. If you are serving your tool, something is wrong. *You are the boss of You, Inc..* Stop and take a different direction if you have to, but also be strong enough in your conviction to recognize when you haven't given a process or technique time to take hold. It can be a fine line.

KEEP IT SIMPLE. YES, KNOWLEDGE IS KEY BUT WE
HAVE TO PUT THAT KNOWLEDGE TO WORK...
PUT YOUR SHOES ON AND GO, CROSS YOUR FINISH LINES.

CHAPTER 8

TRAINING — THE WORK WE PUT IN (INVESTING IN "YOU, INC")

"THE MAN ON TOP OF THE MOUNTAIN DIDN'T FALL THERE."
--VINCE LOMBARDI

"AN EDUCATION IS SOMETHING THAT CAN
NEVER BE TAKEN AWAY FROM YOU..."
--PETE FRANDANO (MY DAD)

Question: What do these two activities have in common?

1. The distance you put in
2. The education you invest in for yourself

Answer: Once accomplished, they cannot be taken from you.

In the business world, education is distance you have put between your competition and you. Your competition can't make distance up over night because it takes time, which equates to the miles you have put in...

From the well-known movie, *Glengarry Glen Ross*, a story about a day in the life of a commercial real estate broker and owner, there was a mantra in the movie: "ABC, always be closing." While certainly entertaining, I will leave you to decide how realistic the movie is, especially if you are a practitioner in the field of commercial real estate.

To that, I would propose another mantra:

ALWAYS BE TRAINING

Which is to say: *always be investing in yourself.*

In a calculus class I took in college, we learned about the term 'infinity'. It was a concept that fascinated me. One of the key learnings for me about the concept of infinity was basically this: *On the curve to infinity, you never truly get there...*

I've often found the world of endurance sports to be remarkably similar to the business world and life in general. On the curve to infinity, you never truly get there. This is to say: once we cross one finish line, we often set our sights on another one up ahead. Continuous improvement should be one of the goals.

Though approximately 1% of the world's population has run a marathon, I would venture to say that once done, that 1% are soon lacing up their shoes and training for the next one. My friend Dewitt once ran a marathon with me, then a week or so later, ran another one. Dean Karnazes, author of *Ultra Marathon Man* once did 50 marathons on 50 consecutive days. Proof that some of us are a bit more *touched* than others. Like life, there is always another finish line to cross. And sometimes, there is no finish line and we have to set our own metrics and goals.

When you think of the word training what word or words comes to mind? Pain? Negative? Hard work? Suffering? Confinement? Joy?

I'd like to suggest a few words or thoughts for you: Growth, Positive, Improvement, Confidence, Strengthening, Freedom, crossing your finish lines...

Webster defines 'training' as: the skill, knowledge or experience acquired by one that trains... I agree with Webster to a point, but modify their definition a bit: *an investment in yourself (or others), either physical, mental, social/emotional or spiritual that betters you and helps your cross your finish lines.*

I would challenge you to think of training, this investing in yourself, as a quiet path to your freedom, a quiet path to advancing *your* ball and crossing your finish line.

For example, when doing something for myself, whether its exercise or a new subject I'm learning about or whatever it may be, often if I substitute out the word *training* for the word *investing* then for me it magically it takes on a whole new meaning. That 5K run I did this morning is an investment in my health (and my mental wellbeing!); that book I picked up to learn a bit more about Big Data and how it will shape the future of most industries is an investment in my knowledge bank.

There are four broad primary categories of training, which can also be renamed Balance, that all fall into what I call the Investing in *You Inc.* category:

In no particular order.:

- Physical
- Mental
- Spiritual
- Social/Emotional

Training (investment) can come in a variety of forms, lets touch on each briefly:

- Physical: where you transform your physical self through exercise
- Mental: educating yourself to expand your knowledge
- Spiritual: working on your inner peace and balance: faith-based or meditation
- Social/Emotional: slow down and find time for you

Training/Investing can could be taking a CE class, working toward a coveted designation, getting your GED, your Associates degree, bachelor's degree or doctorate, reading a book or publication in your field, buying an investment property, going to your place of worship or meditating, taking an online class – and on and on.

How about instead of reading a book, *writing a book?* Instead of reading a blog, *blogging!* Instead of listening to the radio, *how about going on a radio show and sharing your knowledge about your field to help others?* People want to read and hear what you have to say and learn from your experience and wisdom.

How about the 1- or 2-mile walk, the 5K run, the 15-mile training run for your marathon, your 50 laps for your triathlon or your 20-mile training ride, the class you are taking at the community college? These are all investments in *You, Inc.* You are better off at the end and are an improved person once you have crossed that finish line – *and no one can take it away from you.*

Every time I do a 3-mile run, or 15-mile run or swim 50 laps or walk around the neighborhood for a mile or two, it's an investment in me. The common denominator for all of the above: We are better off when we finish than we were at the starting line. I would bet that the people around us are better off as well, due to our disposition!

One of my favorite cycling coaches, Coach Jay, will say early on a Saturday morning: "Just think! You've listened to Led Zeppelin, Billy Joel, AC/DC, Diana Ross and Creedence Clearwater revival all before 8:30am on a Saturday! You've done more in this hour than most will do all day! While the rest of the city sleeps, you showed up, you finished, you're a champion! At the end of this class you will be better than when you walked in here." Coach Jay is animated and a touch dramatic, but I appreciate him *and he's right.* Once done, once that finish line is crossed, whether it's a cycle class or reading that book, taking that CE class or certificate course or training course, or purchasing an investment property, no one can take them away from you. They each are seeds you have planted, seeds planted to advance your ball, making you better.

Training is not confining, it's actually "freeing." While pursuing my MBA at night from 1996-1999, every time I left the Worrell Professional Center after class at night on the beautiful campus of Wake Forest University, I would look up at the moon and I would think "freedom."

Some have joked that watching grass grow or paint dry may be more fun than attending that required continuing ed class. I would argue if that's the case, you simply have the wrong instructor, as my best instructors and coaches have usually kept my interest. For example, if I find my interest waning, I turn continuing ed classes into a game to help maintain my focus. I focus on finding a nugget, two or three, and by doing that, I know I'll be ahead of 90% of most folks who simply complain about the boredom. That new knowledge will put distance between me and the rest of the pack.

I remember hearing Ray Floyd, former Masters winner and Hall of Fame professional golfer, once say that if he had nothing riding on a friendly match, he would flail away at the ball. However, the moment he put as much as a quarter down on the match, he would get focused and his flailing turned into laser like focus. He turned into a game and provided his own motivation for focus.

According to the National Science Foundation, the average person has 12,000 to 60,000 thoughts per day. Of those, approximately 80% are negative and 95% are repetitive. Point being: if we repeat negative thoughts, we think negatively way more than we think positively. It takes focus and an active ongoing plan to keep the negative thoughts and energy out. We know it intuitively, but that small space between our ears. It's a matter of perspective and frame of mind. I'm the first to admit I struggle with this big time, always have but the struggle is worth it: like riding a bucking bronco over the finish line. I'm no *Zen Master*. I have to reach deep on this. The mental side of things is often the toughest.

Take these three statements as examples:

- "I could never run 3 miles"
- "I could never run a marathon"
- "I could never get that degree or designation"

When I first heard our Director of Manufacturing at Hanes, Willard Bullins, say he had run 3 miles, I could not fathom doing so. But, soon after, a seed was planted. One mile led to two, which led to three. The next thing I know, my buddy DeWitt is inviting me to run a 10K (6.2 miles) with him at the Cooper River Bridge Run. Next, we are doing a half marathon, then a marathon, then the next one. All steppingstones. I didn't run a marathon overnight. I built up to it. But once I crossed that 3-mile threshold, the distance I could not fathom, my mental block was lifted. Willard and DeWitt helped me remove that mental block and it became a huge blessing to me. It started, the seed was planted, by someone encouraging me to do something I never thought I could do...I've found that encouragement is a super powerful, almost magical word.

The same with the designation or degree you choose to pursue. The journey of a 1000-miles begins with that very first step.

My father use to tell me: *You can do whatever you put your mind to.* Well, my Dad was speaking to you, too. You just have to take that one step, break down the process into parts that you can overcome, step-by-step.

True story: When my significant other, Mary Soria, set out to do her ultra-hike, a 30.1-mile hike to help raise much needed funding for the Cystic Fibrosis Foundation, she had never participated in a formal endurance event. Of course, she has exercised and worked out her entire life but she had never done a formal 5K walk or a 10K jog. But she was determined to do it. She put one foot in front of the other. One short training hike turned into a longer one, and so on. She built up to it, stair stepping along the way. She crossed that finish line on "game day" for herself and for those she loved.

If she looked out in front of her to that steep summit up ahead and saw how daunting a task it was, she might have been overwhelmed. But when broken down into steps, smaller parts that become the whole, like Mary, you will be crossing finish lines you never thought possible!

The obstacles I have seen people overcome are humbling.

Watch what happens when you change 'training' to 'investing' and you find a reason to become motivated: maybe it's an inner burn or nagging or a goal you simply want to accomplish or maybe it's something you want to accomplish for someone else? Moving whatever it is from the training category to "investment" and making it personal will help you flip that switch.

IT IS A PARADIGM SHIFT.

Below is a simple visual of converting a *training* mindset into seeing it as an *investment* mindset in ourselves:

TRAINING TO INVESTMENT
(Its all frame of mind)

TRAINING "THINKING" (FOR SOME)	INVESTMENT "THINKING"
• NEGATIVE/DEPRESSING	• POSITIVE/JOY-FILLED
• SUFFERING	• HEALING
• UPHILL	• DOWNHILL
• DEFLATING	• CONFIDENCE BUILDING
• CONTRACTING	• BROADENING - EXPANDING
• CONFINING/TIME CONSUMING	• FREEDOM
• REQUIRED BY "OTHERS"	• CROSSING YOUR FINISH LINE

From my experience as a long-time hiring manager, I can clearly state this cold hard fact: If I had 500 applications for an Operations Manager, one of the first "cuts" would be based on college degree. And snap -- just like that -- that pile of 500 applicants is down to 250!

My job just got easier.

Seems cold, doesn't it?

I never met those 250 people I just cut out of the application process, and some undoubtedly could have done the job and are intelligent, hard-working people. But unfortunately, hiring is part numbers game and I don't have the time to talk to all of them. Most managers have an operation to run and people counting on them.

I can be philosophical about hiring all day long, but it is what it is, and my philosophy doesn't change the rules of the game. My point? I play the game, but make my own rules (within reason!). And one rule I suggest is to get that ticket, whatever ticket it is that will grant you admittance to *play the game.*

My Dad always said: "A degree is simply a ticket to play the game."

Are there exceptions out there, those who don't have the degree or the designation or whatever the ticket is and have done exceptionally well? Of course. But they are *exceptions.* The folks I have met who fall into that category are true anomalies, usually brilliant and extraordinarily gifted individuals. We can't all be the next Bill Gates, Jeff Bezos or Dean Karnazes.

So, the idea is to increase the size of our bull's-eye and the probability of our success through higher and continued education. Not a bad weapon to have in your arsenal. It's a return on investment.

The mantra I suggested earlier, *Always be Training,* can actually be translated to mean *Always an Investment in You, Inc.*

Investing in *You, Inc.* is as close to a sure thing investment we can get.

Let me give a personal example of increasing the size of your bull's eye and self-education plus, discuss the use of the CCIM designation and curriculum to highlight the concept of turning training into an investment for *You, Inc.*

CCIM stands for: Certified Commercial Investment Member. In some circles, this is considered the 'PhD of Commercial real Estate'. Approximately 6% of commercial real estate practitioners have obtained this distinguished designation and it's a grind to get it.

I was fortunate to have earned my pin in the fall of 2008 in Chicago. To achieve the CCIM Designation you have to run through the gauntlet of a master's level core group of courses, and then pass a 6-hour comprehensive exam. However, before you get the privilege of sitting down for the final comprehensive exam, you have to close a significant book of commercial real estate business. The idea is that if you are working with a CCIM, you know you are not only working with someone who had the aptitude to get the rigorous course work and conceptual work done, but also someone who has been there and done that in terms of actual experience.

I credit Rob Cheek, my cousin Jeff's former boss, for being the first to tip me off to the designation as I was departing the corporate world. He said, "Pete, if you are getting into commercial real estate, there is this thing called the CCIM Designation, and even if you don't get the designation, the learning and the network will be worth their weight in gold to you." Encouragement. Seed planted.

Rob was right and I couldn't have said it any better myself. I would echo Rob's sentiments to anyone in our industry who is considering making the field of commercial real estate their full-time practice. If you're not in the field of real estate, what designation or training would help you advance your ball? What is stopping you from going after it?

All of the courses in the CCIM curriculum are valuable and insightful and give the recipient tools they can immediately put to work, but the CI 102 class had an instant positive impact on my business.

Doug Sawyer, my CI 102 instructor told me: "If you put this material to work immediately, you will make money with it." He was right. CI 102 is one of those classic examples where 10% of us use 10% of the tools available to us. An example, one of the tools we use in the CI 102 course is called STDB (Site to do Business)[12xii]. It is an amazing tool and saves time, which as we all know, saves money or equates to turning into money for you and your family.

Yes, I hold the CCIM Designation, I earned it in 2008 and am a believer. Thank you, Rob Cheek, for the encouragement and suggestion many years ago.

———

POWER LAND BROKER

The following is an example of someone I know who has turned his motivation and self-education, his drive to create his own system, and his investment in *You, Inc.* to an advantage for himself and his family. His name is Greg and he's a CCIM colleague.

Where many brokers are out driving around looking at or for sites, performing what's known as "site selection", Greg, a seasoned land broker told me: "Pete,, most brokers focus on site selection, I start with site rejection..."

Simple, but brilliant. His system is so refined, he's put so much training and distance between himself and everyone else, he doesn't mind if people know about his system. Through his intellectual capital and tools available to him, he has created a system that creates a completely legal, but unlevel, playing field that tilts toward him.

I could come up with a different system and have a different network, but to duplicate his years of trial and error and refinement? Not going to happen. Do I let this discourage me? Heck no! I use it as motivation because I know that he is in the top .001%.

If you are in the top 50-percent, why not make your next goal to move into the top 25-percent? Then, raise the bar again. Think incrementally.

A personal note on this 'power land broker': like so many of the great ones in our industry, he openly shares his experience and wisdom with others, and he loves helping new folks coming into our industry to cross their finish lines.

We train to sustain. Training can come in the form of networking, educating yourself, and taking any steps that broaden and deepen your perspectives.

Always be training: those three words mean that we are also cultivating our business, networking, and:

MAINTAINING OUR BASE

Like the mountain climber going up a mountain using safety ropes, these are the stakes you are hammering into the mountainside so that, if you fall, you only fall so far.

As I mentioned earlier, my son (and others) have at times proclaimed to me "you are a freak" or "you're like a machine" when referring to my routine, mainly pointing to my workout regimen. Some ask "why do you work out 7 days a week, Pete?" To give you an inner look at one of my "whys" (which is part of what this book is all about!), I'm certainly not pushing my exercise routine, which is basically comprised of four days of cardio and three days of core, on anyone: some do a lot more than me, some less. I do find that many of my life components (work life, personal life, play life, sleep life, etc.) follow my workout routine in terms of my productivity level and my outlook (whether positive or hopefully not negative). It's not just about the workout (or the exercise). It's also the "stuff" that flows from that lifestyle or aspect of my life.

For me, having this routine or discipline component is related to what Navy SEAL Admiral Williams H. McRaven was talking about when he was imploring us to have the discipline to start the day by marking our beds and how good things flow from it. Same for me and my exercise routine. Once I put my last foot down on that 5k or 10K or my 25 mile cycle ride, or my 100 lap swim or whatever it is for the day, no one can take it away from me. I've accomplished that. Put another way, if my day goes to crap at least I have accomplished those two things that day - made my bed and crossed that finish line!

No doubt you know the saying: "Idle hands are the devil's workshop"? Well I say from experience that yes, idol hands are the devil's workshop but an active, focused and healthy routine (discipline) are his enemy...And for me, the word "discipline" can be used interchangeably with the word "routine."

While I'm certainly no psychologist, I recommend some kind of healthy routine (discipline), daily, weekly, monthly in an ongoing and planned manner.

From the Army & Navy Academy website, there is a blog post "Why Discipline is beneficial for Young Men"[13xiii] it says: "Many people associate self-discipline with unhappy times in their lives – training hard for a race, studying for a big exam, and more. However, the truth is that exerting the self-control taught through discipline can improve happiness in both the long and short-term. Research conducted by the

Journal of Personality[14xiv] found that proper discipline can help individuals to manage conflicting ambitions and achieve the goals that matter most to them.

Using a number of different and interesting tests, the study group assessed various participants in matters of discipline and self-control. The research questioned participants on their levels of satisfaction within daily life and a smartphone questionnaire asked volunteers about the desires and moods they experienced. The results of the study found a significant link between high levels of discipline and overall satisfaction in life."

This certainly does not just apply to young men, but to all of us. And it's all a matter of finding your routine, your discipline that leads to your place of balance. Again, its not all about just the exercise "thing." I am using that here as one key example. The above routine (four days of cardio, three days of core) I outlined for me is a base and it works for me. My routine may not be for you.

This falls right in line with what I mean by maintaining my base. Whether your exercise routine, your work routine, your work/life balance routine or whatever and wherever you choose to spend your time. Having the discipline to set a routine and stick with it is critical for my performance and my happiness. Yes, I mix things up every now and then to keep it interesting, but the routine is there and it becomes and remains "my friend." Think about the person in the military or the professional sports world who leaves that disciplined lifestyle and then goes wayward. I bet more often than not, that person who has gone "wayward" was not able to find a successful substitute for their previous disciplined (routine) lifestyle. That routine that may have seemed boring but could possibly be linked to both their positive performance and their happiness.

An example of maintaining our base training level: Even when I'm not training for an endurance sporting event, I am maintaining a steady regimen of cardio and core exercise. Part of my rationale is that if I maintain my base, my next uphill climb is easier. I'm already halfway up the mountain.

Maintain your base and you will have the strength/reserves to navigate the entire mountain. I admit to having a fear of losing my edge, if I don't maintain my base level and strengths, which also translates to my business.

Some coming into the real estate industry underestimate or don't understand the length of time it can take to close a transaction. Nor do they yet understand how many different ways a deal can go sideways. At the end of the day, most experienced brokers focus on their circles of control, those things that are within their purview, and then hope for the best on external forces beyond their control.

In the field of commercial real estate, the length of time to close a transaction can vary greatly. This length of time factor is something that many new entrants into CRE are not prepared for.

Residential real estate deals typically take 90 days or less to close. As mentioned, early in my career, Mary Anne Russ advised I work on the residential side as I built up my commercial business. Looking back, I was thankful for that as the residential transactions put food on my family's table in between the long peaks associated with the commercial real estate industry. The upside in the commercial real estate world with the longer closings can be the pay day.

More often than not, I have found that larger deals do not take a disparate amount of additional effort.

Of course, if the deal is on a 1000-acre land tract near two major highways that has yet to be entitled or have any due diligence performed on it, closing will likely take a significant amount of time. If the land contains a low density, single-family residential zoning designation, and the buyer wants to change the zoning classification to mixed-use category, the process of getting this project over the finish line might stretch to years, not months. I have worked on smaller lease deals that took a substantial amount of effort compared to the pay day, but this is simply a function of the business. My fiduciary responsibility is to do what is in the best interest of my client.

In the real estate industry, the folks I have seen do the best do not treat deal size or clients differently. The professionals I know work just as hard and follow the same basic process for the smaller deals as they do the larger deals. Most have a process and a system and a training regimen and follow it regardless of the event or transaction size.

Whether a 5K run, a 10K run or a marathon, helping a first-time home buyer purchase their new home or helping a client acquire a large office project, I suggest knowing the "event" you are training for and come into the "event" with your eyes wide open.

The following chart highlights a very simple overview based on my experience with different transaction types and the amount of time it can typically take to get a deal over the finish line.

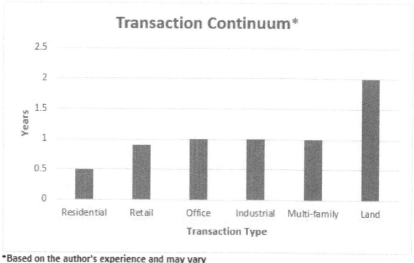

*Based on the author's experience and may vary

Pipeline, meaning the amount of business you have lined up to close, is critical. This is one common denominator in all of the various asset classes above and in any industry. Pipeline, building it up and maintaining it is critical.

As an example, one of our top investment brokers in the region is a machine and churns out a ton of business for himself and those on his team. He has an incredible pipeline, but he is at the tail end of the bell curve; the exception rather than the rule.

While no two deals are alike, understanding the basics of transaction time can be helpful. Some new entrants to the real estate industry are quite surprised at the amount of time it can take to close a transaction (that is "sell") and are not prepared to run from peak to peak.

Some who are in the business think that land for development should be a relatively simple deal. *It's only a piece of land* is the line of thinking. When you begin to take the zoning classification, soil conditions, environmental and other factors into play, the complexity begins to increase significantly. A local municipal planning department review (3 to 6 months, possibly longer). Having a survey and appraisal performed. Obtaining financing.

By the time a broker and all participants shepherd a larger land project through its due diligence phase – that is, move through all of the important tasks prior to actually closing the deal – it can easily be 18 months or longer from start to finish, and before you receive a pay day.

To illustrate some of the items that need to be performed during a due diligence period, let me highlight a partial list created by a friend of mine, Cindy Chandler, CCIM, CRE, one of our elite Commercial Real Estate instructors here in the state of North Carolina.

Cindy has a ton of experience both from a broker and developer's perspective, but also as a consultant and an instructor. I highly recommend visiting her website http://www.cindychandler.com/ for the complete checklist;[15xv*] along with a great overview of the commercial real estate industry. Cindy also has a book: "*The Insider's Guide to Commercial Real Estate*[16xvi] which I also recommend.

Cindy has a due diligence checklist that is extremely helpful to new and experienced commercial real estate practitioners. Due diligence can take a variety of paths, but the basics are the same. The following is an excerpt taken from Cindy's extensive due diligence check list.

Due Diligence Issues in Commercial Real Estate

Land Use Issues

1) Zoning/Planning/General Development Policies
    a) In whose jurisdiction is the property located?
        i) ETJ?
        ii) Sphere of Influence?
        iii) Annexation plans?
    b) What is current zoning?
    c) What does city want there?
    d) Exactly what will it allow?
    e) Is there a "sunset clause" or amortization on current use?
    f) Is current use legal?
    g) Can use be changed?
        i) To what?
        ii) What is needed? Change of Use Permit?
            (1) What is the process?
        iii) Can expansions and/or renovations be done?
    h) What is the rezoning process?
    i) Cost?
    ii) Timing?
    iii) Likelihood?
    iv) Local issues such as politics?
    v) Conditional zoning requirements?
    i) Will a special Use Permit or Variance be needed?
        i) What is the process?
    j) Buffer requirements
        i) Fencing Vs vegetation
        ii) Type of vegetation
        iii) Sizes of berms
        iv) When required
        v) What triggers buffer changes?
    k) Moratorium?
    l) Subdivision process
2) Signage
    a) Is there a sign ordinance?

b) What is allowed?

c) How are permits handled?

d) What triggers a permit?

3) What Acts or local ordinances/policies affect this property?

    a) CAMA

    b) Mountain Ridge Act

    c) Watershed regulations d) Wetlands?

    e) Lake setbacks?

    f) Smart Growth policies?

    g) General Development Policies?

4) Is there any of the property in the Flood Plain? Flood Fringe?

    a) How current are the maps?

Site Issues

1) Size and Shape of site

2) Surveys available

    a) How current?

    b) Any of the site sold off since survey?

    c) Timing to get current survey?

    d) Any encroachments?

        i) Anything look close to encroaching?

    e) What type do you need?

        i) Boundary

        ii) Location

        iii) Topographical

        iv) Subdivision

        v) Construction

        vi) ALTA

3) Easements

    a) On survey?

    b) Can they be moved?

    i) Process, time and cost

    c) How does easement affect land use?

    d) Types of easements

        i) Utility

           (1) Power

           (2) Gas

           (3) Telecommunications

           (4) Drainage

           (5) Water

           (6) Sewer

           (7) Cable TV

        ii) Municipal/Public

           (1) Access

           (2) Greenway

        iii) Private

           (1) Access

        iv) Status of easements

           (1) Recorded

           (2) Not recorded but suspected/visible

4) Rights of Way

    a) Recorded

    b) Not recorded

    c) Transitional rights of way

    d) Additional land taking for slope of road, bridge

5) Local and State transit issues

    a) Transit overlay zoning or additional requirements?

    b) Road improvement programs?

    c) Planned median additions?

        i) Elimination of median cuts planned?

6) Environmental Issues

    a) Environmental Study(s) done?

    b) Wetlands

    c) Watershed

    d) Local issues

    e) Drainage policies

        i) View property during and after hard rain

7) Legal/Title
    a) Title policy available?
        i) Last updated?
        ii) Exceptions? (Schedule B)
            (1) Verified
    b) Legal Description?
    c) Legal Access verified?
    d) Deed Restrictions?
        i) Uses restricted?
        ii) Subdivision issues?
        iii) Setbacks?
        iv) Approvals needed?
            (1) From whom?
    e) Restrictive Covenants?
        i) POA/HOA details
        ii) Enforceable?
        iii) Violated?
        iv) Architectural Review Committee?
            (1) Who
            (2) How
            (3) What are the issues?
8) Taxing Authority
    a) Back taxes paid?
    b) Assessment amount and rate
    c) City?
    d) County
    e) School district?
    f) Utility district?
    g) Special taxing district?
    h) Special Assessments?
    i) Assessment policies & methods
    j) Protest procedures
    k) Next valuation

     i) When

     ii) What's the word on the streets?

9) Interview Seller for property history

10) Services provided by? Additional Costs?

   a) Police

   b) Fire

   c) Emergency

   d) Garbage

   e) Other

*Included sample with permission from Cindy Chandler, CCIM, CRE

From the above list, how many would you guess are truly in your control? Not many. The course book Cindy provides is actually 22 pages long. I have listed only 7 pages illustrative purposes. My objective here is simply to highlight the level of complexity that can possibly be involved.

REAL ESTATE BROKERAGE VERSUS APPRAISAL - SOME BASICS

The key aspects of appraisal and brokerage, as well as the differences between the two, are beyond the scope of this book. There are key differences that vary from state-to-state, so always check before you commit. I only provide a basic overview here and strongly suggest you speak with seasoned professionals in both fields for more information.

Brokerage deals are typically contingent assignments. That is, the fee the broker receives is contingent upon that deal actually closing for her/his client. You will see I use the words typical or typically a great deal because truly, no two assignments or deals are ever the same. If you are not in the commercial real estate field and are considering either brokerage or appraisal as a career, I strongly suggest you do your own research and interview seasoned practitioners in your field of choice before choosing your path. Offering a seasoned colleague a friendly cup of coffee is always appreciated!

A key difference between the brokerage and the appraisal field has to do with compensation. In the appraisal field, the appraiser's fee is typically not contingent upon a deal closing. Like a consultant, an appraiser typically has a high level of confidence that once the client signs a letter of engagement (LOE), the only obstacle standing in the way of being compensated is the appraiser themself. The completion of the appraiser's creditable report following USPAP guidelines (Uniform Standards of Professional Appraisal Practice) typically is the conclusion of the assignment.

The appraiser is typically compensated for what they know and the assignment they have now completed. The appraiser is not compensated based on coming up with a specific value, either high or low, but for putting together a *creditable report* for the client based on the scope of work outlined in the letter of engagement.

Appraisers also sometimes assume the role of a consultant or advocate for their client. In a valuation assignment, it is rare that the appraiser is advocating for the client. Some, who are not familiar with the appraisal industry, feel that the appraiser advocates for their client, meaning they attempt to "hit a number" in the valuation assignment, but this is false.

There are times where a client may disagree with an appraiser's conclusion. This is typically discussed with the client, but ultimately, the appraiser's call stands. The possible exception to this might be that there is a court decision or additional data comes into play that is compelling enough to convince the appraiser to adjust the concluded value of the report.

I once had a veteran appraiser tell me: "Every now and again, my client (in this case, a large municipality) gets upset with me over one of my value conclusions because they disagree with my conclusion. However, they continue to hire me because they know I'm fair and I call it like I see it..."

If you want to understand the two fields in more detail, including licensing and educational requirements, I have included a few links below, including the North Carolina and South Carolina Real Estate commission and Appraisal Board as North Carolina. I've also included links to a few other state and national sites, the National Association of REALTORS® and the Appraisal Institute.

Please check with your local real estate association and your appropriate state licensing authorities to see what your state licensing and educational requirements are, as they vary from state to state. I am sure you will find, whichever state you are in, some very good resources to guide you through the licensing and educational requirements for your chosen field.

For brokerage licensing and educational requirement information, I've included a few state specific examples below my colleagues in North and South Carolina will be familiar with along with a few national organizations:

BROKERAGE LICENSING AND EDUCATION:

- North Carolina Real Estate Commission: https://www.ncrec.gov/
- South Carolina Real Estate Commission: https://llr.sc.gov/re/
- The North Carolina Association of REALTORS: https://www.ncrealtors.org/
- National Association of REALTORS: https://www.nar.realtor/about-nar
- CCIM Institute – Certified Commercial Investment Member: https://www.ccim.com/

APPRAISAL LICENSING AND EDUCATION:

- North Carolina Appraisal Board: http://www.ncappraisalboard.org/
- Appraisal Institute: https://www.appraisalinstitute.org/

BUILD A SIMPLE TRAINING PLAN

A training plan does not have to be complex, whether in the field of commercial real estate or endurance sports. Over the course of my 30+ year career, I have seen that most solid training plans exhibit four basic characteristics: Simple, Focused, Repeatable/Sustainable, and Cross Training.

- **Simple:** Whether a work-out regimen, business process or major project, are you saying it in 10 pages when you could have done so in 1? Put another way: *can you clearly see your vision* – or are you trying to execute someone else's vision? Did the consultant you hired leave a 250 page tome behind for you to decipher and implement? If so, the warning bells, whistles and lights should be going off.

- **Focused:** Cut through the distractions. Don't let the "noise" of your day get in the way of you following your plan. Compile straight-line, achievable goals. Be firm, but not too hard on yourself.

- **Repeatable/Sustainable:** Can you maintain your plan every day without burnout? Does your plan allow you to hit your cruising altitude, your *forever pace* (a concept I discuss in the Chapter13 titled "A Helping Hand"). Does your plan generate recurring income without having to reinvent the wheel? Does your plan consist of strong, simple processes that don't invite or force harmful variations?

- **Employs Cross Training** Cross training, that is mixing things up a bit in your training, helps to keep you fresh: If I'm a runner, I mix in some swimming. If a cyclist, I may go for an occasional run. Your muscles, ligaments, and bones will say "thank you" and gives you a chance to heal while staying fit. In business, think about cross training as "getting away from your business" to refresh every now and again as part of your "cross training." Remember the fourth discipline in the sport of Triathlon: Swim, Cycle, Run and *REST!*

Without some rest, without some creative diversion, you risk an overuse injury. Same on the business side of endurance.

There can be long periods in my brokerage business when I am "swinging for the fences" on a large land deal. Some of those deals can take a year or even longer to close. My consulting business, my appraisal business, my referral network, and smaller deals with shorter transaction cycles help sustain me in the meantime.

Have a plan, have some diversity in your business. If you focus exclusively on a niche, you will need to be laser focused and at the top of your field (the 1%), and then have a diversification plan for the valleys when they come.

With a diverse and ongoing training plan (investing in *You, Inc!*), I have no doubt, you will cross your finish lines.

Training > Investing > *Physical, Mental, Spiritual, Social/Emotional.* The routine of it. The discipline of it. It's all an investment in *You, Inc.!*

TRAINING TO INVESTMENT
(its all frame of mind)

TRAINING "THINKING" (FOR SOME)	INVESTMENT "THINKING"
• NEGATIVE/DEPRESSING	• POSITIVE/JOY-FILLED
• SUFFERING	• HEALING
• UPHILL	• DOWNHILL
• DEFLATING	• CONFIDENCE BUILDING
• CONTRACTING	• BROADENING - EXPANDING
• CONFINING/TIME CONSUMING	• FREEDOM
• REQUIRED BY "OTHERS"	• CROSSING YOUR FINISH LINE

THE NEW DEFINITION OF TRAINING:
An investment in yourself (or others), whether physical, mental or spiritual or social/emotional, which makes you better, and helps you cross your finish lines.

IN THE ARENA

"IT IS NOT THE CRITIC WHO COUNTS; NOT THE MAN WHO
POINTS OUT HOW THE STRONG MAN STUMBLES, OR WHERE
THE DOER OF DEEDS COULD HAVE DONE THEM BETTER. THE
CREDIT BELONGS TO THE MAN WHO IS ACTUALLY IN THE
ARENA, WHOSE FACE IS MARRED BY DUST AND SWEAT AND
BLOOD; WHO STRIVES VALIANTLY; WHO ERRS, WHO COMES
SHORT AGAIN AND AGAIN, BECAUSE THERE IS NO EFFORT
WITHOUT ERROR AND SHORTCOMING; BUT WHO DOES
ACTUALLY STRIVE TO DO THE DEEDS; WHO KNOWS GREAT
ENTHUSIASMS, THE GREAT DEVOTIONS; WHO SPENDS HIMSELF
IN A WORTHY CAUSE; WHO AT THE BEST KNOWS IN THE END
THE TRIUMPH OF HIGH ACHIEVEMENT, AND WHO AT THE
WORST, IF HE FAILS, AT LEAST FAILS WHILE DARING GREATLY,
SO THAT HIS PLACE SHALL NEVER BE WITH THOSE COLD AND
TIMID SOULS WHO NEITHER KNOW VICTORY NOR DEFEAT."
- PRESIDENT THEODORE ROOSEVELT

**VULTURES HAVE TO EAT TOO - THEY
HAVE A ROLE IN THE ECO-SYSTEM:**
No, I'm not a vulture, but I do know a few. Is it immoral that some
folks have money to spend to take advantage of a situation after it
hits bottom or collapses? In the industry, having this kind of money is
called "dry powder", meaning, powder enough to load and fire the gun
when you see the target and can move in for the kill, or take advantage

of a situation; i.e. cash reserves on hand to purchase assets or make acquisitions. An example for clarity: Warren Buffett, known as *the Oracle of Omaha*, Chairman of Berkshire Hathaway has a significant amount of dry powder and employs it as well as anyone in history for purchasing assets (often entire companies!) where he sees a unique opportunity taking shape.

Put another way, let's say you know someone who unfortunately mis-managed an asset and ran it into the ground or out of no fault of their own wandered upon hard times (it can certainly happen to all of us) and went bust and had to declare bankruptcy (thankfully, this doesn't happen to all of us but my experience and front row seat have proven it happens to some very good people. As John Bradford, the Evangelical preacher and Martyr from the 1500's famously said (it is widely thought he was the originator of this quote): "There but for the grace of God, go I," as he watched criminals being led to the scaffold for hanging. I'm not calling people who declare bankruptcy criminals but his message to me is clear:

It can happen to any of us, so who am I to judge?

Let's use a hypothetical example of a problem to illustrate the necessity of having "vultures" in real estate eco-system: in our example here, a housing development unfortunately defaults, let's assume it is going bankrupt, and lets also assume that the cause is due to a severe economic downturn and people have simply stopped buying homes (which is what happened in large part during the Great Recession). In our example, the bank takes a large land tract back (also called "foreclosure") that was only 50% completed, so now we have "stubbed out" piping sitting atop vacant lots that were to be constructed homes and a neighborhood that looks like a scene out of the movie *Escape from New York*. If the damage has been done and someone else, say a well-capitalized developer who has lots of cash and a long time horizon can come in and solve the problem, wouldn't it be better for everyone involved, the neighbors, the community in general, that the new entity could come in and save the day? Yes, of course.

These folks, these entities (who are sometimes individuals) are what I sometimes affectionately call "Vultures." Vultures have to eat too. They have a place in the eco-system.

At the height of the downturn, seasoned commercial real estate friends of mine, Frank Efird Sr. and Frank Efird Jr. and I took a self-guided tour of a then defunct development located in southeastern North Carolina handled by a developer out of the Raleigh market. It was a 700 +/- acre project.

The situation: the market had hit the fan and a large national bank then sued the developer for defaulting on its $22.3 million loan. The project was slated to be a "luxurious Caribbean-theme development. Like many during the severe economic downturn, it was a complete disaster.

When we went in that day in 2009, the Franks and I looked at one another. I pointed up and said, "That's not a good omen." as vultures circled overhead.

Vultures have a place in the eco-system.

I certainly have no interest in seeing anyone get hurt financially, but survival of the fittest states that if someone goes down, and the problem now created can be cleaned up, we have a moral obligation to get it cleaned up. And if possible and feasible, breathe life back into it. I admit, it is an extreme form of help, but it is helping none the less. Vulture capitalists are not always, as some would have us think, necessarily evil people. They can play a productive role. I had a front row seat to several scenarios like this one from 2006 to 2012.

———

As you have probably surmised by now, though real estate centric, many of my lessons learned apply to any small or medium sized business, a manager in the Fortune 500 arena, an endurance athlete or whoever.

The following are a sequence of articles from reputable southeastern North Carolina publications, who, in my opinion, did a fair and thorough job of covering business effects during the Great Recession. I have taken small clips from the articles where I was quoted to highlight some of my time in the arena, which is what I call the battlefield which was the real estate industry during the Great Recession.

2007 - Signs of Trouble. Cracks in the Dam begin to form. Wall Street comes to Main Street. In this article, I was quoted discussing the tightening money situation and this thing we were all learning about called "subprime" (2007 was the year we purchased Southport Realty)

Mortgage loan difficulties hitting home

By Wayne Faulkner, / Business Editor

Posted Sep 9, 2007 at 12:01 AM

Updated Sep 9, 2007 at 2:21 AM

Fallout from the subprime mortgage meltdown - mostly felt on Wall Street - has come to Main Street.

"Mortgage brokers and bankers say, 'We definitely have money to lend,'" said Pete Frandano, principal at Southport Realty. "If you listened to the news you would think" otherwise.

For some banks, the mortgage and credit turbulence has had relatively little effect because they never made some of the riskier loans.

"Our product line has experienced relatively no shock because we did not originate some of the most aggressive products and we have a well-performing portfolio" of loans held in-house, said Jill Shaver, vice president at BB&T in Southport. As a result, "We are pretty much doing business as usual," she said.

2009 - Major Cracks in the Dam. Prior to Wilmington's First Hanover Bank closing in 1991, and then Cooperative Bank failing 18 years later, there had not been another bank failure in North Carolina for over 50 years. Cooperative and Cape Fear banks, located in the southeastern portion of NC, went down during the long war (2006-2012). They were very heavily invested in land loans. I was not quoted in this article, but it highlights the severity of the downturn in southeastern, NC.

Local bank failure started long before Cooperative, Cape Fear

By Wayne Faulkner / Wayne.Faulkner@StarNewsOnline.com
Posted Nov 14, 2009 at 12:01 AM

In 1991, Wilmington's First Hanover Bank closed, making it the poster child for bank failures in North Carolina, state banking experts say.

Wilmington's experience with bank failure started long before Cooperative and Cape Fear banks went belly up this year.

But it appears Port City bankers didn't learn from that experience.

In 1991, Wilmington's First Hanover Bank closed. It became the poster child for bank failures in North Carolina, state banking experts say.

But the closing of Cooperative and Cape Fear 18 years later begs the question: Why was Wilmington home to all three failures of state-chartered banks in the last 50 years?

The mess at First Hanover was borne out a few years after its failure and takeover by Central Carolina Bank and Trust of Durham. Its founder, president and CEO, Dale S. Caines, went to prison for bank fraud.

Outside of the fraud, however, there are striking similarities among the three.

1. Their loan portfolios were overwhelmingly concentrated in real estate development. In the case of Cape Fear and Cooperative, the value of collateral for these loans - land and homes - plunged as the real estate bubble burst. A lot of those loans went bad.

2010 - Steamrolled. By now we are all trying to figure out what has happened to us. Sometimes, after a major real estate downturn, people start looking through the crime scene for suspects and the appraisal field was an easy target. In my opinion, we didn't have an appraisal issue in southeastern, NC. What we had was a speculative bubble where many small, regional and national developers and investors poured in, everyone drinking the proverbial Kool-Aid. Non-feasible projects of all shapes and sizes were converted to large housing developments, with supply eventually out pacing demand. The market tanked and there was simply too much inventory to be absorbed.

Most of us thought it was going to go forever. It never does. The music stopped, there were not enough chairs to go around, and over the cliff we went.

Finding home values in a red sea of foreclosures and short-sales

By Wayne Faulkner / Wayne.Faulkner@StarNewsOnline.com
Posted Feb 13, 2010 at 12:01 AM

Though lenders and real estate agents say bad appraisals are not derailing the closings of home sales.

"Where's the bridge to Bald Head Island?"

The question is part of a story making the rounds in the area's real estate industry.

The answer, of course, is that there is none.

But it was an honest question asked of a Southport real estate agent by an out-of-town home appraiser.

Pete Frandano, principal with Southport Realty, sees money as a motivation to use of AMCs. "A lot of it is being driven by the banks trimming costs, and the consumer is being hurt."

Fees are also a point of contention between local appraisers, bankers and AMCs.

2011 - THE INVENTORY PILES UP:

Home lots recorded –- Brunswick's first batch since bust

By Andrew Dunn / Andrew.Dunn@StarNewsOnline.com

Posted Jan 29, 2011 at 12:01 AM

Brunswick County recently recorded one of the first major sets of new lots since the real estate bust. And while there is by no means another boom afoot, it comes during a precipitous drop in the amount of unsold properties on the market.

While the lots join a still-slow market, the number of unsold lots has been dwindling.

There is still 86 months of unsold inventory on the market in the county – about seven years, said Pete Frandano, president of the Brunswick County Association of Realtors.

That's down dramatically from the nearly 20 years worth that was on the market just two years ago, Frandano said. There was a 64 percent drop in the last year, he said.

2011 - Setting the stage for my year-long "negotiation", alongside several teammates, two I need to specifically mention, as I would not have been able to make it through the year without them working along me and our great team. Steve Candler, our Association Executive and Wilson Sherrill, a friend and at the time, our fearless Treasurer who practically lived in our Association building the year I was President, as we negotiated with Waccamaw Bank (WAC) over our Association building and our membership dwindled (a common phenomenon across our great country). Also, Cynthia, Margaret, Ben, Larry, Charley and team. I appreciated you then and now! (and we all miss you Larry!).

This article is a sign of things to come that year. WAC having to purchase $110 million in home equity lines of credit due to a loan-swap agreement with Augusta Holdings, which purchased $11 million in problem loans (bad debt) from WAC. This article includes a statement of my colleagues humbling and trusting me to be at the helm of our Association that year.

Business notebook - Waccamaw buys lines of credit

Posted Jan 14, 2011 at 6:27 PM

WHITEVILLE | Waccamaw Bankshares said Friday that it has purchased $110 million in home equity lines of credit that are expected to increase revenue and improve the quality of its loan portfolio.

The Whiteville-based parent of Waccamaw Bank said the purchase "comes at a time when loan demand is down across the nation and banks face revenue challenges, particularly community banks."

The purchase is part of a loan-swap agreement with Augusta Holdings, which bought $11 million in problem loans from Waccamaw in the third quarter last year. The two transactions improve the quality and mix of Waccamaw's loan portfolio, Waccamaw said, replacing some of the bank's problem real estate loans with income-producing home equity lines.

The pool of loans Waccamaw sold to Augusta averaged a credit score of 730 with none more than 30 days past due, the bank said.

WILMINGTON | Deloitte Technology has ranked the BioDuro unit of PPD Inc. 22nd among its 500 fastest-growing technology companies in the Asia-Pacific region.

The "Deloitte Technology Fast 500 Asia Pacific" recognizes the 500 fastest-growing Asia Pacific-based technology companies. This is the first time BioDuro has been ranked among the "Deloitte Technology Fast 500 Asia Pacific."

Wilmington-based PPD acquired BioDuro in 2009 and employs more than 1,400 people in Asia Pacific and nearly 1,000 people in China.

SHALLOTTE | The Brunswick County Association of Realtors has named Pete Frandano of Southport Realty as its president for 2011. Margaret Rudd Bishop is president-elect; Ben Styers, vice president; Wilson Sherrill, treasurer; Jayne Anderson, MLS chairman; and Mary Ann McCarthy, past president. On the

2009-2012 - The Ultimate Loss. There were several "casualties of war", folks who literally lost their lives. I will refrain from naming them or posting the articles out of respect for them and their families, but suffice to say, lives and livelihoods were at stake then and now...

2012 - This article highlighted the inventory problem (where supply strongly outpaced demand) in southeastern North Carolina.

Saunders' deal with BOA could flood Brunswick lot market
By Wayne Faulkner / Wayne.Faulkner@StarNewsOnline.com
Posted Dec 22, 2012 at 10:05 AM

A recent settlement between a major Brunswick County developer and Bank of America could have an impact on the residential lot market in an area awash in unsold land.

Bank of America has not said what it will do with the lots and didn't return a phone call Thursday inquiring about its plans.

Lot prices already have plunged from levels when they originally were marketed. Lots that were at one time $250,000 – during the real estate boom of the last decade – are now going for half or even a quarter of that if they are bank-owned, said Pete Frandano, a commercial broker with Southport Realty and a former

starnewsonline.com/article/NC/20121222/News/605048807/WM/

Saunders' deal with BOA could flood Brunswick lot market - News - Wilmington Star News - Wilmington, NC

president of the Brunswick Realtors.

There still is the possibility, however, that the transfer of the 750 lots could have a negative effect on a market that has been improving in recent years.

There are about 2,300 residential lots on the Brunswick County Association of Realtors' multiple listing service, Frandano said.

Though there are many more that are not listed, those on the MLS are a good indicator of the market, he added.

If those lots are already listed on the MLS and Bank of America sells them, it would cut the inventory by 30 percent, Frandano said.

On the other hand, if they are part of the so-called shadow inventory of foreclosed properties that have not yet been released by lenders, it could have the opposite effect and increase the supply of lots dramatically.

But overall, Brunswick's residential lot market has improved in recent years. Three years ago there was about a 140-month supply of lots listed in Brunswick County. That has come down to about 30 months, Frandano said. That means that it would take 30 months to sell all the lots at today's sales pace.

Investors also are starting to re-enter the market looking for deals, he said.

But some lenders are also selling individual lots, and home builders are looking to buy again.

It's not so much local builders (looking) as it is huge companies – Lennar and

newsonline.com/article/NC/20121222/News/605048937/WM/

Saunders' deal with BOA could flood Brunswick lot market - News - Wilmington Star News - Wilmington, NC

D.R. Horton and Pulte – who "are scanning the landscape again," Frandano said. "I definitely think that the amount of interest we have in lots today compared to two, three, four years ago it is markedly different," he said. "It's not up to 2006 levels, but it's quite a bit more than three years ago."

Wayne Faulkner: 343-2329

2012 - "Vulture have a place in the eco-system."...they help clean up the carnage:

Home sales up, but prices lag in Brunswick County

By Wayne Faulkner / Wayne.Faulkner@StarNewsOnline.com
Posted Dec 6, 2012 at 12:34 PM

Home sales jumped in Brunswick County in the first 10 months of 2012.

He saw prices rising 3 to 4 percent over the next six months.

Others were not so optimistic.

"I don't know that prices will go up," said Pete Frandano of Southport Realty and a past president of BCAR. "What we have seen is at least a bottoming out.

"It will take longer than a year and less than five years before we will start to see price appreciation."

Frandano also sees more activity in the new-home market after that segment reached historic lows in the midst of the housing collapse.

"It's certainly not up to that 2003 to 2006 level of activity," but it's not at the low point of 2009-10 either, he said, pointing out that "this area was on par with the worst hurt places in the country."

Prices on the beaches – he cited Oak Island – are now attracting people who want to invest. Southport, also, "will push in the right direction."

"In the outlying areas, the U.S. 17-Supply area, there is way too much inventory. It will be a long time before we see those areas going again," Frandano said. But properties within a couple or three miles of the water will hold their value, he added.

The beaches are holding their own, both Frandano and McNeil said.

Home sales up, but prices lag in Brunswick County - News - Wilmington Star News - Wilmington, NC

"Most of the opportunity deals that investors are looking for are gone," Frandano said.

"Vultures have a place in the ecosystem. The vulture capital is back and has done its job (getting) the ecosystem clean again."

Wayne Faulkner: 343-2329
On Twitter: @bizniznews

2012 - Humbling to the say the least - it does not get much better than being recognized by your peers:

https://stateportpilot.com/news/article_be587614-5421-11e2-987b-001a4bcf887a.html

Frandano is named 2012 Realtor of the Year by Brunswick County Association of Realtors

By Lee Hinnant, Staff Writer
Jan 1, 2013

Pete Frandano (left) is congratulated by Ben Styers, whom he succeeded at Brunswick County Association of Realtors' Realtor of the Year. Both are with Southport Realty.

When he's not selling property, consulting with investors or spending time with his children, Southport's Pete Frandano enjoys running marathons and triathlons. Those sports, he said, are a fitting metaphor for the sometimes-turbulent real estate market.

"Ten or 15 years from now, we can look back and remember how quickly things can go south," said Frandano, who was named Realtor of the Year for 2012 by the Brunswick County Association of Realtors (BCAR). "I told folks (back in the crash of 2008) that they have to weather the storm and look at it like an endurance race or a marathon.

"Now is not the time to throw in the towel. ... Gosh, if we can survive this, we can survive anything."

Frandano, a principal at Southport Realty, got into the business almost a decade ago after working for several years as global operations manager for paper and packaging giant Avery Dennison. Excessive travel helped persuade him to get into real estate, he said.

Read more about Frandano's thoughts on the local real estate business in this week's edition of The State Port Pilot.

NO SHORT CUTS TO THE FINISH LINE

"THERE ARE NO SECRETS TO SUCCESS. IT IS THE RESULT OF
PREPARATION, HARD WORK, LEARNING FROM FAILURE."
--GENERAL COLIN POWELL

A MARATHON AND A SPRINT

Some say life and business are a "a Marathon, not a Sprint..."

I say it's both, *a Marathon and a Sprint...*

As an example, in this data-driven world, if I can't turn information around quickly to help myself or my client make decisions quickly, I am toast.

To put it bluntly, in the real estate industry, or any industry, we all better be darn comfortable or get comfortable with implementing technology and continuously re-assessing our business model to make sure it is relevant... or we will be eliminated.

My experience and observations have shown this to be true. In any industry, there are lions up on the hillside always waiting for us to get fat, happy, lethargic and comfortable so they can size us up and decide how they want to eat us. Those lions may or may not be from my industry (think: Silicon Valley).

Think: artificial intelligence, robotics, technology, exponential changes in data and knowledge consumption, learning, intel and change...efficient versus inefficient.

Some of the best disruptor's in the world, people like Jeff Bezos (Amazon) are experts, sharp shooters at spotting inefficiencies, and then turning those inefficiencies into opportunities to drive efficiency by exacting their new business model on it (you, us). What is a disruptor?

An article written by Caroline Howard in Forbes Magazine, March 27, 2013 titled *Disruption vs. Innovation: What's the Difference?[17xvii]* does a good job of summarizing the definition of disruptor and disruption in the business world. Primarily, a disruptor is someone or some entity that uproots and changes how we think, behave, do business, learn and go about our day-to-day. The article goes on: "Harvard Business School professor and disruption guru Clayton Christensen says that a disruption displaces an existing market, industry, or technology and produces something new and more efficient and worthwhile. It is at once destructive and creative."

If I were to tell Jeff Bezos it's a "marathon, not a sprint", my guess is he would smile at me, before he chewed me up and ate me for dinner. How about Zillow in the residential real estate world as an example of a disruptor in the real estate industry?

I am being dramatic for a reason. It's happening. Simply take a look around us.

I smile when I hear "it's a marathon, not a sprint" because I realize whoever is saying it is probably trying to make themselves feel better. Heck, I get it, I have done the same thing. But when I say it, it means I am giving myself time to catch my breath. I give myself permission to put my head back, hands behind my head, and say, "Whew, this has been tough, but I can take a break now." I am giving myself an excuse to rest and I don't have to move forward with a sense of urgency.

"I HAVE TWO KINDS OF PROBLEMS, THE URGENT AND THE IMPORTANT. THE URGENT ARE NOT IMPORTANT, AND THE IMPORTANT ARE NEVER URGENT."
--GENERAL DWIGHT D. EISENHOWER QUOTING AN UNNAMED UNIVERSITY PRESIDENT IN 1954

In Dr. Stephen Covey's book, *7 Habits of Highly Effective People*, he discusses his 4 Quadrants theory. Prior to Dr. Covey, it was widely known as the Eisenhower Matrix, which was also referred to as

Urgent-Important Matrix. These concept structures help us decide on and prioritize tasks by urgency and importance, sorting out less urgent or important tasks that you should either delegate or not do at all. It is an excellent and simple tool for prioritizing.

Below is a very simple outline of the Eisenhower Matrix or the Urgent-Important Matrix.

	Urgent	Not Urgent
Important	Quad 1 Do it Now	Quad 2 Planning/Decide
Not Important	Quad 3 Delegate	Quad 4 Eliminate

Quadrant 1 activities are Important and Urgent, as in crisis, pressing problems, deadlines. Some call this the hero or firefighter quadrant, as everything must be solved now. This urgency can, at times, get in the way of important planning and strategizing before implementation.

Quadrant 2 activities are Important and Not Urgent, as in planning, strategy building, and preparing for action.

In my opinion, the problem with this matrix -- and don't get me wrong, I respect it, find value in it and have used it throughout my career to my benefit -- is that in today's world, where technology has turned just about everything on its head, this tool can lull us into a false sense of security.

It worked really well a decade ago, but in this age of *Moore's Law*[18xviii] where change and growth due to technology is happening at an exponential rate, I argue we do have to move forward and focus on what's important and place a sense of urgency on it as we have never had to do in our history.

Technology is causing disruptive shifts in magnitudes we've never seen before. In some cases, *it is forcing some incredibly good marathon runners to also learn to be sprinters.* In many industries, real estate included, we sit around and pat ourselves on the back congratulating ourselves for the hard day's work, while these lions (the Disruptors) on the hillside look down on us, thinking about ways to eliminate us, absorb us or make us more efficient.

Here is the positive side of recognizing that life and most of our businesses, whatever businesses we are in, are both a Marathon and a Sprint. When you recognize and reconcile this truth, you become like the endurance athlete who is getting ready to embark on the marathon. You plan ahead on your nutrition, plan where you are going to refuel along the way. You must have the discipline now to balance your plan, to include rest and downtime and re-charging your battery. You must block them out on your calendar, as they are every bit as important as any meeting you will ever participate in.

I call this balance *burnout prevention.* In runner's parlance it's called *hitting the wall prevention.*

I'm sure many of you, like me, struggle with the dynamic of balance. Your spouse and children's schedule, your extended family and close friends' needs, daily life, and your business -- sometimes we get to the end of the day and feel as if we've been sprinting through our day like the Olympic sprinter, Usain Bolt.

If you ever get to the end of a day and simply feel "slap wore out" -- well, that's a marathon and a sprint day.

The disruptors figure out a way to tilt the playing field in their favor and use technology to their benefit to buy back time.

See my friend, who is the power land broker. He is a "micro disruptor" in a specific niche who has tilted technology severely in his favor. While the rest of the world is out there doing site selection, he is doing site rejection. He has already weeded out 18 of the 20 sites I was going to drive around and look at, so he can focus on the 2 sites that are actually feasible. This saves him time; hours or days of work which translates directly to money in his pocket and food on his family's table.

There are no short cuts. All while running our marathon and our sprint, at times the temptation to "short cut" important aspects such as our integrity, self-leadership, discipline and simply *doing the right thing* may crop up.

Denis Waitley, in his excellent book *Empires of the Mind,* explores and points out the integrity factor. He asks, "What is your absolute bottom line?" He goes on to say, "You must consider the bottom line but make it integrity before profit.[19xix]" Cutting corners in ethics or integrity is a slippery slope. I know that if someone will cross the ethics line with me on a small deal, he will do the same on a larger deal...

There are no short cuts.

However not taking shortcuts does not mean I have to do it like everyone else. I may go off road, off course, off track, off whatever and find a new path never discovered before.

Again, to quote Muhammad Ali:

THE FIGHT IS WON OR LOST FAR AWAY FROM WITNESSES - BEHIND THE LINES, IN THE GYM, AND OUT THERE ON THE ROAD, LONG BEFORE I DANCE UNDER THOSE LIGHTS.

It's all in the training and preparation. Yes, intellectual capital and hard work count a great deal, but rarely are there shortcuts to the finish lines we want to cross...

———

A CASE STUDY IN THE SILLY SEASON:
ATTEMPTING TO FLIP THE ELEPHANT

This section is related to the chapter, *To Endure*. I included it here because I think the lessons could be used in a short training course on several topics; including land acquisition, the art and dangers of flipping real estate, turning problems into opportunities, and a few others.

I'm going to tell you a story about a land tract I was involved with that as it turns out, is a solid case study in the "goings on" during the Great Recession.

Pull up a chair...

THE CYPRESS TRACT - OR - WHEN
OPPORTUNITY KNOCKS...

This tale, a true story, spans a seven-year period, 2006 through 2013. It has Endurance Event written all over it. All of the material below is public record, and as such, I did not have to hide identities as I am not disclosing any confidential or fiduciary information. However, out of respect for some of the players, I have in fact done so in certain instances, as some of these good folks are still in the business. In the case where I do mention names, it is because the reference would be deemed a "positive light" or the company is no longer operational.

I met Warren in 2006 through a friend of mine, Jordan, who had met Warren coming off the plane at Charlotte Douglas International Airport.

Jordan, ever the networker, and Warren got to talking about business, and as luck and coincidence would have it, Warren was heading down to a county called Brunswick, the far southeastern corner of North Carolina, right at the border of North and South Carolina.

The land gold rush in this area was well underway and we were pushing hard into the height of the *silly season* (the period from 2003-2008 where real estate values and stock market values as well, simply did not make sense). Many of us were losing our minds and our common and business senses chasing ridiculous deals. Yours truly certainly included at various points during this time period.

Warren was a significant developer in the Denver Metro area and had done a ton of work with a national home builder out there. He felt like he was overweight in that area and wanted to diversify out of the Denver Metro area. By another coincidence, this national home builder had a large land tract in Brunswick County, North Carolina that they wanted to build on.

The tract was owned by a local land and timber guy, Kyle. I was aware of Kyle's legend through my colleague, Brian Quinn, who worked with Kyle off and on during his career. Brian in my opinion, is one of the best land brokers in our state.

So, Warren was on his way down to Brunswick County to check things out.

A group out of Raleigh, led by Mark, a prominent developer out of the Raleigh-Durham area, had the tract (known as The Cypress Tract) under contract to purchase.

Warren and Mark are two folks who defined the signs of the times during this historic downturn: good people, well respected in the industry, involved in their community, highly intelligent. On a personal note, I have to say it was an honor to meet and work with Warren. He taught me a lot. I only met Mark one time in passing but I know folks who know him, and his reputation is sterling.

This downturn did not discriminate in any form or fashion and certainly did not distinguish its casualties based on pedigree or experience. Like so many of us, Warren and Mark got hammered.

We all got hammered. *We were all casualties of this war.*

Mark, like many, declared personal bankruptcy and, according to a Triangle Business Journal article of January 31, 2012, listed $66 million in liabilities and against $1.9 million in assets. The article stated that banks foreclosed on properties in northeast Raleigh and the Wilmington area, which was actually Brunswick County and included the Cypress Tract.

At the time, I was chasing deals for one of the largest land developers in both the Carolinas. I will call them "LC." They had been doing a ton of work for a large regional builder, we will call *Fine Homes.*

I had many deals under contract for LC, (which is to say, had we closed them I could have retired at around age 40) and we were still chasing projects even when things started ticking back, but because Fine Homes was still going, so was LC. Unfortunately, when the musical chairs stopped; LC had no seat at the table.

Sixteen projects filed Chapter 11. Fine Homes was one of their Creditors. LC had sold more than 1200 lots in 72 neighborhoods in 2005. Projects went down like dominos.

From a Charlotte Business Journal article of December 15, 2008:

"LC Management and/or the LC principals suffered economic losses on certain projects, cost overruns, delays and other materially adverse changes which weakened the enterprise as a whole and endangered individual projects as well," said the attorney who was representing creditors in several of the bankruptcies, said in a court filing." The article goes onto state: "The major creditors in the bankruptcy cases include (*four large banks were listed, I've withheld them here*) and local home builder Fine Homes. Total debt on the 16 projects is $101 million, with assets of $150.4 million, according to court filings. The attorney who represented LC expects at least another three communities will file for bankruptcy in the next few weeks."

The attorney quoted is the bankruptcy attorney we selected during my year as President of the Brunswick County Association of REALTORS to help us negotiate our Association Building with Waccamaw Bank and its officers. WAC went under in 2012.

List of banks failed in North Carolina in 2008/09/10/11 (7)

#	Bank	Location	Date Closed	Assets	Deposits	FDIC Cost
7	Pisgah Community Bank	Asheville	May 10, 2013	$21.9 million	$21.2 million	$8.9 million
6	Parkway Bank	Lenoir	April 26, 2013	$108.6 million	$103.7 million	$18.1 million
5	Waccamaw Bank	Whiteville	June 08, 2012	$533.1 million	$472.7 million	$51.1 million
4	Blue Ridge Savings Bank, Inc.	Asheville	October 14, 2011	$161.0 million	$158.7 million	$38.0 million
3	The Bank of Asheville	Asheville	January 21, 2011	$195.1 million	$188.3 million	$56.2 million
2	Cooperative Bank	Wilmington	June 19, 2009	$970 million	$774 million	$217 million

LC had an interest in the southern most portion (area in white below, south of Gilbert Road)

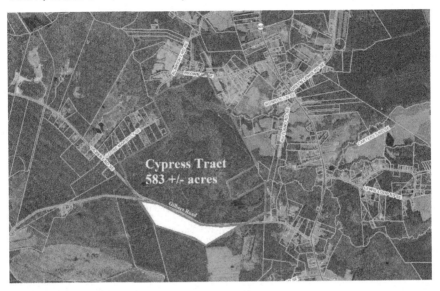

Cypress Tract
583 +/- acres

Gilbert Road

THE CYPRESS TRACT

Continuing from the Article above:

"Nobody on the bank side or the development side ever thought this would happen," says (LC's attorney). "Builders can't get construction loans, and home buyers can't get mortgages." . . . Local real estate analyst says developer's troubles likely arose from bad timing. "He continued to buy land after the residential market had already started to decline in the fourth quarter of 2006. Why he's crashing and burning is that he could have gotten land at the wrong time. The straw that broke the camel's back is that he got too many projects going in 2007." This analyst expects (partner in LC) will recover from his financial difficulties and legal battles. "(Partner in LC) has been around for a long time," she says, "and I think he's good at what he does."

An article from the Charlotte Business Journal of July 21, 2008, LC Projects in Bankruptcy stated:

Troubles in the banking and real estate markets have caught up with prolific local developer . . . The total debt on the five projects is

$53.8 million, with assets -- primarily partially developed land -- listed at $85.3 million.

The projects total more than 1,488 residential lots. The largest creditors named in the lawsuits are (five banks of varying sizes, a few large and a couple of small regional).

"I fight the banks, but I feel for them, too," says attorney for LC. "The bank people are doing the best they can under the circumstances, and we appreciate they are trying to work with us." Attorney for LC says LC has faced challenges with financing because of the fallout from the subprime mortgage crisis. "This is the most difficult economy I have seen in my 35 years representing mostly debtor companies or individuals who have problems with banks or other creditors," says attorney for LC. "In particular residential real estate has been hit the hardest."

Fine Homes may purchase most of LC's lots, per LC's attorney. The company focuses on the starter home and move-up market, with prices ranging to the low $300,000s. It is already involved with all five developments. But according to bankruptcy court documents, Fine Homes has filed an objection to LC's intention to go forward with lot sales in some of the projects. . .The company contends LC failed to deliver lots in the communities on time.

In the case of (two developments), Fine Homes says it's unclear how LC will be able to finance completion of the developments. In a prepared statement Thursday, Fine Homes says it "has been actively monitoring the business reorganization efforts of LC management, which represents about 10% of the communities where Fine Homes builds in the Charlotte market.

"Fine Homes hopes to continue and support a long-term relationship with LC management and is optimistic LC will weather the recent economic downturn," (author's note: they did not).

LC had been founded in 1986. A local developer (name withheld) says he is still partners with founder of LC in a variety of commercial real estate ventures across the city, including the (names withheld) says associates in Charlotte will understand that times are tough, especially in the residential development business.

"There's really no one in the business that hasn't been affected in one way or another by the banking crisis and the residential real estate industry crisis," developer and friend of found of LC says.

As a broker and co-owner of Southport Realty, I was in the middle of the real estate maelstrom, chasing land all over southeastern, NC for LC's local acquisition manager, Michael. Michael and I became friends and he went on to start a construction and maintenance company from June 2008 to July 2014, then joined a national real estate firm. As I have said, people much smarter than me were also caught up in the tsunami.

Prior to the Great Recession's onslaught, Warren closed on this land for $9,000,000. My client, LC, was interested in the lower portion of the land for around $6 million dollars; however, LC as previously mentioned, had their own problems and went under in 2008.

Not longer after, Warren introduced me to a person who is still a friend of mine to this day, a veteran land broker, Keith, with a national firm out of Columbia, SC. Warren wanted Keith and I to work together to help sell this piece of property, highlighted below, called "The Cypress Tract." Together, we co-marketed the tract at a price of close to $18 million. (see flyer)

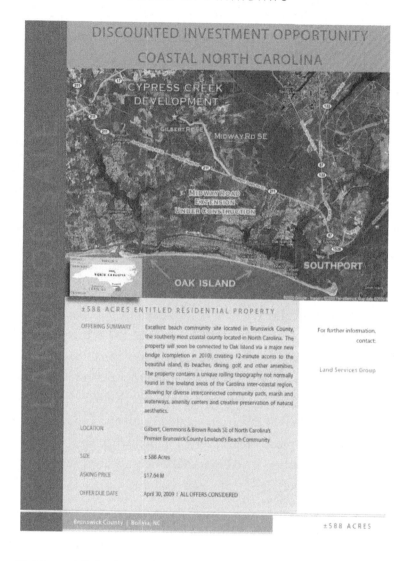

Keith and I had a co-brokerage agreement and did our best for sure, but we were swimming upstream against a very heavy current unfortunately. The downturn rolled in, getting deeper and tougher and Warren eventually gave the tract in 2011 back to the Bank.

By happenstance, when 2012 rolls around and I am working for a land banker client of mine, Francesca, an intelligent, well capitalized person out of the New Jersey area, who has since relocated to North Carolina. She was looking for land tracts in southeast North Carolina.

We had been searching for months and in the fall of 2013 I receive a call from a colleague of mine, Spruill, with a well-respected commercial firm out of Wilmington, NC.

The call went something like this:

"Pete, this is Spruill!"

"Hey Spruill..."

"Pete, I have a tract of land I want to get your help with, its one that you know really well."

"Which tract Spruill?"

"The Cypress Tract Pete"

"I *do know* that one Spruill...How can I help you on that one?"

"Pete, the bank wants me to unload it for them..."

"Define *unload* Spruill..."

"$850,0000...." [long pause]

"Spruill, I'll call you back in 15 minutes..."

I call Francesca, give her the quick back story, and we close on the land December 30, 2013 for $650,000. *Happy New Year!* Francesca still owns the land. It was good timing for her, as her land was on the mainland and a new bridge to Oak Island (a beach community) in close proximity, opened in 2010 which reduced the time to get to the beach from 30 minutes to 10 minutes.

So, in summary:

1. The property was owned by (name withheld, LLC) who was put onto this tract by National Home Builder whose principal of (name withheld) had done a significant amount of business with (we will call them Awesome Homes (a very large national builder) out west). (Name withheld, LLC) acquired the tract from XYZ Investment Group on January 12, 2006. This was a transfer between related parties and no revenue stamps were recorded.

2. XYZ Investment Group, LLC purchased the subject property from Kyle's, LLC for $9,000,000 ($15,306/gross acre) also on January 12, 2006

3. (Name withheld LLC) submitted a 1,409-unit subdivision plan for PUD approval with Brunswick County in June 2006. At this time, it was conditionally approved with some site plan changes requested by the County.

4. The intent was for (Name withheld, LLC) to pad lots out to National Home Builder, but as previously indicated, the market cratered, and this builder abandoned the market.

5. LC (administratively dissolved May 25, 2010 according to the North Carolina Secretary of State's website) had interest on the lower 60 acres with intention of assembling 140 more acres and had under contract for $6,000,000 prior to the market going south ($30,000 per acre). LC backed away and eventually went under.

6. We attempted to co-market the Cypress tract with Keith out of Columbia for close to $18 million with no success.

7. 2011 –Owner gave property back to Bank. Elephant unsuccessfully flipped.

8. Fall of 2013, I receive call from my colleague with Wilmington firm which he was marketing for Bank for $850,000.

9. My client closed on the property December 30, 2013 for $650,000.

10. Now - we are patiently waiting to flip what once was an elephant, no longer an elephant for Francesca, given her much lower cost basis in the real estate.

The Silly Season was in full swing and I was getting the education of a lifetime. People, giants in our business, were falling like Red Pines and taking smaller trees with them. It was brutal. The intent here is to demonstrate the magnitude and the breath-taking velocity of the plummet, as a warning and learning for others, certainly not to celebrate anyone getting hurt financially.

I thought *if you put this in a book, no one will ever believe it...*

Well, here it is.

————

RISE AND SHINE PORCUPINE! - A WORK ETHIC AND OUTLOOK REFINED

My youngest son has at times said, "My dad is a freak. He gets up and goes to run at 5am in the morning when he doesn't have to..."

Well, what my beloved son doesn't quite get right in his sentence is I *do have to.*

While I enjoyed my college years, as the old cliché goes they were truly some of the best years of my life, jumping into the world of textiles, more specifically textile management and working for Hanes, helped me put those days and their free spirit, not so disciplined life-style quickly behind me. Those days helped me quickly learn to relish waking up and getting shaking well before the sun came up, a 'new day' excitement I still enjoy today.

When you're working with textile managers, 'old textile men' as some refer to them, there is no waking up at 6am or 7am in the morning.

Heck, half the day is gone by 9am. As the old U.S. Army commercial used to say: *"We get more done before 9am than most people do all day."*

That certainly applies to those textile managers.

Half of those good folks had farms that they had to tend to and they were already out the door at 3am, having tended their cattle prior to heading down the road to the plant (factory). I never had the privilege of serving in the military, but as you have probably surmised by now, I greatly respect all who have and are currently serving for our great country. Although I never served, I like to think that my nine years working with those salty and seasoned managers in the textile mills helped make me a more disciplined and better person.

It sure as heck helped develop in me a love for waking up early and being out the door. This quality didn't hurt later in my endurance sport world either, where I developed a love for *flashlight running*.

Those good folks in Forest City, NC, Galax and Hillsville, VA, Sparta and Winston-Salem, NC helped me develop my work ethic. Not just working hard but also efficiently. Striving to work as efficiently as possible, working as a team to get massive amounts of product out the door to our customers stayed with me in life.

From when I was managing a Distribution Center and going to business school at night, relishing a long workday helped me a great deal in terms of helping me build up endurance to keep going.

My father was a good, firm and fair disciplinarian. My mother was the cheerleader, so they worked well together. I respected and appreciated them both tremendously, but those nine years at Hanes in those manufacturing and distribution operations gave me something that my dad could not: an assumed work ethic. In other words, you did as the group did, you pulled your weight or better, or you got eliminated quickly. I never wanted to let my dad down and that desire carried over into my role on the team with my fellow management group. I had a fear of letting people down.

Dad 'toughened me up'. Hanes helped finish the work.

One of the other aspects I appreciated about being at Hanes was that we were under the Sara Lee Corporation umbrella, where one of the best and most progressive management training programs in the Fortune 500 arena, which is to say the world, existed. They were a leader and a pioneer in Workforce Diversity training.

In the early 90s, Sara Lee Corporation "coined" and invested in education and awareness of diversity in the workplace before most companies even batted an eye at the importance of it.

It was interesting for me to be an early "20-something" watching an African American female lead a room of mainly older, white male textile managers through the aspects of diversity, and the strengths and positives it could bring to an organization. It was also great to see the "light come on" in many of their (and my) eyes. I'm grateful to the company for showing me early on that *within our differences lie our strength.*

Most of those seasoned and salty managers got the message and appreciated it. Most of our management team understood the fact that within diversity you could achieve levels of performance you'd never achieved before, that there was strength to be found within diversity.

Combined with my Wake Forest B-school stuff, one of the key lessons learned was if "everyone thinks like me and looks like me" we will only be able to go so far. That is to say, if everyone agreed with me, the training I received taught me to go seek out a dissenting view. A diverse team could take us higher and further. Surely, in a room full of intelligent people, not everyone agreed. The path forward here is to make sure the team knows it is safe to disagree respectfully.

The ongoing training was an eye-opening, awareness-gaining journey for me and I like to think it made me a better and more broadened, welcoming, talent-seeking manager and person.

My days at Hanes and the fine tuning of my work ethic and, in some cases, enlightenment, along with my time at Avery Dennison, where I was given the opportunity to take it even further and help others with their supply chain management initiatives, were a blessing to me. I'm grateful for my teammates, my days, the training provided and all of the experiences at both Sara Lee Knit Products and Avery Dennison Corp.

CHAPTER 9

A HELPING HAND – GRATITUDE AND ATTITUDE

"NO ONE HAS EVER BECOME POOR BY GIVING..."

--ANNE FRANK

Let me ask you a philosophical question, one that may make you raise your right (or left) eyebrow:

Do you believe in Guardian Angels?

I do.

I think they are all around us. I've posted a few quotes from others throughout this book.

Well, here is one of mine:

"I'M NOT WORTHY, BUT THROUGH HIS GRACE, I'M LIFTED UP AND I AM FOREVER GRATEFUL"

or the shorter version:

"I MAY NOT BE WORTHY BUT I'M SURE GRATEFUL..."

I'm not pushing my religious beliefs. This is simply a humbling realization I have had over the past several years.

GRATITUDE AND ATTITUDE

I've had the good fortune to participate in a Wounded Warriors Cycle ride, a 46-mile ride with soldiers, all heroes to me, who had been wounded in combat. If you've never had chance to do it, I encourage you be involved. It's a blessing.

Several years ago, for our Wounded Warriors ride, a Marine Lieutenant Colonel kicked us off with a sunrise pre-game pep talk. Part of what he said:

"Every day, I start with two words: *Gratitude and Attitude.* The Gratitude that I've just been given the gift of putting my boots on the ground another day, and the Attitude to make the most of it for myself and others."

His words sent chills down my spine and made me proud to be there in the presence of all of those amazing warriors.

During the ride, many of these wounded warriors kept up or passed me, and I'm not slow. Witnessing this, it washed over me about 15 miles in, watching one soldier who kept up with me with only the strength of his arms and upper body, riding a modified bike. He was powering along without the help of anything but his own mojo, no legs to help as I found out later he had lost his lower body in an IED explosion during the Gulf War.

The parallels between Endurance Sports, real estate, business, and life are evident to me. To follow the good Lt. Colonel's mantra: I have a deep Gratitude that God has revealed these parallels to me, and I have an attitude of wanting to do the best I can, for myself and others. So many have helped me along my journey, on every finish line I've crossed. Endurance sports probably saved my life at one point, as I was staring into the Abyss...

At one point, as I was writing this book, my son made a comment to me, "So Dad, you're writing a book about how to make money in real estate right? What has your production been?" Great questions. His question landed in my "why are you qualified to write a book and who should listen to you?" zone. He certainly didn't say that, but that's where my head took it.

If I go with that line of thinking for a second – *who is actually worthy to write a book?* Are you qualified? Am I qualified? Is only the best person in any given field at some specific point in time qualified? Is there a top tier? Hey, for the record, I've seen folks write books about my industry (and other industries) that have never stepped one foot inside our industry or the industry they were writing about. No knocking them at all, I'm just stating facts here.

To make a technical point, if the question above is the case (*is only the best person in any given field at some specific point in time is qualified*), this means at any given point in time and in any given category, there is only one person who should be writing a book, *right?* If so, look out Amazon and Barnes and Noble, there is going to be a shortage of books for sale! And a shortage of ideas and TEW shared...

It is a fact that at any given time, there is only one best – marathoner in the world, world class sprinter, commercial real estate practitioner, sales exec in the software world, CEO of a Fortune 500 company, small business owner, entrepreneur and on it could go. I realize this is an extreme example, but it made me wonder how many people don't share their story because a) they don't think they are worthy or b) don't have or take the time? My point: there is no rule that says who can and cannot write a book or share their knowledge (whether gained firsthand or well researched) with others.

As an example: in the endurance sport world, we compare ourselves all the time to one another on time, distance, number of events completed, etc. But here is a fact: though we were all endurance athletes, in any one category, there is only one BEST at any given time, *in the entire free world...* But does that stop the others from competing?

Enjoying and sharing the experience and the journey? *From helping others on their journey??* Heck no!

How many great stories that could help others are not being told? How are you sharing your story to help others?

Sometimes we wonder if we are worthy...

There have been plenty of times I have been asked by others or organizations to do things on an order of magnitude that pulls me up short with the question: *you sure you got the right guy?* Plenty of times I have felt I'm not worthy to give that talk, say that prayer, or whatever it is I'm being asked to do.

But I've found comfort in this realization: Sometimes God selects the least worthy to make a point.

So, am I the best? No. (One of the best? Well, in my humble opinion, I think so!). And yes, at times I do feel I'm the *least worthy.* But in this book, I tell the truth. Sometimes the truth is awesome, sometimes it's ugly, but it's my truth. Sometimes it's me or someone else triumphing. Sometimes it's me or someone else falling flat on our faces and having to pick ourselves up to keep going, but it's real.

So, to answer my son's question...I've given a few tips on how to make money in the real estate industry (and as a small business owner) in this book. At other times, I'm discussing how not to lose money. My goodness, there are times I sure wish I would have heeded my own advice and the good, sound and caring advice of others who gave it to me without charging me one penny.

TEW = TIME*EXPERIENCE*WISDOM.

No one can do it all by themselves, right? The Beatles had it right when they sang, "We get by with a little help from our friends..." I've been fortunate to have many good people provide me with their advice and counsel along my journey, whether in real estate, business, training, endurance sports, you name it. I try to pay it forward and do the same for others.

Let me share another of my "Guardian Angel" experiences with you...

MYRTLE BEACH MARATHON: FEBRUARY 13, 2010 IN MYRTLE BEACH, SOUTH CAROLINA.

I look back and I don't think it's a coincidence that this event was scheduled for lucky Friday, the 13th day of February.

I had been training for 16 weeks...

The forecast in Myrtle Beach SC was for ... snow and ice.

My good buddy, DeWitt Brown, was there with me at our family beach condo; and although he had run several marathons previously, he was not running in this one. He was there to support me. DeWitt and I had run in countless 5K and 10K runs, a few half marathons, and a triathlon or two together, but never a marathon.

We did the traditional carb-loading pasta dinner the night before, and then we each headed off early to our beds. With our 4:30am wake up call, I wanted to make sure I was down to the start line in time. I was pumped up and ready. All that training and it was finally game day. I thought a little dusting of snow would be great because it would keep things nice and cool – and for runners, cooler is generally better.

When my alarm jarred me out of bed, DeWitt called from the living room and told me to look outside. I didn't get up but looked at my phone to check the local Sun News and other news apps.

I quickly found the announcement from the marathon organizers:

"The city staff has monitored weather conditions and delayed making a decision as long as practical, in hope that the forecast would improve. Unfortunately, the forecast consistently calls for snow accumulations overnight, raising concerns about the safety of all involved in the marathon. The BI-LO Myrtle Beach Marathon is valued by the entire community, and we do not make this decision lightly.," the statement said. "We are disappointed by the cancellation, but believe this action is necessary to ensure the safety of our guests, volunteers and staff members."

This was the first snowstorm in the Grand Strand area in a decade and right before my eyes, it was forcing the City of Myrtle Beach officials to cancel the 13th annual BI-LO Marathon.

Apparently, the statement had been issued about 10:30 p.m. the night before but we had been long since off to sleep.

I was crushed. I rolled back over and had tears in my eyes. Sixteen weeks of training --gone.

I definitely told myself to get over it and asked, *what's the big deal? It's a canceled endurance event...* I could even hear my Dad saying, "If that's all you got to worry about you've got it pretty darn good..."

It was a first-world problem to be sure. If that's all it was, I would've stopped right there...

"What's the big deal? A canceled endurance event? Get over it, dude..."

But that's not all it was for me...

———

For most of us, no matter what we're doing, it's usually a little deeper than what most folks see on the surface. Simple and deep are different to me.

Deep has an underlying meaning, it's what it means to you or what it means to me.

Simple means just that. I put on my running shoes and I go. I don't overthink it. I go. People see me running and think "Oh, he's running..."

But what they don't see is the underlying *reason* I'm running.

And there's not just one, but a variety of reasons. Because I want to live and feel alive, because I want to push myself further than I think I can go, because I want to live long enough to see my sons have their children. Or maybe because I'm trying to raise money for people who are battling cancer or to help raise dollars for a soldier who had his legs blown off defending us.

Some may see me in the heat of the summer running in 90-degree weather and think *"what a nut"*, but what they don't realize is: I have no choice.

If you've run distance or participated in any endurance sport, you know that when you are training, you keep to a training schedule. If you missed your 5am window and now you're running in the middle of a hot summer day, your training plan still calls for 15 miles that day, regardless of the time or temperature, so you press on.

We push ourselves, sometimes for us and sometimes for others. And sometimes our largest critic, our most demanding drill sergeant is staring back at us in the mirror.

What many don't see is the pain you endure, how deep you have to reach when training or during an actual event to cross that finish line.

For me, on this snowy day in Myrtle Beach, I had been gearing up to prove something to myself and had just gone through the previous two years of hell at the start of the worst downturn in our history since the Great Depression. And in this event I was raising money to help people fighting through cancer. This race was to prove to myself I could cross this finish line, no matter what I had been through the previous two years. *To prove to me, myself and I* that I could reach deep and still have the strength to put one foot in front of the other.

Veterans who laid their lives on the line for their brothers in arms or those who struggle to defeat cancer or fight hunger or enable cystic fibrosis research or whatever circumstance of bravery and perseverance is being overcome, in a similar way, I wanted my efforts to say:

No matter what, I will push through for you, I will leave it all on the table for you, I will put my life on the line even if I fall flat on my face and collapse; whatever obstacle I must endure, I will crawl across the finish line for you.

No way am I attempting to place myself on par with our heroes, our military service members. But, when I put myself on the line for someone who has a battle far greater than mine, I am less likely to throw in the towel for a cause greater than myself. My dedication to running and endurance sports is a small way for me to help others, no matter what I'm going through, to push myself outside of myself, to move myself outside of my comfort zone.

In my talks with those who have served or are serving in the military, I've learned that the credo of "no man left behind" creates an extraordinarily strong and positive psychological impact.

When I speak with fellow endurance participants, most have something to prove to themselves, to others, or demons they are attempting to overcome and almost without exception, they are doing it for someone or some group that needs help. A cause outside of and higher than themselves.

Maybe they are swimming, cycling or running for someone who can't? Maybe, in their own personal way, they're trying to keep someone's memory bright and alive? At times, when I'm cycling, I feel close to my cousin Jeff, like he's there riding along with me. Whatever the reason, it's usually deeper than what we see on the surface.

I don't confuse "deeper" with "simple." I keep things simple by throwing on my shoes and training. My deeper reasons are the *who* and the *why* I am doing it.

I keep in mind the old adage about someone being in a bad mood, but we never know what they've been going through or have yet to face that day or what obstacles or demons they are trying to overcome. Just because we can't see their storm raging doesn't mean it doesn't exist.

The same holds true in our business.

The real estate closing that fell apart. The new account you didn't land. The sale that fell through or the production goal you didn't make. You're not just disappointed because you didn't get a check, you're disappointed for your client and for those depending on you.

You're trying to close that deal for your client, but you're also trying to close it for your family, who is expecting you to keep the electricity on.

Back in my Operations Management days, as a manager, I always knew that under-performing plants risked being shut down. Poor performance could lead to a plant closing, and outside of someone getting hurt on the job, that was "the unthinkable."

Of course in that instance, if a plant was going to be shut down, it meant the entire management team was out, but also "out" were 1000 or 1500 people, who had likely never worked outside of their small rural North Carolina, South Carolina or Virginia town. The livelihoods of all of those good folks were at stake.

This is how I would justify "making a coaching change" if I were not being able to *coach a manager to improved performance*. Letting a manager go was always a last resort. It was never an easy thing to do, and any manager or leader or business owner who has had to terminate someone and said it was easy or they enjoyed it is either lying or heartless.

I always knew my actions not only impacted that manager, but also impacted those who depended on that person to bring home the dollars for their food and shelter. I knew that person had a story behind him or her...

Marathons, real estate closings, life in general. Endurance sports, all of them? You bet they are!

———

So yes, it was more than just a canceled endurance event for me.

I was out to prove I could make it across the finish line. And no matter how hard things would get; this marathon was going to be a proving ground for me.

I came out of my bedroom and DeWitt was standing there in the living room.

"Man, I'm sorry..."

Of course, I said, "No worries, I'll do another one at some point." But talk about feeling deflated. Believe me, I get it was certainly not the Super Bowl, but for the 1500 to 2000 of us who had trained for weeks, and then – poof! – the 'big game' is canceled, it was tough. We understood the cancellation was for good reason.

Instead of working through my normal morning routine, DeWitt and I loaded up and went out to Stacks Pancake House on restaurant row in the heart of Myrtle Beach for a big breakfast. Nothing drowns your sorrows better than a big ol' stack of pancakes with some sausage (ha!). My intention was to eat, and then go on a 13-mile (about a half marathon) training run to keep my edge.

We had made it to Stacks with no problem, although the roads were slippery and definitely had a good coating of snow/ice/slush, but for the most part passable, which also made the cancellation feel like a punch in the gut.

As you who do it or have done it know, after your training, waking up at 4 o'clock in the morning, running through driving rain storms, freezing temperatures, getting chased by rabid dogs, raccoons, or you name the creature, there is pretty much nothing outside of hitting the wall or injury that will stop you from *crossing your finish line.*

One of my main goals is to always get to Game Day somewhat healthy (it's rare that you are 100%), and then enjoy the reward of the next day. Usually, in most of my events, whatever the day my event was on, my mantra was the next day. Meaning, if I was running a marathon on Saturday, in my head during my run, I would chant: "Sunday, Sunday, Sunday..."

Hey, we each have our own personal mind games to get us through. That mental space between our ears can be our biggest hurdle.

I have a chant I do at times when I'm "trotting", a cadence, in the spirit of the Marine Corps, and what they do when they are marching, which is:

THANK YOU GOD FOR GIVING ME STRENGTH
THANK YOU GOD FOR GIVING US THIS DAY
THANK YOU GOD FOR EVERYTHING
THANK YOU FOR YOUR BLESSINGS!

Simple and it picks me up...Any "can't do" or negative thoughts or gremlins inside my head simply vanish.

When we got back to the condo, I put my running gear on and took a few of the jells out of my fanny pack because I was only going to be running 13.1 miles and would not need the nutrition for 26.2. DeWitt and I exchanged high-fives. He was driving back to Southport and I was running south from the Brigadune Condominiums to Grand Dunes in the heart of Myrtle Beach.

I hit the elevator, reached ground floor, walked outside and stretched, watched my frosty breath for a minute then took off, pressing the start button on my Garmin GPS watch. It was about 28 degrees or so. The sidewalks were slick, actually slushy. My feet were going to be soaked.

Out Shore Drive to Lake Arrowhead Road, I turned south on US 17. Trotting along the sidewalk, the roads were fairly desolate. I headed through the Dunes Country Club neighborhood that I knew would wind around and down to the Grand Dunes area and further on into the heart of Myrtle Beach. Once out of the neighborhood, I could see the Grand Dunes Marriott down the street and saw some runners coming my way. I could tell they were not just runners out for a casual run and bellowed out to them, making inquiry as to what was going onto the south of us.

One yelled back, "There are a few still running it!!"

A vision blossomed in my mind: a scattering of humanity. runners who were not going to be denied, regardless of the event being canceled, regardless of no tents, no water, no food along the course...

YES! I was back in the game! It wasn't about having 'an official time', it was about proving something to myself. I was going to cross that line or die trying. In the deeper recesses of my mind, the actual message was *"this real estate downturn was not going to crush me, and neither was some stupid snowstorm..."*

I went from depressed to adrenaline overdrive. And there it was, that "others" factor – others, complete strangers, picked me back up without knowing it and motivated me.

I was alive again, out in the elements and pushing forward. Five miles clicked into seven, then nine, then eleven. And then I met Richard Hefner, who happened to be a 60-and-over Grand Prix winner, and a veteran half-marathoner for years. As we were cruising along, he and I started chatting. I told him how disappointed I was the event was canceled. He understood and shared several of his running stories. He was going to be running the half marathon that day, Richard was a seasoned half marathoner and was doing his run effortlessly (unlike me!).

When he learned that I had just made up my mind to attempt to run the full marathon, unsupported, I could hear the concern in his voice. He looked down and saw that I had no water bottles, no fluid, and no nothing outside of my little fanny pack. He earnestly said, "Pete, you're going to have to get some kind of water or Gatorade or something..."

I remember telling him I had no money with me, but I would be just fine and laughed and mentioned that I had been scraping snow off fences along the way, my sophisticated method for extracting water that day. He chastised me, a bit like a father would a son, and told me *there is no way that is sustainable for 26.2 miles...*

"You're gonna have to get some actual fluid in you, outside of that snow you're eating, or you won't make it. I'm buying..."

I resisted at first, but he insisted and as we continued along the main portion of the Grand Strand, he pointed to a little convenience store up ahead right off the street with an "Open" in bright red letters and basically forced me inside. He bought me a Gatorade, looked me in the eyes, gave me a combo hug/chest bump, and gave me a sincere *God bless you and good luck*. I thanked him and our paths diverged...

Later, outside of being grateful for his help, I was grateful I remembered Richard's name and was able to find him on Facebook.

As it turns out that day, Richard was my guardian angel, one of many in my life, from inside and outside the world of endurance sports, acting as a set of gentle guard rails along my way.

———

Thirteen miles turned into fifteen, which turned into twenty.

That's when the cramps started hitting me.

Welcome to the Land of Cramp Valley Pete.
The road ahead will truly suck now.

They were excruciating. I learned the hard way over the years that there's a science behind cramping and its actually quite simple. If you run out of nutrition, if you don't sustain yourself along the course or trail or wherever you are, there's nowhere for your body to go but the dreaded Land of Cramp Valley.

After hearing about one of my early cramping experiences, a friend back in Southport, a father associated with my sons' local Cub Scout troop, explained my problem to me and offered the solution. I packed enough support nutrition and hydration for two hours and I needed enough for four, so I cramped. I did some research later and he was right. I was well-versed in the science behind cramps after that.

My brilliant move of emptying out my fanny pack "for weight" (had to shed those ounces!) now returned to haunt me.

As I approached the Dunes neighborhood, 4 or 5 miles out, the neighbors in the Dunes probably thought they had some crazy man outside, as I would cramp, scream, cover my mouth, and then take off again. By then, my running had slowed to a stumbling trot, having been assaulted by a snow, ice and slush covered 20 mile nutrition deficient run.

By the time I got back to our condo, I had actually put in 26.5 miles, according to my GPS watch. I wanted to make sure that I put my stamp on the 26.2 and it was my way of exacting retribution on the snow event that had occurred.

When I looked back, I actually had two guardian angels with me that day:

1. Dewitt: with me and my big breakfast, there's no way I would've made it had I not fueled up and had him there with me
2. Richard Hefner.

The Beatles are still right: *We get by with a little help from our friends...*

My poor neighbors at the Brigadune probably thought some crime was being committed next-door with my howls and screams from the cramping. This meant that two subsets of the population that day were assaulted with my cramp screams. Apologies, folks...

My lessons learned from that day – and none are about me being a "tough guy":

- Accept help, we can't do it all by ourselves
- There are angels all around us and sometimes we know they are angels. I'm convinced Richard was an angel that day for me. God put him in my life for a reason. Without Richard I would not have been able to cross my finish line.
- Help others; give back..
- Be grateful and kind,
- Have faith no matter how imperfect or faltering the faith may be at times
- Be humble
- Don't ever give up, it's not over until you say it's over, push yourself,
- Don't let the course or weather conditions of life determine your outcome.

As Dr. Stephen Covey put in his book, one of my favorites, his classic *The Seven Habits of Highly Effective People*: don't let external weather conditions (external factors, no matter what they are) dictate your mood, tone or outcome. That day was a literal example of this for me.

Snow? Ice covered course? Canceled? No support? God put support out there for me, another example of how He has at times carried me in life, and certainly many of those times I did not realize I was being carried. We rarely do...

As I take time to look back beyond that day, I see there are so many who have helped me along the snow-covered course of my life and it's quite humbling.

I've come to realize:

I've crossed no finish line in my life
without some help from someone else.

Yes, of course, I had to exert my own energy or effort to get over the line, whether in endurance sports, business or life, but someone, some "thing" or some being (and I'll leave it at that) has often, if not always, helped me somehow, somewhere along the way.

Once at the condo that day, I called my mother, my life's angel and cheerleader, who was experiencing pre-dementia. We learned after my Dad passed away in 2008 that he was doing a truly magnificent job of shielding all of us from the fact Mom was slipping into pre-dementia. Mom was my biggest cheerleader and I remember hearing the joy in her voice when she heard me scream, "I did it! I did it!"

"I'm so proud of you, son!!!"

My dad was an exceptionally good athlete, but he was not a distance runner. He always thought I was crazy for doing distance, but always said, "You are built for it." If only he could have seen me that day! Ha! He would have told me to "get tough." It makes me chuckle.

My sister had actually made a sign for me, a collage of support, she was and always has been my other cheerleader. My family was hunkered down back in Southport and I checked in with them to let them know I was alive. Their message: "Glad you made it!"

I was glad I made it, too. I had work to be done and a lot left to do. I had more finish lines to cross and I still do. And no doubt, you do, too. Remember the Curve to Infinity? We never truly get there do we? But the journey is what it's all about.

If you could have heard my carnal scream when the hot water hit me in the shower, you probably would have chuckled (TMI = too much info?). I admit though that the warm water after I got over the initial rawness was grand. And the metal ceremony that night at the Myrtle Beach House of Blues was a true gift.

What Ice? What Snow? What canceled, unsupported event? The Land of Cramp Valley?

Bah...

Trotting along Ocean Drive in Myrtle Beach (the following year!) Note: No Snow...
Atlantic Ocean on my right

Oh, and the next year? I decided to make a run at it again. I was training in cold; it was an awesome training season. However, the game day event was the opposite from the year before: SPRING DAY! Cool, huh? No, not cool!

Training in 40 degrees and running on event day in 70 degrees is a big difference. People were yelling (literally) "MEDIC!" at the finish line. I had a great run (around 4 hours, which is decent for me) but as usual when I was done I had to run off to use the facilities.

Only there was one ridiculously small problem. Sitting down on the toilet was easy. Getting up? Well that, my friends, was a whole different matter. I couldn't get off the dang toilet.

"Ummmmm, a little help over here!" Thankfully, DeWitt heard me, busted in and helped me, actually almost carried me to my car. Now, *that's* true friendship — busting into a toilet stall to help your friend get off the seat! Ranks right up there at the top for me...

———

Through the years, in the events I have participated in, I've had the good fortune and opportunity to help others in a small way, whether cancer survivors or future cancer fighters or our wounded veterans or the Cystic Fibrosis foundation, as a few examples. I have found in life that going beyond myself and keeping others in mind, having that higher cause is a huge motivator and helps me get out of bed at 4am for a 15- or 20-mile run in the cold dark days of winter or hot dark days of summer. I always find I do better, my focus gets heightened, if I have a higher cause or am doing something for someone else. The thought of letting myself down is bad, but the thought of letting someone else down is much worse for me.

The "in a small way" is always significant for me, and the old Starfish parable comes to mind:

One day, an old man was walking along a beach that was littered with thousands of starfish that had been washed ashore by the high tide. As he walked he came upon a young boy who was eagerly throwing the starfish back into the ocean, one by one.

Puzzled, the man looked at the boy and asked what he was doing. Without looking up from his task, the boy simply replied, "I'm saving these starfish, Sir."

The old man chuckled. "Son, there are thousands of starfish and only one of you. What difference can you make?"

The boy picked up a starfish, gently tossed it into the water and turning to the man, gently smiled and said, "I made a difference to that one!"

It's true isn't it? We *all* make a difference, and if we all chose not to act, then the world in my humble opinion would be a much different place. If we choose to sit on the sideline, not send a hand down to help give someone a hand up, then what?

———

YOUR SAG TEAM

Accomplishing big things in any business or endurance event usually involves a team. When you look around, you have all probably been helped by more people than you realize. More people than you realize care about you.

As Mother Theresa points out above, I have lost count of the number of people in my world, many I know, some I met or encountered once and never saw again, who took the time to cause a positive ripple in my world.

We all have a SAG Team. In the world of endurance cycling, SAG stands for "Support and Gear", the group who is there for you when your tire blows and you need a quick change. In the corporate world, SAG may stand for "Special Applications Group", which is a group of trusted advisers you have assembled to solve a problem. Either way, they are especially important people in your world.

As I have mentioned before, I know there has not been one finish line I have ever crossed in my life without help from a member of my SAG team.

Some, I may never do a deal or any type of business with. Some, their voices in the back of my head telling me *not* to do the deal, may have saved me from going over a cliff. Their advice, counsel and friendship are invaluable. These folks, if we listen to them, can help reduce our "trial by fire" time significantly. And time is, of course, one of the most valuable commodities in our world.

Those others that I call our Guardian Angels are people like Richard Heffner who just show up, and later you realize they were put in your life for a reason. Some are mentors, Cooper or Ray, friends like my buddy DeWitt, or complete strangers (my angel on the plane, telling me my cousin was always going to be with me; Linda, the day of 9/11, giving me a lift back to Boston; and on and on)

Remember DeWitt helping me off the toilet? Well, I have to ask: Who are you going to help off the toilet of life today when they cramp up??

Throughout my career, typically, the best deals I have done have been as part of a team, not flying solo.

And speaking of key members of our SAG Team...outside of my family, friends and peers, I've been fortunate in my time in leadership to work with some incredible Association Executives, including Steve Candler, Mike Barr, Cynthia Walsh, JoAnna Edwards, Theresa Salmen and Andrea Bushnell. In every association, the association execs are the common thread through their teams. Part of their job is to keep the association between the guard rails and ensure that we leave it better than when we came into it.

I never underestimate the impact I may have on someone's life at any given moment, because it's happened to me! I'm grateful for the people along the way who have taken time to give me a word of encouragement or a coaching session, especially when I didn't even realize I was being coached.

One such instance that occurred in the locker room at the YMCA comes to mind.

THE LOCKER ROOM

You can learn a lot in the locker room. I was at the Harris YMCA here in Charlotte after a really good cycle class. I did my pool stretch (no laps this day), and then went right into the dry sauna. The room was crowded when I first got there but soon cleared out and a young gentleman and I were in there alone. He was very fit, and from what I could see, had quite a few tattoos. I'm a sports fan, so those of you who are the same may know the name John Wall of the NBA's Washington Wizards. Well, this young man had a striking resemblance to John.

I'm doing my meditation when I hear a quiet voice say, "Can you tell me what time it is, sir?"

Having just had my meditative moment broken, I cut my eyes over at him and see him looking at me with piercing eyes. I looked down at my watch and said, "9:35am..." He said thank you.

I put my head back up against the wall, gently going back into my meditation.

A minute or so later, probably not even, I hear a quiet voice again. "You doing okay?" It was my John Wall's (JW Jr.) almost look-alike.

I smiled without looking over at him, my face still upturned and my eyes still closed, and said, "Yeah, I'm doing good now." I chuckled. He also chuckled.

He said, "I know that's right."

I told him, "I try and enjoy the workout, but I swear my favorite time is when it's over. I'm always doing better when it's over and behind me..." I let my new friend know I had just had my butt kicked in a cycle class (thanks Coach Jay!), hit the pool to stretch, and ended up here in the sauna to recover.

JW Jr. asked, "Did you do the pool first, and then come in here?"

I clarified. "Yes, did the cycle, hit the pool, came in there. Just stretched out in the pool."

He said, "Man, the pool is great... I love to hoop it up, then go run, sometimes I do the pool...I'm 30 years old, but I feel like I'm in great shape."

Yes, he was.

"Basketball is awesome for you. It's agility and endurance all combined and rolled into one. It will wear you slap out..." I said.

JW Jr. said, "It sure will, just the stops and the starts and the squats and the jumping."

I replied, "People don't realize what an incredible workout it is, all that rolled into one."

JW Jr. explained that he runs five miles.

I said, "That's a great run, any run, like 5 miles or whatever, is a great work out."

He said, "Even 3 miles! You ever run on the trail around here?"

I said, "Heck, yes. A 3-mile run is awesome and more than most do! And I love the trail, the lower impact compared to being out on the streets. Running is my first love, but I had to have my hip replaced a few years back from running a bit too much, including a few marathons along the way...so, I've gotta watch the runs. Actually, [whispering] I'm not even supposed to be running, so I call it trotting."

JW Jr. chuckled and said, "Oh, so you are sneakin' them in?"

I said, "Yeah, you can say that... just getting my "fix." Too many marathons and other runs, pounding the pavement over the years. I guess you could say I'm addicted..."

————

Just in case Dr. Bo Mason or Mary, or anyone else in my world that cares about me and knows the "program" I am supposed to be on is reading, I do not encourage hip surgery patients to run.

Dr. Bo Mason told me to "flip that page...put it behind you, Pete. If you have to come back in here and I have to grind that artificial implant out of you, almost like having to jackhammer a steel pole out of concrete, it won't be good."

That image stuck in my mind, so I do what I call the "old man shuffle" now, I call it "trotting."

Dr. Bo had recommended Olympic-type walking. I do something that is very close to that. What I hadn't realized over the years, until Dr. Bo informed me, is that running, by definition leaving the ground, exerts up to about seven times our body weight every time one of our feet reconnects with the ground. Look it up for yourself. I did, and from a simple search I found the following from Dr. Matthew Klayman, PT, DPT, SFMA Certified, Barefoot Rehab Specialist's article, *The Ground Connection: Why You Should Be Aware of Your Foot*, of October 29, 2018: "Every time that we take a step on the ground, we get a force exerted by the ground. This force can range from being equal to and up to 7x our body weight."

The goal after hip surgery is not leaving the ground, which is what the running motion does, you actually depart the earth for a split second. In contrast, when walking we do not depart or literally liftoff from the earth.

I honestly think that the medical community is concerned more with my nutty colleagues who, after surgery, go back to trying to post a 7- or 8-minute mile, 3 or 4 or 5 days a week. Not those of us who are focused on not having our feet leave the ground, and are hitting a 12-mile pace, one or two times a week. There, that's my rationale and I'm sticking to it.

But please, hear this! I am not a medical professional and I'm certainly not encouraging anyone who has had hip surgery to run, trot, or jog! Follow your doctor's orders please … and don't tell mine on me? Ok, deal!

———

"How long is a marathon?" JW Jr. asked.

It's funny how I still, even to this day, take certain things for granted. Like, I assume everyone knows that a 5K is 3.1 miles, an 8K is right at 5 miles, a 10K is 6.2 miles, a half marathon is 13.1 miles, and a marathon is 26.2 miles.

"26.2 miles…"

JW Jr.'s mouth formed almost a perfect 'O' and contorted his face like he had just smelled something really bad, almost grimacing. "Oooooooooohhh Weeeee!"

I laugh. "Yeah, like I said, I guess I'm a bit addicted, that's probably too much running, but I love it. I think any of it's good for you. Heck,

I've heard some say that walking is probably better for us than running. I think walking is great exercise."

"Man, that's so right."

"I always encourage anybody who's choosing not do anything to try and get out and at least do something ... like walking."

"That is so right, I got a buddy of mine, maaannnn, this dude is so big I can't even see him in Facetime. I just tell him to get out and walk..." JW Jr. says, grinning widely but with an almost pained look

"That's a great start. I have someone in my world like that and I let them know to just get out and move. Get some walking in and you'll be amazed at how quickly that will begin to improve your shape, your health, your outlook and your life. I'm worried about my friend's size, straining his heart..."

"My friend has kids. I tell him get out and do it for them!"

Ahhh, the doing it for others theme...

I said, "Tell him we need you here..."

And he repeated it back. "Yeah, *we need you here...*"

JW Jr. got it and he helped reinforce it for me again that day, right there in the locker room. I know that young man was an angel in my world that day and he was not going to be denied having that conversation with me.

———

FOREVER PACE

I would like to tell you about a concept I call my *Forever Pace*.

I define it as that pace in which, once achieved, I feel like I can run forever.

When I'm running distance, I always try and get to that plateau, to find my Forever Pace. It's my cruising altitude. Hey, pilots want to get to that level, so why shouldn't we? At my Forever Pace, I feel I am exerting maximum effort or, in my mind, what I would call 'perfect effort' and I am receiving maximum return for my effort: you could call it a *maximum return on effort*.

Maximum *return on investment* to me is similar to *maximum return on effort*.

In your business, in your life, and in your endurance sport event, not everything is going to be an "investment" so you want to get to a place where you are achieving a maximum return on your effort. It's that place where you're not getting flat exhausted because you've been going at a full sprint for half a mile. For example, a marketing program that is so costly you can't sustain it – it only gives you a big splash with no long-term customer follow up or sustainability.

We've all seen it, right?

At the marathon start line, the guy that takes off at a 6.5-minute pace and at mile 14 you're passing him and he's breathing so heavily you're concerned for his health and safety. He was training at an 8-mile pace, and due to the excitement or ego or whatever, he got dragged into running someone else's race.

Or how about that person or new business that pops up out of seemingly nowhere and is doing something to gain short term attention, causing you to make a short term adjustment off your value proposition, the basic things that "brought you to the dance" in the first place.

It's easy to get sucked into the idea that someone might know something you don't. Or the feeling that you have to run a race that is not your own. If you feel someone does know something you don't, investigate the situation, do your own research, have a process to vet it. My advice is to not come out and try to replicate a system you truly don't understand, or run at a pace for which you have not been training.

If you stop and think about the times you have performed your best, whether it's in business or an endurance sport, you've probably looked up at some point and felt like it was almost effortless. I bet if you analyzed your performance at those times, you were probably running at your *Forever Pace.*

This is a concept, a mindset, that can be applied practically and will help guide you in any effort you need to sustain. Don't get sucked into a pace you have not been training in or something you haven't researched. It can be a long way to the finish line and your ultimate goal is to cross that finish line. Stay your course. Run your own race. Believe in your system.

Let's face it, the business of real estate, your business, and your life are all truly marathons. If you don't achieve your Forever Pace, you will wash out or burn out or hit the wall or at the very least, be miserable.

Yes, Marathon and a sprint – but we still have to manage our pace.

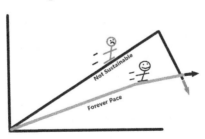

MY SUPER SOPHISTICATED CONCEPTUAL GRAPHIC OF "FOREVER PACE"

COMPETITION: RUN YOUR OWN RACE: YOUR LOYAL CIRCLE

"IT'S VERY HARD IN THE BEGINNING TO UNDERSTAND THAT
THE WHOLE IDEA IS NOT TO BEAT THE OTHER RUNNERS.
EVENTUALLY YOU LEARN THAT THE COMPETITION IS AGAINST
THE LITTLE VOICE INSIDE YOU THAT WANTS YOU TO QUIT.
—GEORGE SHEEHAN

With your own client base, you are not competing, the game is yours
to lose. Don't get me wrong, one of the quickest ways to lose a client is
to take them for granted. But once the relationship is formed, it truly
is your game to lose.

In the real estate industry, we compete, and we compete hard, but
we also have to work together to get deals done.

I enjoy applauding other's successes. I don't fret over them. I try
and learn from them. If you feel someone out there is doing something
you would like to be doing, or achieving a level of success you would
like to be achieving, invite them out for a cup of coffee, figure out how
to partner or do more deals with them.

One philosophy I always keep in mind has helped me: if there
are four quarters on the table, I would rather have one than none.
I don't want to be the person who wants all the quarters. I've seen
that before and its ugly, and most people can spot those folks. If
people work with me, they know they are going to get paid. If you
and I were to do a deal together today, I would make sure you knew
very clearly that I'm happy to be working with you on this deal

today. But I also want you to trust me enough to know that we're not just working on today's deal, but 20 years from today (Good Lord willing).

I'm always *trying* to think long term. I have told some of the newer folks coming into the real estate industry that no client or deal is worth your license or your reputation. Walk away with your integrity and ethics whole, if you have to do so. It's worth it.

––––––––

LESSON FROM A PRIEST

We were in St. Gabriel Catholic Church for a service and I heard our awesome new Pastor Father Richard Sutter (who replaced our long time awesome Pastor Father Frank O'Rourke) talking to the kids about the "twelve fruits of the Holy Spirit."

He said, "If there is one thing I want you to take away from my talk today, it is this: *What is the Thief of Joy?*"

And one youngster yelled out, "Comparison!"

Father Richard said, "Right on!!!"

Be your own person, run your own race, the thief of Joy is Comparison.

Father Richard was not saying that we shouldn't be competitive. Far from it. He was telling us to run our own race. To me, competition is a great thing, it can make me better and it is part of what makes our country great. It is a significant part of our foundation.

But unhealthy comparison, to the point of distraction, is not a good thing. And Father Richard's overarching message is that true joy, true happiness, is not found in money or possessions, but by knowing the Guy who, as real estate people can certainly appreciate, canceled our debt for us, and to be true to ourselves.

In line with my "every finish line I've ever crossed, I realize I had some help along the way" theme is the famous story of the person who failed to heed the help that was being sent to him as the river was rising in the great storm. Remember this one?

Yes, at some point we have to exert our own energy, I have to take responsibility and be able to spot when I'm receiving help and act on it.

THE PARABLE OF THE FLOOD

A man was trapped in his house during a flood. He began praying to God to rescue him. He had a vision in his head of God's hand reaching down from heaven and lifting him to safety. The water started to rise in his house. His neighbor urged him to leave and offered him a ride to safety. The man yelled back, "I am waiting for God to save me." The neighbor drove off in his pickup truck.

The man continued to pray and hold onto his vision. As the water began rising in his house, he had to climb up to the roof. A boat came by with some people heading for safe ground. They yelled at the man to grab a rope they were ready to throw and take him to safety. He told them that he was waiting for God to save him. They shook their heads and moved on.

The man continued to pray, believing with all his heart that he would be saved by God. The flood waters continued to rise. A helicopter flew by and a voice came over a loudspeaker offering to lower a ladder and take him off the roof. The man waved the helicopter away, shouting back that he was waiting for God to save him. The helicopter left. The flooding water came over the roof and caught him up and swept him away.

He drowned.

When he reached Heaven he asked, "God, why did you not save me? I believed in you with all my heart. Why did you let me drown?"

God replied, "I sent you a pick-up truck, a boat and a helicopter and you refused all of them. What else could I possibly do for you?"

I don't want to be the one who doesn't act. My interpretation of this is: we need to put our own (God given) fortitude and endurance to work.

God Helps those who help themselves.

———

On a practical level, as relates to ground cultivated and your effort put in, take your network as a great example. These are relationships that you have formed and cultivated. You have a circle that knows you, trusts you and will do business with you. I tell people when they are new and coming into the real estate business to start with your friends and family or your small network and grow it from there. Let people around you know that you are in the real estate business (or whatever business you are in). Your own sphere of folks, when you are loyal to them and keep their best interest in mind, will give back to you over and over again through the years.

In the real estate industry, one can go bankrupt quickly if the wrong decision is made, due to the sheer magnitude of the financials (i.e. the dollars, aka "the dough") involved.

The long view, on the relationship side will get us through...

We had a CEO of Sara Lee Knit Products, Kirk Beaudin, who once put "running your own race" to me another way. He would say:

"Measure your own curve."

This was his way of asking: are you seeing steady improvement in your operation, in your business? Or are you stagnant?

We want to be consistently measuring our performance and doing a "maintenance check" on our business and performance, using our competition only as guard rails on the ride up the mountain.

Once, during the Beach to Battleship Triathlon in Wilmington, NC, I looked up to see that I'm getting smoked by a guy who was a tad overweight, dressed as the devil (the event is near Halloween so some dressed in costumes). At first, I'm thinking *there is no way in Hades I'm letting this chubby Satan guy beat me.* But he was flying! (I'm assuming he made it to the finish line way ahead of me!)

If I would have tried to keep up with him, I knew I would put my finishing the event at risk. I almost got sucked into running his race because of my own ego and pride.

This is one of many times over the years that reminded me to never judge a book by its cover. Sometimes the chubby devil will go flying right by you. Let him go. It's not all about the external, is it? Heart, soul and mental. What's inside is every bit as important as what's outside.

Keeping up with the Joneses doesn't work well in triathlons, marathons or business. Besides, *who the heck is this Jones guy, anyway, and why do we want to keep up with him?*

We can't do it all by ourselves. Be grateful for our SAG team. We shouldn't forget about our *Forever Pace*, our cruising altitude. *Run our own race (measure our own curve).*

———

Gratitude and Attitude. I do my best to keep this in mind and at the forefront of everything I do. I firmly believe these concepts will help you cross whatever finish lines you choose to cross in your business or life.

CHAPTER 10

HITTING THE WALL - YOUR SECOND WIND

"MOST PEOPLE NEVER RUN FAR ENOUGH ON THEIR
FIRST WIND TO FIND OUT THEY HAVE A SECOND..."
--WILLIAM JAMES

The first time I bonked, it was ugly.

What is bonking, some may ask?

Wikipedia defines 'hitting the wall' or 'bonking' this way:

"In endurance sports such as cycling and running, hitting the wall or the bonk is a condition of sudden fatigue and loss of energy which is caused by the depletion of glycogen stores in the liver and muscles. Milder instances can be remedied by brief rest and the ingestion of food or drinks containing carbohydrates. The condition can usually be avoided by ensuring that glycogen levels are high when the exercise begins, maintaining glucose levels during exercise by eating or drinking carbohydrate-rich substances, or by reducing exercise intensity."

For the curious, it goes onto say:

"The term bonk for fatigue is presumably derived from the original meaning "to hit", and dates back at least half a century. Its earliest citation in the Oxford English Dictionary is a 1952 article in the Daily Mail.[1]

The term is used colloquially as a noun ("hitting the bonk") and as a verb ("to bonk halfway through the race"). The condition is also known to long-distance (marathon) runners, who usually refer to it as "hitting the wall." The British may refer to it as "hunger knock,."..

It can also be referred to as "blowing up."[2]"

And it even goes onto to tell us what our German friends think of it:

"In German, hitting the wall is known as "der Mann mit dem Hammer" ("the man with the hammer"); the phenomenon is thus likened to a man with the hammer coming after the athlete, catching up, and eventually hitting the athlete, causing a sudden drop in performance."

And from an insightful Runner's World article ("The Science Behind Bonking"[20xx]) on bonking, March 1, 2004 by Paul Scott:

"And then there's the little-purple-men bonk. "After about 20-K, I started to see little purple men running up and down the sides of these cliffs," says Mark Tarnopolsky, M.D., who wears hats as both a leading sports nutrition researcher and an endurance athlete. "I knew it was an hallucination, but I stopped in the middle of the race to look at them anyway," he says. "It was kind of crazy."

On the day of my inaugural bonking, I wasn't seeing little purple men, but I wish I would have known about bonking, whether in English or in German! Of course, I knew of it but not the science behind it. I must say, regardless of the language, based on my experience the above is very accurate indeed. I had a bit of a different reaction caused by overdoing it after a run one time.

There is the blood-sugar crash, and then the insulin spike. This particular day, I had an insulin spike, whereby I consumed a combination of the wrong foods, ye' old too much, too soon phenomenon. In the unsupported Myrtle Beach marathon, I experienced the blood-sugar crash, by not providing my body with enough fuel at the right time.

During the training period for my first half marathon, I had just wrapped up my 12-mile training run.

On this day, with my training run over, I was famished, which is to say I had not properly fueled ahead of my 12-mile run. Over the years, I have had a bad habit of "going low" on hydration and food intake, with the idea I would catch up on the backside, which is simply not a good idea. That tended to work for me on the shorter distance runs (5K, 10K) but I was about to find out that my good luck and fortune did not extend to the longer distance categories.

The Runner's World article mentioned above goes on to say:

"Then there is the larger question of people, and how we may be bonking for far less metabolic, far more goober-headed reasons"

And yes, that was definitely me most of the time, the scientific, "goober-headed" reason, usually describing the category my rare bonks belong in during my endurance sport journey.

After this 12-mile run, I managed to do a reverse bonk, I had under fueled pre-run and was fortunate to have not bonked during my training run. The result, however, was something bordering on what felt to me like near starvation, as I had the urge to chew my left arm off, I was so hungry after the run.

I came into the house, took off my running stuff and proceeded to scarf down a full yogurt, some fruit and peanuts, slammed down a Gatorade or two, a water, tossed in some peanut butter crackers for good measure, eyeballing anything to take the edge off quickly.

My youngest son Joe and I went into the backyard to play a little kickball. I would roll him the ball and he would kick it back to me.

I don't recall when it hit, but I do remember looking up one time and watching the trees suddenly sway. If I was asked to describe it using a term, it would be a *WOMP...* Then a longer *WOOOMMMMP...* It was as if I was walking into a fun house, *only it wasn't fun.*

The next thing I know, the globe as I knew it, my surroundings seem to take a drunk-like spin. I remember hearing my son say, "Daddy, you look green, you don't look so good." and chuckling at me uncomfortably.

And then, here it came: me spewing a few chunks right then and there, and running toward the house, as the land seemed to take on a strange sloping gradient ("hey, I don't recall adjusting the grade of our backyard?") , and into my bedroom master bath and it was full on...

I can't even imagine what it must have looked like to my son, who probably now thought his father had been taken over by some evil demon... "Daaaad?!!"

It wouldn't stop for a while and I thought to myself, "Oh no, what have I done? I've blown it, I'm going to die..."

This was a Saturday, but I still called my doctor, Mick Palagruto. Mick and I had coached together and our kids were same age range, so we all ran in a similar circle, which is to say, in this very small town, he was more than just a "doc" to us, he was also considered a family friend (a group of us, including Mick, actually ran the inaugural Oak Island half marathon together). I explained to him what had happened. My body temp had spiked to 104. Dr. Palagruto got more details and when we got to the food part. I could hear him chuckle a bit. It turns out that I had basically spiked my sugar levels and, as I understand it, had gone into an almost toxic sugar overload.

According to the Mayo Clinic (and Dr. Palagruto) a symptom of High Blood Sugar levels can include nausea or vomiting. Bingo! *Good to know...*

I can hear you saying, "Okay, Pete, great, I'm sorry you bonked, but what the heck is the point of all of this?"

Here's my point: At times in life, we will all bonk. In endurance sports, business and life. What do we do when we bonk? How do we handle it and get back up in the saddle?

Oh, and at times, we will witness others around us bonking on the course we are running, either in our sanctioned endurance sport event, business or life. How will we respond? Do we leave them behind and keep rolling? Or do we hold and help?

Bonking in the real estate industry, or just about any business, can mean not training, not investing in yourself or your business, not watching expenses, not making the tough decisions. Like removing that one client because they are draining you or your team or your company, and the return on time and real dollars is simply not there. It can result in you running out of steam in your business.

Bonking in your business can mean chasing deals that take you over a cliff, hurt you in the short run, or worse: bankrupt you. Bonking can mean not taking some time off to recharge and recover, think scheduling in rest, downtime and vacation. Trust me, your loved ones and your work colleagues will appreciate it when *you take some time for you.*

Sometimes in a half or a full marathon, I would see fellow runners passing by first, second or third water stations and I would know it was a mistake because I'd learned the hard way. *Hey, You! Don't pass on the water stations of life!*

The research on this is solid and it basically confirms this "technique" to be a big mistake. An old runner's axiom (and, as I understand it, what most doctors say): if you start to feel thirsty, it's too late.

How does not fueling as we should translate into our business?

In the above scenario, we will most likely eventually lose time on the course, thinking we've saved time passing the water station. It will come back around to haunt us. Not fueling properly, not investing in our business and in ourselves can lead to becoming stale and lethargic, creativity, passion and joy go out the window. However, if we take time to fuel properly along the way, we will more than make up for the time we diverted to the water station.

The reason I hit the wall in the unsupported Myrtle Beach marathon was because I did not fuel properly. I left half my stash back at the condo. It was self-imposed. I brought it on myself.

There have been plenty of times that I have been out on my feet and it's then I realize someone, something is carrying me. Think about the famous poem "Footprints in the Sand." Second winds and being carried are very much related.

But sometimes, it happens. We bonk. It's okay. I've learned that on the days I bonk, and it's tough to do, but I typically need to toss the towel in and live to see another day. It's a setback for today, and today alone. We shouldn't let it shake our confidence.

Lack of investment in ourselves, lack of fueling (or training) will end up costing us in the long run. Refueling along the way will help us avoid "hitting the wall" and reach our finish lines.

As William James eloquently put it all the way back in the late 1800s:

"Most people never run far enough on their first wind to find out they have a second..."

To give yourself a higher probability of achieving your second wind means properly refueling yourself along the way.

Yes, it's both a *marathon and a sprint*. And when I'm hitting the hills on my run or in my business or in life, my goal is to do my best to maintain my effort, but not necessarily my pace. If I'm trying to maintain the same pace on the hills as I did when I was on flat land, I could encounter trouble along the way. I may burn out, bonk, hit the wall or not make it the rest of the way. Maintaining solid effort on the hill becomes the goal, not maintaining the same pace. Effort, not pace becomes my mindset...

Adjusting our pace at times in anything we are doing will give us a better shot at hitting the finish line, which is always the goal, isn't it?

ENTER THE NO BONK ZONE

Of course, at times, we will encounter some pain along the way. That will always be a part of the journey, especially when we reach deep. Bumps in the road or major sink holes. Remember *"no pain, no gain"*? Though, at times, doesn't it seem we live in a *"No Pain, No Pain"* world? My Mom used to tell me "what doesn't kill you will make you stronger!" Seemed extreme, but Mom had a point. I had no idea that Mom was giving me a modified quote of the German philosopher Friedrich Nietzsche. In 1888, Nietzsche wrote "Aus der Kriegsschule des Lebens.--Was mich nicht umbringt, macht mich stärker," which can be translated as "Out of life's school of war--what doesn't kill me, makes me stronger." It appears in his book of aphorisms, Twilight of the Idols, and no further explanation follows.

I always love it when I'm in a hotel workout facility and I see the sign that says "At the First Sign of Discomfort, Discontinue Use." Heck, if I followed that rule, I'd never make it past the first mile, en route to hitting my Forever Pace!

The graphic below is actually a picture I took and posted on my Facebook page several years back:

Pete Frandano
January 17, 2013 · 👥   ...

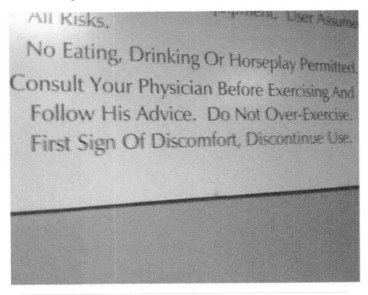

This s always comical to me...if I followed this 'advice' I would never get far into any workout, run, swim, cycle, etc...heaven forbid we push ourselves to the point of discomfort...

All Risks.
No Eating, Drinking Or Horseplay Permitted.
Consult Your Physician Before Exercising And Follow His Advice. Do Not Over-Exercise.
First Sign Of Discomfort, Discontinue Use.

👍 Like   💬 Comment   ↗ Share

No Pain, No Pain! Nah, I am fine with the old "No Pain, No Gain..." I know when I reach deep, the reward is there. (author's disclaimer: I understand these signs are there for liability purposes, not exercise advice - so, please heed your doctors advise for sure and those signs as you see fit!)

We will hit the wall... It happens...

Our goals in any endurance effort should always include learning our limits and refueling properly along our journey so we can enter that "No Bonk Zone" and give ourselves the best chance of getting our second wind en route to our Forever Pace.

So here is a toast to your second winds: whether swimming, cycling, running, in your business or in your life.

CHAPTER 11

RECOVERY AND CROSS-TRAINING

"EXERCISE IS FOR PEOPLE WHO CAN'T
HANDLE DRUGS AND ALCOHOL."
--LILY TOMLIN

In a book that is endurance and real estate centric, I would be remiss if I did not touch on the important topic of recovery and cross training. In his classic book, *Marathon: The Ultimate Training Guide*[21lxxi], Hal Higdon quotes David L Costal, PhD of the human performance laboratory at Ball State University in Muncie, IN. Doctor Costal mentions that runners often trained too hard in the weeks immediately preceding a marathon. "They feel they need one last butt-busting workout and end up tearing themselves down."

In fact, in Chapter 15, *The Magic Taper*, Hal says, "In the critical, final weeks just prior to the race, many marathoners make a serious mistake. They failed to utilize one key ingredient in any training system as mentioned many times in this book: rest."

The concept of tapering, in the case of a marathon, is that you never really peak and hit the 26.2 miles you will be doing on event day. I like to joke that a marathon is simply a 20-mile warm-up run followed by a 10K.

In tapering, you peak at about 18 to 20 miles for 2 to 3 weeks prior to your event. Then, you come in on a slow and steady downward slope to event day, decreasing in miles and increasing rest. Think of a plane coming in for a smooth landing. The idea is to give your body recovery for what you're getting ready to put it through. Unfortunately, most of us don't know how to take a break. We are pros at wearing ourselves out and not the best at scheduling rest or downtime periods.

A friend and colleague and national franchise owner here in Charlotte is consistently in the 2% club nationally for performers within his franchise. At a top-performer conference in Florida, attendees and their spouses took to the beach for a break between sessions. Looking around and down the beach, my friend noticed that nearly every colleague owner of his was on the phone while their significant other stared out at the water.

Most of us, me included, have a hard time "unplugging", turning it off.

In the marathon world, there is a concept known as "Taper madness" which highlights this and essentially means we don't know how to rest.

In Hal's book mentioned above, Dr. Costal notes that research with swimmers has shown that when they tapered properly as much as 3 to 6 weeks before an event, they more often set personal records. He also found that swimmers performed better when under-trained.

Dr. Costal also worked with a group of runners, starting their taper 3 weeks before a race. During their taper period they only ran 2 easy miles a day. He found that two problems developed. Psychological testing revealed that runners' significant concerns about losing conditioning resulted in anxiety, sometimes severe. This anxiety is the essence of "Taper Madness."

I call it being obsessive compulsive and not disciplined enough to force oneself to back down. I feel comfortable making this very blunt statement because I've been there and paid the price for it.

The bottom line is that those who taper, for those who make time for rest and recovery, and who cross train properly, also will perform better. Being disciplined enough to incorporate recovery time on a systematic basis is as important to your success as any of your other disciplines, whether an athletic activity or working on that report into the wee hours of the night.

This backing down on your training before you come into your event day is called the *Magic Taper...*

The magic taper is basically that phenomena that brings you up to the peak of your training, and then winds you down, backing off and tapering your training until you come in for a smooth landing on your game day.

To the person who is new to the endurance sports world, this can be counter intuitive.

"DON'T I NEED TO BE TRAINING RIGHT UP TO GAME DAY?"

No, your training, when done properly, will hold and your tapering off will actually help you do your best on event day because you allowed your body to properly recover. Magically tapered, you are a thoroughbred ready to roll full steam ahead.

Over-training, not tapering properly is remarkably similar to a workaholic. The bridge between over training or not tapering properly and being a workaholic is very short. As an endurance athlete, rest and recovery and cross training have to be scheduled into your plan.

Aches and pains in the endurance world are part of the journey, as they are in whatever business you're in, but there is a fine line between pushing through pain haphazardly and being smart, recognizing your pain threshold and veering off before you encounter an overuse injury, or before you reach burnout.

In chapter 7 of his book, *Triathlon Training: Race programs for Sprint distance through Ironman*[22xxii] (another book I recommend, especially if you are entering into or are already in the Triathlon world),

Michael Finch Carmen says most people think that triathletes, because they are tackling three different sports, actually encounter three times the amount of injuries. Research has proven that injuries are actually less likely to occur because the triathlon is a form of cross-training.

In the Tri World, it is often said that there are four disciplines: swimming, cycling, running and ... rest.

There are times we experience overuse injuries in the sport and the pain derails your training. We train ourselves to push through pain. We become martyrs in our business ("they can't go on without me") and then, the setbacks come.

In our day to day industry work, we can encounter parallels to physical injuries due to overuse or overtraining and lack of rest. Mistakes, some critical or at the wrong time in our business, irritableness and confusion, immune system breakdown and illness from not enough sleep, alcoholism, divorce and, in the extreme, suicide.

And in your quest to cross all the finish lines in your life, it's okay to be exhausted and worn out and tired. That's normal. Don't beat yourself up over it or tell yourself you're getting too old. You are not alone...

It's a grind. Remember, it's an endurance event, it will wear you down at times, that's why recovery, the fourth discipline, is so important.

BALANCE IN RECOVERY – FINDING MY QUIET PLACE

We touch on it in more detail a little later in the book, but this topic is so important I wanted to provide a brief intro here. Consider this the "teeing it up" part. Or, if you are a volleyball player, this is the "set" before the spike! As we all know, its' not *all* about physical is it? Whether in training for an endurance event or working in our business or whatever it is we are engaging in, we often neglect the all-important "balance" side of our personal equation.

One useful tool I stumbled upon is *meditation.* I am far from perfect in the use of this tool, but I find when I employ it I'm more productive, more creative and more energized.

Similar to my take on massage, which at one point I thought was for people who were soft, not tough. I admit my ignorance led me astray. I had no idea the healing and recovery benefits that can come from massage.

I saw an article a year or two ago by Ray Dalio about how Transcendental Meditation (TM) helped him recover from financial ruin. I was intrigued. Anytime a billionaire says something helped him recover from financial ruin, well, let's just say it sparked my attention.

TM is a technique from a movement created in the 50s by Maharishi Mahesh Yogi out of India. Dalio had recommended a book I picked up and recommend by Bob Roth, *Strength in Stillness: The Power of Transcendental Meditation*[23xxiii] I got copies for my two sons also. I'm not pushing it on you, but I recommend it if you want to learn about TM and its' benefits.

Strength in Stillness resonated with me.

A quick review of WebMD online mentions that "studies have found that regularly practicing meditation can reduce chronic pain, anxiety, high blood pressure, cholesterol and the use of health care services. ... Meditation, both TM and other forms, is generally safe and may improve a personal quality of life. But experts agree that meditation shouldn't be used as a single treatment for any particular health condition, or instead of conventional medical care."

TM requires a seven-step course, but there are some forms of meditation that do not. I have not taken the course, but I do practice a modified version of TM and have adopted it to my lifestyle and routine. I'm not trying to tell you how to approach it, only that it has made a difference for me.

If you decide to wade into this arena, I recommend doing your own research and, if you are so inclined, seek a professional for advice. WebMD states responsibly: "A few reports suggest that meditation can cause or worsen symptoms in people with certain psychiatric conditions. If you have an existing mental health condition, consult your doctor before starting TM."

I will say that having incorporated meditation into my life, I credit it for making a positive difference in my attitude and outlook, focus, and my ability to deal with situations that arise in a more level-headed way. It has not removed my "type A" tendencies but I feel it has taken the edge off at times. I have also often found that I'm not as "short" with myself or with others. I definitely seem to sleep better, as long as I don't meditate right before I go to sleep (which is not recommended by many experts).

Meditation, rest, recovery are all part of a larger theme. You have to make time for yourself. It's a simple fact we can only run so far and for so long without having to make time for recovery.

The same thing in business. At times, we need to remove ourselves from the personal dictates of our world, remove ourselves from being available to everyone, including even those that we love and move into a period of self-reflection or meditation. It has proven invaluable to me.

I become infinitely more productive when I have to force myself to jump off the treadmill of my everyday cycle. Many of my best ideas have come when I have gotten away from my everyday routine. I'm not in the business of advising on when and where to take a vacation; although, if you haven't had a vacation in three years, it's probably a good idea to do so.[24xxiv]

My point is that just like we need to have the discipline to work hard for ourselves, our clients and our families, that same discipline needs to transfer and apply to our recovery time. We have to have the discipline to force ourselves out of our current situation on a systematic basis. If we don't do this, we will hit the wall and we will be no good to anybody, including ourselves.

At times, we all take on what I call the heroine/hero mentality, the martyrdom syndrome, pushing ourselves to the brink of exhaustion or passing out. Hey, nothing wrong with hard work and I'm certainly not afraid of it, but after I've been training and pushing myself for five days, my body then tells me: *"Dude, it's time to take a break."*

If I don't listen to my body, my body will definitely get the last laugh.

Make sure you get off your treadmill. Stop and smell the roses. Read something that might spark a creative thought. Do something you normally wouldn't do. Take a walk, get a cup of coffee or cappuccino with somebody you haven't seen in a long time. Do anything to break with your routine and give your mind, body and soul a chance to rest and recover.

AN EXAMPLE OF OVER-USE INJURY:
TAKING MY OWN ADVICE

When training several years ago for the Beach to Battleship triathlon in Wilmington, NC, about halfway through my 18 week training cycle, I woke one morning, tried to get out of bed and -- locked up. I was now the tin man from the Wizard of Oz. I could barely move. I literally was clanking along, and had no idea what was going on. With my tin man-like motion, I thought, *"I'm done, all this training for nothing."*

I went into see my doctor (Dr. Palagruto), who I had called, thinking I was headed to a state of paralysis. I'm so grateful to have had a great medical team in my corner throughout all the years of participating in endurance events.

My doctor referred me to an Orthopedic Specialist, Dr. Joanne B. Allen who, coincidentally, was going to be our "Doc on the Dock" at the Beach to Battleship Triathlon. Most triathlons, especially for the iron events have a doctor there on the dock to observe the swimmers as they come out of the water.

Dr. Allen informed me I had an overuse injury. *A what?* I had strained something called my "IT bands." In layman's terms, these are bands that run the length from your hip area outside stretching down to almost your ankle. They had apparently seized up on me because of overtraining (no doubt from not taking time off and not performing proper stretching). I had to give them a chance to heal now.

The doctor also introduced massage therapy and pedicure. I thought massage was for sissies. I'm ashamed to say this, but I had no idea about the science behind massage therapy and the fact that it can release toxins in your body that buildup, like plaque, and prevent you from performing at your best. *Silly boy...*

Dr. Allen then prescribed a rigorous program of physical therapy that had me back out on the road and in the water again in less than 10 days.

———

This year, 2011, it was 38 degrees with a nice, hard driving, cold rain when we donned our wet suits and hit the water in the Banks Channel at Wrightsville Beach. The swim (1.2 miles) was a walk in the park compared to the 56-mile bike ride, which was one of the coldest I had ever recorded. Thirty degrees or so, with a nice hard driving rain that felt like needles hitting us. The wind was whipping, which also made it extra fun. During the ride, an ambulance blew by us. Someone up ahead had "blue leg" and didn't know it – hypothermia – and one of the volunteers had spotted him. They had to pull him off the course.

———

On event day, I got out of the water, having completed the swim portion of the triathlon, and saw Doctor Allen as I was running down the dock. I stopped, gave her a hug, pointed her out to the news crew standing there filming us wackos coming out of the Banks channel in a 38 degree hard driving rain, and yelled out, "This is my miracle worker!"

Thanks to Dr. Allen – and Dewitt, for allowing me to tuck in behind him on that hellishly cold, wet and windy bike ride – I crossed that finish line.

One lesson learned from this near fiasco: put ego aside and perform self-maintenance. Have the discipline to slow it down or stop, and reflect and do the things you need to do springboard to the next level. Sometimes what we consider to be one step backward (in my case above, rest) will help move us three steps forward.

Your loved ones will thank you, and they actually may thank me, too! (Ha!)

CHAPTER 12

WHERE THE RUBBER MEETS THE ROAD

"DO NOT ACT AS IF YOU HAD TEN THOUSAND YEARS TO
THROW AWAY. DEATH STANDS AT YOUR ELBOW. BE GOOD FOR
SOMETHING WHILE YOU LIVE AND IT IS IN YOUR POWER..."
--MARCUS AURELIUS

This is what I call the ROI Chapter. Return on Investment. I certainly
hope you have found this entire book has been worth your while and
I'm especially hoping this chapter alone is your return on investment
for the time you have spent with me on this journey.

Here, I put a collection of my thoughts, advice, suggestions, observations, et al. from my combined years in the Fortune 500 management and real estate arenas.

I'm hoping this chapter will be a deposit in your TEW (Time *
Experience * Wisdom) bank.

This is the section where I lay it out, at times providing cold, hard
advice, my "straight from the gut" observations, concepts or ideas I
hope will help you. Some of these are practices I have used, some may

be practices I have seen others use that brought them success, and some fall into my "what to do" and "what not to do" categories.

The information here, like the other chapters, are grounded primarily in my experiences and I'm hopeful one or a few of them will help you run from Peak to Peak.

As we all know, whether real estate or some other industry, business practices good and bad are "transferable." Some of these business practices (concepts, ideas) will apply to just about anyone in the real estate or general business arenas, endurance athletes or whoever you may be!

Some of the information in this chapter is geared to helping you identify and mold your "value proposition." Say, for example, you are a small business owner of a real estate firm. What is your "value proposition" to your brokerage team? Why should they partner with you and not another firm down the street? How do you build and maintain a positive work culture and environment? Do you recognized the fact your teammates, the brokers who are hanging their license with you, are also a *You, Inc.* and they have chosen to partner with you?

It's the same if you are in a Fortune 500 organization as say, Director of Operations. Do you recognize that your managers are the CEO's of their own *You, Inc.* and have decided to invest their time and talent with you?

We had a CFO at Avery Dennison Corp. who would say, "We vote with our shoes ." Which is to say: people can come and go from any company as they please if they don't like the environment, most companies don't lock the gate from the outside. It's true isn't it? Of course, there are some "switching costs" to exiting a company, but ownership and pride of work are key factors for all of us in what we do to make a living. The best managers and leaders I have seen apply that concept wherever they are and with whomever they are working. The best managers, leaders and business owners spark the pride of ownership with their teams. People that work with them (we all work first for ourselves and our family, right?) have a sense of ownership. They are not just punching a clock.

Many of my fellow small business owners are small business owners for a reason – because they want to work for themselves and their clients. Maybe you also were previously in the Fortune 500 arena and departed because you were pursuing your entrepreneurial dreams?

Maybe you are thinking about doing so and want to take what you have learned in your years of experience and apply it to your own business? If so, what's stopping you?

Maybe you are a manager within a medium-size company or larger and want to help improve your and your team's performance? What's getting in the way of your team's performance? Whatever the route or path or role, I'm hoping a nugget or two in this extensive chapter helps you in your business and your life.

INCREASING THE SIZE OF THE BULL'S EYE

In any industry and in life, there is no such thing as risk free.

One of the goals we should all have is to widen the size of the bull's eye for ourselves and our clients. By understanding our value propositions, our strengths and weaknesses, where we should focus on our training, what we bring to the table and who we choose to partner with, we inherently widen the bull's eye.

As I'm sure you are aware, there is no "free lunch", no such thing as a risk free investment. Whether you are purchasing a piece of real estate or are taking a course of action in a large manufacturing operation to help improve process performance, there is risk and cost involved.

The wider the bull's eye, the better. And by widening that bull's eye, we increase our probability for success.

CEO OF YOU, INC.

Throughout this book, there have been some recurring themes. One is the idea that we are all *CEO's of You, Inc.* You are your own "Inc." and you are the CEO of that "I-N-C." It's not about acting, thinking or impersonating a CEO. It's arriving at the realization that you *are a CEO*.

Whether you are a manager in a company, a school teacher, the owner of a small business, a nurse on a certain floor in a small or large hospital or specialty within a hospital, a Police Officer responsible for the safety of citizens in a certain section of your town, a clerk in a grocery store or whatever -- you are the CEO of one important and major corporation, *You, Inc.*

YOU KNOW A LOT, BUT WHAT ARE YOU DOING WITH THAT KNOWLEDGE?

The *Knowing-Doing Gap* first introduced by Jeffrey Pfeffer and Robert Sutton of Stanford is very real. It is called many things. Zig Ziglar put it this way: *"First you have to Be, then you have to Do, then you can Have."*

Three simple words: *Be, Do, Have.*

I had the pleasure of seeing Zig in person once when I was at Hanes and he yelled that at us and my colleagues and I were jumping up and down by the end of the session, pumping our firsts in the air, giving each other high fives. Zig had that kind of impact on people and he was special for sure.

No matter what you call it though, it's all about execution and taking action on what you know. Knowing is great, *doing is better.* Perfect is great, but *Done is better than Perfect*...Because let's face it, with perfect, although a great goal, we may never get there. Ye' old curve to infinity. Don't get me wrong: that's not an excuse for shoddy work. I'm just saying get it done right, get it out the door and move on.

"A GOOD PLAN VIOLENTLY EXECUTED NOW IS BETTER THAN A PERFECT PLAN EXECUTED NEXT WEEK."
--GENERAL GEORGE S. PATTON

Part of the art of being a CEO is also recognizing the fact that you have to be cordially ruthless at times. That does not translate into mean spirited. For example, people might intentionally or unintentionally steal from you. I don't mean by performing the actual act of larceny, rather I mean they might steal your time, knowledge, business idea, etc. I would argue that someone stealing your knowledge or your time is one of the quietest yet most significant of all acts of thievery, either intentional or unintentional.

I don't get angry about this kind of loss though because, most often, it is purely innocent and I actually enjoy sharing and helping others, as I'm sure you do as well.

But there is a fine line between someone asking for help, advice, counsel, and wandering over into the "stealing" of time or knowledge or information from you. I actually use this as a motivator. And I feel obligated to help people *not* steal my time. I have gotten better at that over time. It takes practice.

General James Mattis is a highly decorated, 40-year Marine Corps Veteran, who rose to the rank of 4-Star General, former leader of our U.S. Central Command under Presidents George W. Bush and Barack Obama and was Secretary of Defense for a while under President Trump. His troops adored him.

While serving in Afghanistan as a brigadier general, he was quoted as saying, "Be polite, be professional, but have a plan to kill everyone you meet."

It's an extreme example, but the point translates nicely to the real estate world and most any business, large or small, and to any endurance sport or life situation you may be involved in.

We have many decisions to make every day involving our time. How do we choose to make those decisions and spend our time? Who do we let shift or re-direct our day over to *their agenda?*

Obviously, Afghanistan, the Bad Lands, are much different than our civilian worlds, but this is how I would translate the General's word to apply to those of us not in Afghanistan: Be polite and professional and recognize that you may have to be cordially ruthless in guarding two of your most precious assets: *time and knowledge.*

Yes, sharing your TEW (time, experience and wisdom) is important, but it's okay to guard your time and knowledge, as you have to take care of You, Inc. first, before you can help others. And I'm here to say that we should all do so unapologetically and maybe even with a smile on our faces.

To help you understand where I'm coming from, part of my mentality is genetically encoded (as it is, in part, for all of us). As mentioned previously, my father grew up in Harrison, NJ. Dad let me know he had to be tough to grow up where he did. Football was his way out and he knew it. It was his path to education, and education was his path to a better life, to freedom.

So, my Dad looked at every tackler as someone who was trying to keep him at his station in life. There were times, he admitted to me, that he turned toward a defender to run over them rather than trying to go around them. He ran with anger, with a chip on his shoulder, with the intention of delivering the blow rather than receiving the blow. I saw that in his eyes my entire life. He was always afraid someone was going to come knocking on his door and say, "I'm sorry Mr. Frandano, but there has been a mistake...You have to go back now..."

Not that Harrison is a bad place. It was just a place he never wanted to return to full time. That poor defender on the football field wasn't just a defensive player trying to tackle him, he was trying to keep Dad from achieving his goals. In Dad's mind, that defender was trying to take something from him, trying to hurt him and his family. *So, run over him he did.*

Though he made sure I (we) had it much better, I had some of that same edge. I was grateful to get into college (thank you, Joe Ward, at Appalachian State University, for taking a shot on me!). Once I got there, I was ruthless about staying. 24-hour study room here I came. The rest of my life was driven by several factors and fear of failure has certainly been one of them.

When I eventually got into endurance sports, I attacked hills as if they were the enemy and those long roads my nemesis, both trying to keep me from crossing my finish line. And if I didn't cross that finish line, if I quit, well, in my mind, that is a slippery slope and can spiral out control. What else would I quit or give up on?

My thinking would be along these lines: *my two sons, John and Joe and my family needed me to keep going. If I can cross that finish line, I can cross any finish line.*

Cordially Ruthless. Guarding my time and my knowledge to advance my ball first, so I can then help others. I don't apologize for it and I don't see anything wrong with it. I hope you don't either, for yourself or others in your world.

A DIVERSFIED, YOU, INC.: OWNERSHIP VS BROKERAGE, EQUITY VS TRANSACTIONAL:

One common denominator: almost everyone I know in the real estate industry who fall into the category of what most would deem "successful" and who truly put themselves into a position to run from peak to peak, are diverse in their business. That means if they are a broker, they most likely have a hedge, something that can counter the drop off in their income stream if the transactional side of the business slows down or falls off.

There are some brokers in the real estate business who are laser focused and have a pure niche, but I have found them to be the exception.

Another example: if you are a commercial real estate broker and your only focus is in office and if, for some reason, demand for office-related transactions drops off, you better have a Plan A, B or C or eating is going to be hard to do.

The point is, if you are focused purely on any niche segment and demand in your market segment dries up, you'll face a very long valley to run through. You darn well better have some support and re-fueling stations set up along the way so you can make it to your next peak.

Common sense? Yes...

Common practice? Not at all.

When I was first getting into the real estate business, one of my mentors, who is a talented multi-family developer, let me know that the "transactional side is great but it is the equity side you really want to get to..." This tidbit translates to: Transactional side = Brokerage or sales, Equity side = ownership. If you are on the equity side, that means you have equity in the deal, you are an owner. His over-arching point was to have recurring income.

RECURRING INCOME - THE GOOD OLE "CLICK, CLICK, CLICK" SOUND OF THE PRINTING PRESS

This click, click, click sound is much better than that roller coaster I was riding up back in 2003, only to plunge off the cliff on the other side of 2008!

What my mentor was referring to above is known as having a source of recurring income, income that throws off cash after you own it. It's the good "click, click, click" and it's a blessing and powerful thing to have.

Some of the best income is income that makes you money while you sleep.

Warren Buffett, Berkshire Hathaway's Chairman, would call that compound interest. Compound interest is just that, an investment that "compounds" or grows over time for you due to the interest you are earning on your investment. Mr. Buffett uses the S&P 500 as a great example. If you invest in an S&P 500 index fund, for example, it has been proven that over time there is generally a reliable return to you from your investment.

Let's take an example, the Rule of 72, to help explain this.

FROM INVESTOPEDIA.COM (THEY DO A GOOD JOB OF EXPLAINING THIS SIMPLE YET POWERFUL CONCEPT):

The Rule of 72 is a quick, useful formula that is popularly used to estimate the number of years required to double the invested money at a given annual rate of return.

While calculators and spreadsheet programs like excel sheets have built in functions to accurately calculate the precise time required to double the invested money, the Rule of 72 comes in handy for mental calculations to quickly gauge an approximate value. Alternatively, it can compute the annual rate of compounded return from an investment given how many years it will take to double the investment.

The Formula for the Rule of 72 is:

Years to double = 72 divided by a selected interest rate where Interest rate = rate of return on an investment.

CALCULATING THE RULE OF 72

If an investment scenario promises an 8% annual compounded rate of return, it will take approximately (72 / 8 =) 9 years to double the invested money. Note that a compound annual return of 8% is plugged into this equation as 8, and not 0.08, giving a result of nine years (not 900).

The rule applies to the exponential growth of an investment based on a compounded rate of return.

The summary of this is that if you begin early enough, the time value of money invested builds up quickly due to the compounding effect and will, at least in theory (and in practice if done properly), make money for you while you sleep due to this compounding. You are "employing" the use of compound interest to work for you.

The real estate world sets up very nicely for this concept. Rental income from a small duplex property in the world of real estate is another way of applying this concept. Say you purchase the duplex by getting a loan and, over time, you pay that loan off. Now you have the underlying real estate as an asset, and you have the recurring income coming into you monthly from your tenants. Cha and Ching!

In both cases, you can hear the "click, click, click" ticking off both while you are working and while you are sleeping, with dollars flowing your way. Think "pre-printing press." Yes, you had to earn the dollars and put in the thought up front, but now, they are making money for you while you sleep. A nice thing for you and your family or anyone in your world you are wanting to help.

A friend of mine, a residential appraiser, started about fifteen years ago purchasing one residential property a year. His goal was to have thirty of them and have them paid off by the time he retired. When I had lunch with him a couple of years ago, he was well on his way.

Having those thirty properties and collecting, in theory, a rent check every day of the month will be better, in my opinion, than relying on the folks behind the curtain on Wall Street to deliver returns for you.

By the way, this person will probably be collecting the bulk of those thirty checks on the first day of the month. I used collecting a check every day only as an example, since his goal is thirty properties and there are thirty days, give or take, in any given month.

BE THE OLD GUY IN THE COFFEE SHOP:

I remember my first real estate licensing instructor (we'll call him "Pete") talking about the coffee shop he would go to in his small town. Every day, an old man was there when he got there and was there when he left.

One day, Pete asked a friend who knew the old man, "What does he do? Every day, when I come in and when I leave, he is here the entire time and yes, he's older, but he doesn't look so old that he's retired?"

His friend replied, "He owns real estate...his job is to pick up a rent check every day from one of his tenants. So, he drinks his cup of coffee, then a second one, then goes and picks up his rental check, deposits it in the bank. And if it's a sunny day, he goes to the park and watches the ducks around the little lake. If it's raining, he goes home and reads the paper on his screened in porch."

Being the old guy in the coffee shop doesn't sound like a bad goal to me, but you have to be methodical about making that happen by setting goals and adding to your portfolio over time.

EXAMPLES OF PEOPLE I KNOW WHO HAVE DEVELOPED DIVERSE INCOME STREAMS:

- Prominent commercial broker who also owns a successful gasket franchise, and is a sales coach, motivational speaker, and author.
- Broker friend (college roommate and fellow Myers Park High School Alum) who is also a highly active residential appraiser

- Broker/commercial developer who owns 50+ Autozones, as well as apartments, among other various projects.
- The residential appraiser friend of mine whose goal is to accumulate 30+ homes as his retirement for rentals and is almost there at age 60. Based in Gastonia, NC, he has served in leadership in our great state.
- My client, Jack Cargile who was an apartment developer and also owned a logistics company.
- I perform appraisal/valuation work which is much different than brokerage work. Commercial real estate appraisal typically does well in an up market (due to the volume of transactions and bank financing that is required) and in a down market given the amount of work that needs to be performed to assess the value of real estate assets > people (or banks) need to know the value of what they have when the market "hits the fan."

Here's another real example of "the Hedge" or diversification of your business and how it may help save your backside, like it did mine.

During the Great Recession, Southport Realty, the company I co-owned, had a great team and a very sound system in place for property management. This was a lifesaver for us when homeowners couldn't sell their homes and had to rent them instead. Thankfully, we were set up to handle this segment of business and focused on long-term rentals.

Ask any property manager and they will let you know that the property management segment of our business is hard, detailed work. To put it bluntly, it can be a pain. It typically requires you or someone on your team to be on the clock 24/7 and requires meticulous record keeping, months-end reconciliation, owner reports and documentation, etc.

If you are in the real estate industry and you do not have a property management business in place, you may want to consider referring this business to a firm that has a property management business already set up. We gladly paid referrals to other brokers who brought business to us and most firms will pay referral fees. A referral is just that, if you and I are both licensed real estate agents and I refer a client to you, and you close the transaction (i.e. consummate the deal), then you pay me a referral fee.

Some in the real estate industry feel that referral fees are "easy money", but whatever it is, it is essentially rewarding you for your network, which holds a great deal of value.

No doubt there are others, but here, I list two benefits of having a great property management business in place:

1 – The rental income keeps clicking (click, click, click) – month in, month out. It's a nice and secure feeling.

2 – Property owners who want to sell their property will often turn first to their property manager, who they typically know and trust, and that property manager will in turn take it on and list it or will refer it to another broker.

Diversification, in the stock and investment market and in the real estate world, is typically a wise and prudent path to follow. I'm certainly not saying focus and having a niche is a bad thing, far from it. If you are the best industrial broker or one of the top industrial brokers in your market, high five! I am only suggesting checking your revenue streams and see if there is another one you can add as a compliment or offset. And don't forget to loop in your accountant, or financial adviser or attorney for advice. Someone with the CCIM designation would also be a good person to have on your team.

From my experience and observations, only a small percentage of real estate practitioners have figured out and actually put this concept into practice.

What about you if you are not in the real estate business? Is there a complimentary product or service you can add to your business that will act as a hedge or offset if things bump back slightly? It's always good to do a health check on our business model. The COVID-19 pandemic has certainly taught us a hard lesson in checking for strengths, weaknesses, opportunities and threats (SWOT analysis).

When you are standing on one peak and looking across to the other peak, you need to have a plan that will get you there. How can I get through the valleys when I set off on a marathon if I don't have a nutrition and a pace plan? I'm not going to make it to the end if I don't have both. You can't run a marathon without fueling your body along the way and without a sound nutrition plan, you will eventually hit the wall (bonk). It's the same in your business.

In summary on this point, unless you are so well entrenched in your market segment and are in the top 1% to 10%, and even if you are in the top tier, I recommend your business model include some type of hedge and recurring income that can weather severe downturns; otherwise, you will have a difficult time running from peak to peak.

ON DEAL SIZE

I have experienced first-hand that some smaller real estate deals take every bit as much time as the larger deals. Sooo, why would I take on small deals if I can pursue other, larger deals?

At times, we have no choice, there is a client need and we may feel a responsibility to help. Acknowledging the fact that some larger deals have a much higher level of complexity (for example, having a large, 1000-acre land tract, rezoned and taking it through the entitlement process to move it from a residential land tract to one that can be used for a mix-used project)...

Just some food for thought.

ON OWNING YOUR OWN FIRM (OR SMALL BUSINESS)

Owning a firm sounds very prestigious doesn't it? It's all good until something like the Great Recession rolls in and the *defecation hits the oscillator*[25xxv], at which point you have to plug every red cent back into the business to keep it floating.

Try this on for size...

The first four years of ownership of our real estate firm, we did not take an ownership draw. I liquidated a significant chunk of my 401K from my days in Fortune 500 land and reinvested every cent into the business. Had we not done that, had we skimmed off the top like so many others had done (hoping the market would soon turn for the better, which it did not) to provide us, as owners, with an ownership draw when those dollars desperately needed to be going back into the business to prop it up, we would not have survived. We would have gone down like so many brokerage companies did.

Instead, we put ourselves into a position to scoop up some incredibly good people from firms who did not reinvest in their business and did not survive. For those first few years in the tsunami, we lived off of whatever business I closed, which means being on 100% commission-based income. Pay for performance. You close a deal; you get paid. You don't close a deal; you don't get paid. No excuses and shame on us for buying a real estate company at the top of the roller coaster, not many saw it coming, we certainly did not.

But in 2007-2009, when some went down, we survived.

As an owner of a firm, in addition to your own hard work, it's not a bad thing to have others working hard to add to your income as well. This is simple math: there are only so many hours in a day, so you have limited *time and resources*. If you can leverage, in a positive way, other people and resources to add to your income stream, there is nothing wrong with that! Are you good at motivating people? Do you like to coach? Are you a good manager and prefer not to sell? If you do like to sell, will you be competing with your brokers or teaming with them? How will you funnel leads when they come into your sales team? All beyond the scope of this book, but things to think about for sure. Call me or email me if you have questions![26xxvi]

Hey, what author of a book do you know would give you his contact information?

TO MY FELLOW FIRM & SMALL BUSINESS OWNERS:

At one point during the height of the Historic downturn, I had a friend of mine who had broken away from a competing firm (I was friends with their owner). This person, David, was a very active commercial broker in our market. At the height of the Great Recession, I asked David how it was going with his new firm. He looked at me and said *"Pete, I'm like a country club with no paying members..."* I laughed, but I could see he didn't think it was funny; he was serious.

If you are a firm owner, I'm assuming you are in it not out of charity necessarily; although, that may be an important part of it for you. But I hope you are also planning and executing on some component of your world that is going "click, click, click", making money for you while you are sleeping. Part of that is of course to ensure you have folks on your team who are producing.

As a firm owner I can tell you this: *it's fun having other brokers make money for you.*

Think about it...

As an independent contractor, when you are working for others, whether for a brokerage firm or an appraisal firm or whoever, you are effectively getting taxed twice. Once by the firm you are affiliating with on your split and again by Uncle Sam. I call it double taxation because that is exactly what it is. The general public doesn't understand this, a few firm owners don't want you to know this.

If you are a residential broker, I bet many of your clients think that if you close a deal, you got a certain percentage fee, and that you just pocket 100% of that fee. Most do not understand you are paying a significant portion of that fee back to the house; that is, the firm where you have chosen to affiliate with and where you hang your license.

This is not me advising you to leave your firm. I am just pointing out that as the CEOs of *You, Inc.,* we should choose and continuously check our partnerships wisely because that's what they are – *partnerships.*

Most firm owners tilt the table toward themselves, which is fair and normal. They have to bear the burden and risk of owning the firm. It's what we do. I'm not calling this Vegas, but similar to Vegas, *the House usually wins.* In fairness, the House also bears considerable risk and has bills to pay. Of course, so do you! Many people who are not small business owners do not realize how expensive it is to run a full-service real estate firm (or any firm) ... not to mention the legal liabilities that go along with it.

Solid companies, that is, firm owners who are confident in their value proposition and culture, typically attract and keep good team members (i.e. partners).

We vote with our shoes, right?

Some suggestions to Fellow business owners:

- Invest in the business
- Don't take short cuts
- The Basics: Your competition has'em, you better have'em or else (MLS, information, subscriptions, tools, technology, support, etc.)
- Technology? Don't be afraid of it. In this category of business ownership, there are two types of people: the Quick and the Dead. We all need to be aware of the exponential changes and shifting going all the time on the technology side of any business. You have to be quick and agile or your business will be dead and left behind.
- Help your team close deals – Are you actually helping by removing some of the administrative or paperwork burden or are you bogging your team down with burdensome processes?
- Make team meetings productive and collaborative. Are you the movie *Glengarry Glen Ross*? This is a movie about a day in the life of a commercial real estate broker and owner. Much of the public thinks this is real estate. It's not, but it is entertaining. One of the mantras in the movie is: "ABC, always be closing." If as a firm owner, this is the environment and culture I have and is my sole focus, *I am doomed!* To reiterate a previous point: selling a piece of real estate, unlike some other "products" is a long term and serious financial proposition that can bankrupt our clients if not done thoughtfully and with every attempt to mitigate risk.

- Does the "Tax" on your team, meaning the fee split that you are charging your brokers, match your value proposition? Is the fee split you are charging your brokers worth it? Are the tools and the environment you are providing to your brokers worth the fee split to them? Most reasonable brokers in the real estate industry (or managers in a company as another example) understand there is no perfect firm, *no broker or firm utopia*. Some firms who provide a nice high split for their brokers also may load a ton of unforeseen expense on the broker, so broker beware.
- As the firm owner, are you generating leads or does the broker have to generate all of her/his business?
- Are you helping remove the administrative load?
- Are you helping your team cross finish lines or are you putting up roadblocks to those finish lines? If you are weighing your partners down, slowing them down, putting a drag on them, remember, we all vote with our shoes.
- Do your brokers need an advanced degree to understand how you share fees or expenses or is it straight forward?
- Does your "system" allow for progressive splits or do what expenses you split shift with the wind? Is your system consistent year over year?
- Turnover is always a great indicator of culture and environment in any business. If you are a turnstile, a training house that trains brokers (or other key people if you are not in the real estate business), then sends them on their way to other firms shortly thereafter, this is an indicator of something gone seriously awry in your culture, in the environment you have created. In seven years, we had one broker leave us. When I was in Fortune 500 land, I was certainly not a perfect manager, but I always had very little turnover on my teams. Is your firm a training ground for others? A Farm Team for other firms? If so, why? It's okay to ask folks when they are leaving why they are

leaving. If you feel you may be the problem, then have someone you trust do the "exit interview."

- Play to your strengths. At times, my son, who was an exceptionally good baseball player, would shade over from centerfield. Many broker owners are rain makers, great deal makers, but due to their personality traits are lousy at managing others, much less motivating or uplifting or coaching others.

- We need to recognize where we are strong and where we are not. We need to get team members and leaders who complement us. And if we are poor motivators, we need to step back and get a great sales manager or coach.

- If you're an analyst or an introvert, you should have somebody on your team who knows how to generate business and talk to people.

- If you are a great talker, a great communicator and you hate the details, you better have somebody that's willing to dive into the details and take care of the paperwork, administrative, organizational "stuff" for you. The administrative component of this business (or any) can bury you. It is critical not just to run the business, but to make sure you are in compliance with, not to mention following the law. I had a great arrangement with a colleague of mine some say I gave too much to, but it was worth it to me. At one point, our arrangement was she would receive 25% of every deal I brought in. Though I'm ok with detail, it was bogging us down and she loved the detail. Her handling the detail freed me up to go get more business. Well worth it!

- Your environment? Culture? Managing by the numbers or creating an environment that knocks down walls, picks people up? Long term vs Quarterly Wall Street type environment? I was determined when I left corporate America that I wasn't going to manage only by the numbers, but rather to do my best to think long term, beyond the next quarter. When you are working for a public company, you are somewhat strapped by Wall Street and earnings expectations. Being outside of the "grasp" was a liberating thing for me!

My message here?

If you are an independent broker and you are thinking about opening up your own "shop" with an actual office (even if it's a "virtual office"), be aware that there are inherent risks and rewards. Regardless, if you are in the real estate business, you are the CEO of *You, Inc.* But if you decide to expand outward and take on other brokers, that presents its own set of expenses and challenges but also may have its own set of rewards and revenue streams!

ON BANKS SHARING THE LOSS WITH YOU ON A LOAN

I can hear my Dad, the lifetime banker, up in Heaven chuckling right about...now!

I recall someone (many someones actually), borrowers from banks, complaining to me during "the long war" about the banks not cutting them (the borrowers) slack when they were under water (typically, this means the owner owes more to the bank than the property is worth).

Our clarifying conversation would go something like this:

Me: "Do you share your profit with the bank on the upside?"

Borrower: "Heck no! Why should I? They are making money off me every month in interest..."

Me: "Then why should the bank share in your downside? You signed a contract with them and they are holding you to it..."

PURCHASING INVESTMENT REAL ESTATE - APPRECIATION VERSUS BUYING AN INCOME STREAM

I had a senior CCIM Instructor once say: "If you are buying real estate for anything other than purchasing an income stream, than you are speculating. If you are purchasing real estate with the hope of being awarded by price appreciation, that is speculation."

It was very good advice.

No such thing as risk free, but the idea is to increase the size of your bull's eye (for you and your clients). Buying real estate that has a good income stream is a way to mitigate risk.

Owning real estate can be a viable tax shelter. This in-depth topic is well beyond the scope of this book, but for more information I strongly recommend taking a CCIM Course (CI 101 would be a great start) or a GRI (Graduate REALTORS Institute) course or pick up a book that focuses solely on this topic.

One of my apartment developers (apologies to my friends who are doctors - this certainly does not apply to all of you!) once said: "I watch where doctors pool their money and buy apartment projects, then I wait. They raise the rents over time, then their vacancies shoot up, and eventually, they panic and have to unload the project. Coincidentally, I'm there to buy it. I fix the project up, lower rents, make the project more efficient and Voila!! I'm leased up in a very short period of time."

The point here: don't go in cold, educate yourself and understand what you are investing in and if you don't have the knowledge or know how, consider partnering with someone who does.

ANOTHER COMMON DENOMINATOR: INTEGRITY AND ETHICS AND THE LONG VIEW

By long view I simply mean no one client or deal is ever worth losing your license or reputation over. Do the right thing even if it kills the deal. Profit, yes, but integrity over profit if you have to decide on one or the other. Take the high road every time.

Remember my reference to Denis Waitley earlier and in his excellent book *Empires of the Mind?* He asks, "What is your absolute bottom line?" He goes on to say, "You must consider the bottom line but make it integrity before profit." Cutting corners in ethics or integrity is a slippery slope. Again, I know that if someone will cross the ethics line with me on a small deal, he will do the same on a larger deal...

SIMPLY THE BEST

In observing one of the best land brokers in our real estate industry (I'm talking about you, Greg), understand that the best do not play the same game the rest of us are playing. They are not breaking the rules but instead have done what I call 'shifting the curve' or the playing field in their favor. They are on a different plain, playing a different game. While the rest of us are chasing sites, getting in our car and driving the client around all day to "tour", this broker is doing a "reverse tour." He's weeded out the sites that don't work via technology and his market knowledge. He uses "site rejection" versus "site selection."

Put another way, Greg is using his intellectual capital to leverage the tools he has taken the time to create and turns this into a major time advantage, an advantage he has over the rest of us. He has put distance between himself and the rest of the field.

I've heard a best-selling author and seasoned real estate investor/owner (Grant Cardone) and a few others put it this way: *Don't compete, dominate.* They are not saying be unethical or break the rules. It makes sense: there's nothing illegal about it, you don't have to be a monopoly and you don't have to hurt others.

Grant also says: The market crushes those who compete.

Well, I understand what he is saying, and I agree to a point, but at the end of the day, we all have to compete.

In every segment of our field I know someone who dominates or at least has put a great deal of distance between herself/himself and the rest of the field, while the rest of us 'compete'.

In his excellent book, *Brokers Who Dominate*[27xxvii] Rod Santamossimo, CCIM discusses some brokers in our field who dominate and he touches on some of their business practices... Most successful people I know in our field or any field adopt a system and strategy that suits their style and personality and then have others who compliment their style.

EVERY MISTAKE SHOULD YIELD AN OPPORTUNITY:

I had a really good boss at Hanes once say: "If you are never making mistakes, then you aren't doing anything. You aren't pushing the envelope." This was his way of telling me it's okay to reach, to make decisions, and sometimes to fall flat on my face, as long as I learned from the mistake. His other message: find opportunity in the mistakes!

I have found sometimes I learn the most when I fail, pick myself up, dust myself off and keep moving, this is also where I grow the most.

BEWARE OF DEBT

Another topic I have learned the hard way on. On this topic, I have a seasoned friend and mentor that basically says "if you owe a million dollars to the bank, they own you, but if you owe the bank $800 million, you own them!." (To be sure: that $800 million number has shifted upward significantly over the years!). Strategic debt can be a positive thing. Too much debt, not incorporated strategically, can be an insidious monster and should be treated with caution. If used properly, debt can leverage your business and take you to higher places. If not used properly, it can be catastrophic. I know this from experience. The old saying "live within your means" applies to us and our firms.

TECHNOLOGY AND TOOLS

In this day and age with the exponential increase in data management, data science and technology in general, you will be rendered the next "buggy whip" if you don't leverage technology. To put it bluntly: You will be left behind.

Are you using these tools to help you leverage your business or are you getting mired down in which one to use? Or worse, are you having to manage your tools? Are you working on your tools instead of on and in your business?

Incorporate technology into your business and daily life. Use technology. If it's not your game, it's also nothing to be afraid of; and by all means, please don't get stuck and never start.

CRM (Customer Relationship Management) software is the perfect example of this. I see so many of my colleagues get bogged down in managing the software that they forget about the client. CRM is a software platform to help the user manage client contacts, leads, manage the sales process from start to close, and so on. Selection of the perfect platform is a common conundrum in the real estate industry (or quite frankly, any industry that has clients, which is to say, all of them!). My suggestion is to do a quick review, interview a few users, and then pick one and go. Keep it simple.

If you find yourself managing the technology and spending what you perceive to be a disproportionate amount of time with it, it may not be working. Of course, there will be start up and learning curves; however, if a good chunk of time has passed and you are still fighting that piece of technology you selected and it's distracting you from generating business or closing deals, get rid of it. It's now an obstacle to you crossing a finish line. It's not helpful, it's hurtful to your cause. Be bold enough to make the executive decision and cut your losses if the tool is too complex and not yielding what you need it to yield.

In the commercial real estate world, ARC GIS (www.esri.com) and STDB (www.ccim.com) are great examples of tools that, when you are trained properly on them and implement them, can save you a ton of time and thus money. They will help you cross your finish lines.

The following are a few articles I recommend that provide technology overviews or a discussion on the concept. I suggest you do your own search and take an hour or two and immerse yourself in the topic as this is such a dynamic, ever changing component of just about any business. I think you will come up to speed on the basics very quickly. This segment of our real estate industry, like any industry, is changing so fast that some of these articles/books are outdated by the time you get done reading them (not literally, but almost!). So, the idea is to get the basics and to take that first step if you have not already done so.

- *Real Estate in a Digital Age* (2019) published by The National Association of REALTORS® :
  https://www.nar.realtor/research-and-statistics/research-reports/real-estate-in-a-digital-age
- *Commercial Real Estate Trends to Watch in 2020* published by Wall Street Journal written by Deloitte Risk and Compliance:
  https://deloitte.wsj.com/riskandcompliance/2019/12/30/commercial-real-estate-trends-to-watch-in-2020/
- *Moore's Law* (an overview on the speed at which computing power is advancing) published by Investopedia
  https://www.investopedia.com/terms/m/mooreslaw.asp#:~:text=Moore's%20Law%20states%20that%20the,growth%20of%20microprocessors%20is%20exponential.

My bet is that if you take the time to invest in it, use it, and incorporate it properly in your business, whatever your business is, technology and some of the associated tools out there will a) save you time/free you up to do other things with your time; b) put more money in your pocket; and c) enhance your quality of life. If those three things are not happening, I suggest something has gone awry in your strategic technology journey.

A WORD ON DESIGNATIONS

A designation, should you choose to pursue one or more, should be a means to an end, but it should not be the end. There are some great designations in the field of real estate that in my humble opinion are tops of the industry education-wise, networking-wise or both.

For the commercial field:

- CCIM: Certified Commercial Investment Member (www.ccim.com)
- SIOR; Society of Industrial and Office REALTORS (www.sior.com)
- CPM: Certified Property Management, through IREM, the Institute of Real Estate Management (www.irem.com)

- For Appraisal: MAI (Designated Member of the Appraisal Institute (www.appraisalinstitute.org)

In the residential world according, a few key and well-respected designations are:

- GRI: Graduate REALTORS Institute, https://www.nar.realtor/education/designations-and-certifications/gri
- CRS: Certified Residential Specialist, https://www.crs.com/about-us/contact-us
- SRES: Senior Real Estate Specialist, https://www.nar.realtor/education/designations-and-certifications/sres
- SRS: Seller Representative Specialist, https://www.rebinstitute.com/
- RSPS: Resort and Second Home Property Specialist, https://www.nar.realtor/education/designations-and-certifications/rsps-certification
- ABR: Accredited Buyer's Representative, rebac@realtors.org
- CPIS : Certified International Property Specialist, https://www.nar.realtor/education/designations-and-certifications/cips-designation
- e-Pro designation that focuses on technology and digital media > Contact e-PRO® at epro@realtors.org(link sends e-mail) or 877-397-3132.)
- For Appraisal: SRA Designated Member of the Appraisal Institute, https://www.appraisalinstitute.org/our-designations/#MAI_Designation

TO PROSPECTIVE BUYER OR SELLER CLIENTS, WHETHER RESIDENTIAL OR COMMERCIAL:

For the residential real estate client, I recommend strongly that you find someone with the designation like GRI or ABR, or in the commercial world CCIM, SIOR or CPM. They have invested in themselves and their own education and have access to networks that the other 90% of the field simply don't have.

In some cases, like the SIOR, CCIM or CPM designations, they have not only passed a rigorous curriculum of coursework related to the industry, they have also had to actually close a significant amount of commercial real estate transactions: rigorous academic level work combined with practical experience.

A competent professional in the residential world or in the commercial world should translate into an extra set of guard rails for you in your real estate journey.

AS CEO OF YOU, INC, HAVING TRUSTED AND DIVERSE SOURCES OF INFORMATION IS CRITICAL.

We all need to have our trusted sources of information. I jokingly say at times that I find it baffling that some economists and weather forecasters can be wrong 50% of the time and still remain employed, but if you or I are wrong 50% of the time, we're probably out of business.

To me, this translates into conducting my own research, using a few, focused and trusted resources, preferably also obtaining a dissenting point of view (the "devil's advocate") just to make sure I'm not missing something and then moving forward with my now well calculated decision.

A note on Experts:

As CEO of *You, Inc.,* we need to know and develop finesse as to when we are wandering outside of our area of expertise. If we need legal advice, we should hire an attorney. If tax advice, a tax adviser. If investment advice, an investment adviser. And if real estate advice, we hire a real estate professional, preferably one with an earned designation.

Sometimes, with more complex situations or deals, we may need all of the above on our team.

MY MANAGEMENT PHILOSOPHY HAS ALWAYS BEEN:

Coach to performance if you can... It's easy to fire somebody and I don't mean that in a cold callous way, because it's tough and you are dealing a major short-term set back to someone and their family. Show me an ongoing and consistently problematic employee, in any field or industry, and I will typically be able to show you a lazy or incompetent manager who failed to step up and do their job. Coaching is tough work. If coaching doesn't work, then you have a moral obligation to terminate the person, especially if they are bringing your organization down. Remember: you did not cause this problem, the "offending" individual brought it on themselves, by their action or lack thereof. If you have an employee or team member that is sinking the ship, then it's your job to save the ship and those who are on the ship. The good news is you are now solving the problem. Onward, upward...

LARGE PROJECTS VS SMALL PROJECT - I.E. SCALE AND YOUR TIME: BE THE SAME PERSON, EVERY TIME.

I have found during the course of my career that the $2000 fee job often takes as much time, if not more, than the $100,000 fee job. Yet the true professional treats them both with equal importance. If we start adjusting our work style and intensity around the size of our deal, we'll slip and not perform at our highest level on any deal. In other words, our work effort cannot be conditional on the deal. Our work effort needs to be unconditional and the same on every deal.

CHECK YOUR BUSINESS MODEL:

Periodically (now more than ever in this post-Pandemic world), check your business model to make sure it is a) relevant and b) sustainable. If not, as the CEO of *You, Inc.*, don't be afraid to change it, shake it up. What goods and services are needed? What mechanism and logistics and marketing channels to you need to use to deliver these goods and services? Take learning, restaurants and sporting events as three examples from our COVID-19 experience. How do you think these three segments will be impacted in the post COVID-19 world? Are there opportunities to serve customers in a different way within these segments? Some will win, some will lose. Why not be one who wins and take others with you across the finish line?

SOME OF YOUR MOST TRUSTED CONTACTS WILL COME FROM YOUR VOLUNTEER OR LEADERSHIP WORK:

The same applies to the work we all do at times, pro bono. This is part of the reason why I enjoy the volunteer (non-compensated), elected, industry leadership roles. There we get to see our peers and colleagues and how they operate when they are not getting paid for anything as they play a leadership role within our organization. I call it a window into the soul. Some of my best relationships have been by working alongside peers who are volunteer leaders and seeing the heart and effort they put in while serving those organizations. At times, I have even done deals with some of those folks. We negotiate hard, and then we work together to get those deals over the finish line for our clients. Not to mention that it opens up the referral network, so I now have trusted colleagues, professionals who are at the top of their game, who I never would have met in other geographies that I can refer business to. This is why some of my mentors and other industry leaders have said that when you give, you get back much more in return, and this has proven to be true for me.

TAKE THE LONG VIEW AND DELIVER VALUE.

In his classic book, *Permission Marketing*[28xxviii] in 1999, Seth Godin gave me permission not to be a *salesy guy*, not to use cheap sales tactics to try and woo business. If I was meeting with the Vice President of Logistics for a major corporation, and I used cheap, short-term sales tactics when she was putting her livelihood on the line by giving me access to one of their most precious assets: their supply chain, I would have been run out of the industry on a rail. If I couldn't deliver value to my client, I was out. Don't be afraid to say, "Thank you for your time but I'm not (we're not) for you." This will come back to you in ways you can't even imagine.

STAY THE COURSE/ADJUST YOUR COURSE/ABANDON SHIP:

As the CEO of *You, Inc.,* we need to simultaneously have the courage and conviction to stay the course, but also the vision to change the course if we need to. As the CEO of *You, Inc.* we need to give a well thought out process and business model a chance to "take hold", to gain traction, to let your drip marketing campaign do its' trick. How do we know when? Well, that is where finesse and our own business judgment come in to play. It also assumes a sound business model at the outset. If a sound business model doesn't exist, the ship goes down, regardless of our course. At that point, it's abandon ship!!! I have seen, over the course of my career, whether managing a large manufacturing operation or embarking on a new marketing campaign, that sometimes we don't have the appropriate patience or trust in our process to give it the necessary time to take hold, to gain traction. It can be an exceptionally fine line to walk for sure. An *Abandon Ship* call is the last resort but sometimes on rare occasion, its necessary to do and requires strong fortitude with the understanding you are "living to see another day." It may sound cold, *but cut it, don't look back and keep the lesson learned in the back of your mind!*

BEWARE AND BE AWARE: THE UNETHICAL OR UNHANDED ARE ROAMING THE COUNTRYSIDE, ALWAYS SEEKING THEIR NEXT VICTIM; ALWAYS TAKE THE HIGH ROAD AND USE LEGAL ACTION AS A LAST RESORT

Remember, in any industry, there are a small percentage of people who will attempt to take advantage of our good nature (including some clients!) and will steal from you, be it $1.00 or $100,000 or your time or knowledge. Stealing time or knowledge is one of the oldest forms of often unintentional larceny in the world.

MY LESSONS LEARNED:
1. Be aware and Beware
2. Always take the high road, stay positive, you are a Pro, reach deep and be the Pro
3. You are not the only one who has had a crazy client, we all have, you are not alone

4. The client (even the crazy one) is always right, even when they are wrong (although as mentioned previously, sometimes we have to fire our clients)

5. If someone does the wrong (unethical) thing, bite your tongue, get the deal behind you, move on, never to do business with them again, and chalk it up as a lesson learned. If it was a simple mistake, remember second chances can be a good thing.

6. Trashing or slandering someone will do us no good and will only come back to bite us and always makes the "sender" look smallish, teeny, tiny...

7. Never, ever, ever, never use social media to vent. I've seen people do it all too often and I'm stunned when I see it. It makes the "poster" look ridiculously small and unprofessional. Again, smallish, teeny, tiny... *Did I say never, ever?*

8. If the action is truly egregious (I get it's a matter of perspective, dollar amount, of course, etc.), then consult your attorney and take legal action if you have to, but only as a last resort.

9. Finally, email and text are both easy to hide behind and easy to get "twisted" and can be a rich source of misunderstandings. Many a misunderstanding can be resolved by picking up the phone and having a quick conversation – remember those? One trick I have used: type the pithy email you want to send, then send it only to yourself and walk away. I bet dollars to doughnuts when you look at it later, you will revise it to the more toned down, professional version, based on the professional you are! (calm, cool and collected, as my Dad used to say)

Oh, and did I mention taking the high road and staying positive?

It will sometimes take your best effort, reach deep, breathe, take a walk around the block 200 times, hit your head against a wall if you have to and cross that finish line, you can do it! (don't forget to breathe deeply and laugh with or at yourself from time to time)

CASH CALLS SUCK! THEY ALSO COME AT THE WORST TIME...

Heading into the downturn, I had a conversation with one of my mentors mentioned earlier, Ray, a seasoned multi-family developer who at one point was a partner in one of the largest multi-family development companies in the country. On that bright spring day in 2007, the market was starting to hit south, we were talking on the phone and I asked him how business was going.

He replied, "Pete, its good, but with some of my long-term financial relationships, with some folks I have worked with for many, many years, it's very tough. Everyone is running for cover. Relationships I've had for decades are out the window. In some cases, they are even doing cash calls on my developers performing projects...".

A cash call is when you have to go to your bank account, pull out money and put it into the deal. If it's a real estate deal, that means the bank may be requiring you to put more of your dollars in, and it is most likely in a contract you have signed with them (a great example of when to consult an attorney). Some enter into deals and think the only cash outlay they have to put out is up front. Uh oh. Be careful with that. Often, there can be more cash outlays required on the partnership, depending on economic circumstances or the fine print.

You know that queasy feeling? How about when the room begins to spin slightly? Ray's words created one of those moments for me.

"...cash calls on my developer's performing projects..."

At that moment, time froze and that phrase echoed loudly as it bounced around the empty chamber of my inner cranium.

"If that's happening to guys like Ray, what's going to happen to the rest of us??" I thought...

I got my answer soon after... and over the waterfall we all went...

WHICH FIRM TO PARTNER WITH?
DECISIONS, DECISIONS...

(Author's Note: As I have pointed out periodically, when this book was initially submitted to my editor for its "round 1 edit", the COVID-19 crisis had not hit. No doubt due to the pandemic this list is likely to be altered and possibly altered significantly. Regardless of the pandemic, the lists here are for illustrative purposes only and were researched from public domain; these lists will change year over year so I highly recommend you do your own new and original search and due diligence if exploring.).

When coming into the business, many new folks have asked, "Where should I hang my license?" That is a great question and my answer is always, "It depends..."

There are many well-managed real estate companies out there with varying business models and value propositions for their brokers, how they handle fee splits, expense share. etc. So, I advise everyone to set their own parameters and wants, then conduct the necessary research to narrow down where they ultimately land.

Do you want a widely known name, a national or regional firm or do you want to work for a boutique, niche or independent firm? Every firm you interview should be able to provide you with a) their value proposition and b) how they handle their broker partnerships in a two or three page summary of those elements.

If they load you up initially with more than a two or three page Executive summary, that should be a major caution light. It probably means they are already bogged down in administrative quicksand and will most likely be bogging you down as well.

Of course, there will be the larger "operating documents" or resource manuals, which should come later, but an Executive summary of the basics should allow you to make a well informed decision. Certain basic metrics should be important to you.

In addition to speaking with the Broker-in-Charge and/or owner(s), I always recommend you also meet with several of the current brokers.

My sample template below can serve as an example of how to rank firms as you meet them, gather their information and analyze it. Categories can be added or taken away from this simple spreadsheet. The purpose is to create a qualitative way to move from a subjective ("this place just feels right") to an objective process in your selection decision.

A FEW TIPS...

If you are going into the field of commercial real estate and the industrial sector is important or interesting to you because you have a corporate logistics background, that bit of definition will help you quickly narrow your search.

If you are going into the field of residential real estate and you want to focus on a certain area or a certain niche market (affordable housing, first time home buyers, luxury homes, etc.), that qualifying information will also help you narrow your search.

Keep your mind open and don't weed out a firm if they don't focus on your niche, you never know what opportunities might be available for you to grow that niche with your new firm!

On a personal note, when I spoke with Mary Anne Russ, the founder of Southport Realty, the firm my two partners and I eventually purchased, she wanted someone to start up her commercial division and I wanted to focus on commercial real estate, so it was a budding opportunity that became a win-win!

LOOKING AT THE PARTICULARS...

In my sample template below, I have entered information on three 'firms' to show how this ranking system can help, and why.

If you scan through the categories and entry rankings, you can see how quickly you can ferret out a fact-based determination of each firm. As mentioned, you can change, take out or delete categories to best suit your preferences (the wish list).

For me, a firm with team availability, in other words, internal teams I can join within a firm where the broker in charge does not compete against me is important. The latter means the broker in charge or owner does not sell real estate, thus possibly funneling inbound leads to herself, but rather her primary roles are support, coaching, compliance and management.

In the sample below, Firm 2 might get my nod, depending on which categories are most important to me and whether I care or not about working with an independent (boutique) firm or a national firm. For my "sample system" below, I use a 1-5 ranking system with 5 being "most positive" and 1 being a major negative, so the higher the score, the better.

A few categories that mean a lot to me in this sample scenario:

- How a firm handles their commission split with me – do I think it's fair?
- A strong Internet presence – in my mind, this offsets the fee amount they keep on each of my closings
- Great location
- Outstanding Admin support
- My startup costs will be lowest with a firm that ranks high in the expense share/fees category
- Objective lead generation system

This is just one example of many you could create for your search, tailored around what is important to You, Inc.!

As you prepare for any interview with a firm, always remember that this is a dual interview and they need to meet your criteria as well.

Brokerage Firm Evaluation			
Categories	Firm 1	Firm 2	Firm 3
Commission split	4	3	2
Internet presence	3	5	3
Expense Share/Fees	3	4	3
Brokerage size	4	2	2
Facilities	3	3	1
Location	2	5	4
Training	1	4	3
Mentor program	4	1	5
Management support	3	3	4
Administrative support	4	5	2
Culture	4	4	3
Specialties	3	5	3
Broker's reputation	5	4	3
Referrals and leads	2	4	3
Total	**45**	**52**	**41**
Independent, Franchise/Corp?	Ind	National	Ind
Team Openings?	Yes	Yes	No
Broker in charge compete/sell?	Yes	No	No
*Rank 1-5 with 5 being most positive/highest			

A quick internet search, whether you are interested in the residential real estate world or the commercial real estate world (or both!) will yield plenty of ranking and information on various firms. If you are contemplating coming into the real estate industry, I recommend using multiple sources as a "cross check" and speak with people you know, respect and trust in the industry. Most of us in the business are always willing to help!

One company, MEGA 1000, publishes an annual ranking brokerage firms and Associations.

To access the full MEGA 1000 report click here[29xxix].

A NOTE ON POLITICS:

Business and politics go together. They simply do. It's a fact.

Just as I'm passionate about real estate and endurance sports, I also am passionate about this topic, with a caveat: I'm not passionate about it to the point of beating you down on my points of view -- that's not my style.

Winston Churchill once said that *"if two people agree on everything one of them is not necessary."* I agree with Mr. Churchill's statement to a point for sure.

I always smile when I hear someone say they are "not into politics." For those who say "I'm not into politics" three questions enter quickly into my mind: 1) Are you in business or working? 2) Are you breathing? 3) Do you like to eat or help others to eat?

If the answer to any of these questions is "yes", then you are into politics. To not acknowledge this, in my humble opinion, is to bury one's head in the sand.

Just like I told the assembled group of colleagues the day I was installed as President of the Brunswick County Association of REALTORS®, whether they admitted or knew it or not, *they were all endurance athletes*, the same applies to politics. You are in it, whether you want to be or not, whether you realize it or not, so why not play a role or be involved, even if that role is small?

In the real estate industry we have something that is known as "RPAC", the REALTORS Political Action Committee. The National Association of REALTOR® website, states:

Since 1969, the REALTORS® Political Action Committee (RPAC) has promoted the election of pro-REALTOR® candidates across the United States. The purpose of RPAC is clear: voluntary contributions made by REALTORS® are used to help elect candidates who understand and support their interests. These are not members' dues; this is money given freely by REALTORS® in recognition of the importance of the political process. The REALTORS® Political Action Committee and other political fundraising are the keys to protecting and promoting the real estate industry.

I can say from experience this is a bipartisan group: meaning it supports political candidates of all parties without bias. Political donations are divided almost evenly among Republicans and Democrats based on their support of real estate issues (private property owner rights).

In addition to my other leadership roles within our industry, at several points I have served as our state's Legislative Chair for the NC-CCIM Chapter; served on our state level North Carolina Association of REALTORS® legislative committee; the Charlotte Regional Commercial Board of REALTORS® legislative committee; and have been a long time major donor to RPAC. This is to say, I've been involved and I put my money where my mouth is.

For me, it's quite simple. RPAC watches the proverbial "gate while we sleep" to make sure some of our Legislative leaders don't do anything inadvertently or purposely to hurt private property owners across our great nation. In many cases, it is also a resource of information for these same Legislative leaders. My (our) hats off to those Legislative leaders who choose to serve at our local, state and national levels.

Hey, let's face it, over the course of history we have all seen people do strange things when in power and real estate is an especially important component of our economy. So, if we are in the real estate industry, we have a responsibility to help educate and better our communities and be a resource to our Legislative leaders.

Within the realm of *Endurance Real Estate*, there is little doubt that an important component of our business lies within the political sphere, whether at the local, county, state or national level, and being able to navigate and understand it, and contribute to the discussion is critical in being able to run from peak to peak.

So, if you haven't already, I suggest you dip your toe in this arena and have a voice, extreme right, moderate right, center, extreme left, moderate left, whatever your political affiliation (or lack thereof), have a voice! I've seen first-hand how we can all work together to move forward and I have seen individuals who thought they could not make a difference end up making a huge difference in our industry. If you are not in the real estate industry, no doubt there is room for you to get involved and have a positive impact to the legislative process. Your involvement certainly does not have to be "industry specific."

The most popular book in the world, The Bible, in Isaiah 1:18 says it best:

"Come now, let us reason together..."

————

MY MAGIC 80: SOME SHARED WISDOM BASED ON MY EXPERIENCE...

The following are tips, advice, insights gained or suggestions. There is no particular order on these. Some are related to one another either directly or indirectly.

Some are directly related to the real estate industry and some are not. If you see something you already know and your first reaction is "duh", *it's probably not for you* and hopefully you can benefit from some of the others. These are yours to do what you want to with them; use them or don't use them. Just keeping it fun and real....I call these my "Magic 80" because magically, there are 80 points that follow!

1. **On communicating with your sphere on a regular basis:** Whether you are commercial or residential real estate focused or in another industry all together: you need to be touching (i.e. communicating with) your clients and your sphere on a regular basis. Some recommend daily, some weekly, some have focused lists.

   Never forget your sphere is broader than your clients. Your sphere can include folks who view you as an expert and may be a referral source for you, someone you may never do a direct deal but are in a position for you to collaborate with (attorneys, bankers, general contractors, etc.).

   I happen to have a Commercial A list, B List, C list (which means something to me). I have seen a variety of systems over the course of my career and just about all of them are different but work for the user. Please, for the love of Pete (Ha!) you need not wait until you find the perfect CRM system to do this. Set a reminder and do it.

A GRI (Graduate Realtor Institute) class taught by Zan Monroe here in North Carolina opened my eyes many years ago now to my "fabulous 50" - call it whatever you want, whether you have a fabulous 10, 50, 100 or 1000: these are the folks who are loyal to you; make sure to "touch" them regularly, you'll be glad you did. I try and give people some useful information when I reach out to them. Call, email, send handwritten letters whatever works for you.

As it relates to taking that first step, I agree with the immortalized words of Phil Knight from Nike: *Just do it.*

2. **Work from Anywhere - be mobile:** Some have asked me if, due to the COVID-19 Pandemic, I am "mobile." I've been mobile since the first day I joined Avery Dennison back in 1999; and truth be told, I was actually somewhat "mobile" back to my days at Hanes and traveling through Latin America. My first day on the job with Avery Dennison I was on an airplane to Hong Kong. They had recruited me away from Sara Lee Corp on the premise of 25% travel, which quickly turned into 90%. They taught me, thankfully, how to work from anywhere: airports, train stations, layovers, Boston, London, coffee shops. As indicated earlier, if I waited until our global team was together to get it done, we never would have gotten anything done. I like to use this example: Some owners of brokerage firms get nervous when they don't see their brokers in the office. I would say the opposite, that I'm nervous when I do see them! The clients aren't in here, *they are out there.* Go where your clients are and engage!

3. **On Inventory levels:** Knowing the inventory level in a certain market area or segment (e.g. single family homes in the $150,000 to $200,000 price range) is invaluable and will help you zero in on supply and demand gaps. A basic rule of thumb is that six months of inventory is considered to be a balanced market; anything over a buyer's market and anything under a seller's market. Here's a simple example of how to gauge inventory levels:

Take the previous years' closings in your category of interest. Say there were 100 closings previous year. That's 100 closings divided by 12 months = 8.33 closings per month. If there are 50 listings presently on the market in your category that means the supply is balanced (50/8.33 = 6.0024). Again, the rule of thumb is six months of inventory equals a balanced market. Greater than six months equals a buyer's market (over supply) and less than six months equals a seller's market (under supply, higher demand).

4. **Use technology:** No matter your industry, if you are not using technology, you will be left behind. If it's not your game, don't let it spook you, hire someone or add someone to your team who can complement your style.

5. **Save some dollars every month and from every paycheck you make**; Sock it away for the downturn because the next one is always coming. The idea is being able to run from Peak to Peak...We never know when the rug is going to get pulled out from under us. 2006-2012 taught us that. So has 2020. *Boom, out of nowhere.*

6. **On staying in your lane, Bro (or Sis) - Dishing to the experts**: Typically, you can't be an attorney, general contractor, asbestos expert, soils expert, rezoning expert, environmental expert, and all for your clients. Maintain a list of experts and recommend 2 or 3 to your clients.

7. **No deal is worth your license or your reputation** Remember that, especially if you have clients steering you that way. Communicate clearly with them and hopefully it's rare, but fire them if you have to.

8. **Advise your clients as you would your family members or those you care about:** Those clients will come back to you and they will tell others about your professionalism.

9. **I've waived more people off deals than I have put them on deals.** Sometimes, you have to be that military scout who was sent up ahead on recon, and calls back to the inbound troops, flying in by helicopter: *WARNING! Landing Zone is hot, abort mission, I say again, abort...* What this means is you care enough about your client to wave them

off a deal that may not meet their needs or accomplish their goals. Sounds simple, doesn't it? I know it's not. Live to see another day, they will appreciate you for it. The flip side of this also applies: sometimes you have to have the guts to stay with a deal when you know in your heart of heart of hearts it's the right deal for your client and they may be getting weak kneed. It can be a tight rope to walk.

10. **Your network is one of the most valuable assets you have, guard it with your life:** Use it, get paid for it. Referral business is the some of the best money ever. You wash your hands and forget about it, then a check shows up. A friend of mine, David Berne, is an expert on Bald Head Island Real Estate. Bald Head Island (BHI) is a wonderful town right across from Southport, in the far southeastern corner of our great state. I call it "Nantucket without the winters." When I was co-owner of Southport Realty, our firm typically would not practice real estate on BHI because we didn't really know the island at that time. (We stayed in our lane!). David always liked to deliver referral checks in person; he's old school like that. I once referred David to a client and forgot about it. Five or six months later, I hear David's booming, cheerful voice come through the front door. I go out and he hands me a check with a thank you and a big smile on his face. Cha-ching. Satisfied client, satisfied broker colleague. Thank you, David!

11. **Don't over think things,** keep it simple, focused, put your shoes on and go.

12. **Train, Execute, Take time to Recover.**

13. **Always take the high road** - it will come back to haunt you in an incredibly good way.

14. **Bite your tongue,** send ghost emails or texts to yourself to give you a chance to cool off before sending a hot-head communication out to your intended recipient. Go for a walk around the block, ten times if you have to.

15. **I went into several deals knowing I was getting ready to get "had."** On one deal, I was warned by a colleague "he's going to hurt

you on this deal..." He did, and I have not done business with him again. The great majority play fair, a few bad apples don't. Sometimes we learn the hard way. Onward, upward. Life's too short.

16. **One foot in front of the other will get you home.** *It will...*

17. **Advance your ball, every day.** Don't let other people and their agenda get in the way of your agenda, freedom, your goals! If even for a few minutes every day, advance your ball...

18. **If you can keep your head when all about you, are losing theirs and blaming it on you...** Think about the poem, *If,* by Rudyard Kipling.

19. **Don't get too high with the highs and too low with the lows**

20. **Be the same person, everyday** Routine, stay loyal to it. Come up with your system and trust it. Stay the course. Have faith in your system: it will payoff for you.

21. **With the above in mind, don't be afraid...** To change course, direction or make an executive decision. Knowing when to do so is an art unto itself. This goes for your business model, too. Be ruthless on your business model. Have others poke holes in it. Always Remember: Jeff Bezos (Amazon CEO) or Zillow or other disruptors want to eat you...

22. **Take some risk but make sure it is measured risk** Who is your Obi Won Kenobi? Who's on your shoulder saying, "Don't do this deal!" or "Do this deal!"

23. **Read some every day** I heard HUD Secretary Dr. Ben Carson say, in person, once that "my mother stayed on my brother and me to read. We always complained, but now she's got one son who is a brain surgeon and another who is a rocket scientist. Not bad. I'm glad she made us read..." We may not all become Neurosurgeons or rocket scientists, but we'll be more intelligent and better informed if we read regularly and widely. We will pick up on a nugget or two and be ahead of 90% of the rest of the pack.

24. **Seek dissenting points of view**: As an example, if you consume "political" information, I encourage you to read stuff that is counter

to your grain or goes against your normal belief system or is not in agreement with you. You'll be surprised at what you'll learn, and it may even make you smile. Oh, and it's ok to have a cup of coffee or grab a drink with someone who disagrees with you. It shouldn't be personal. (In the world of politics, sometimes I have to remind my far right wing leaning and my far left wing leaning friends of that fact). The same applies to ensuring you have people around you who are willing to offer a dissenting view. It helps prevent Group Think. While attending Wake Forest's B-School, we studied *the Abilene Paradox - The Management of Agreement*[30xxx]; It changed my life... "We're going to Abilene!" thank you Dr. Bill Davis, one of my awesome and favorite profs at Wake Forest!

25. **Related to above, "If two people agree on everything, one of them isn't necessary."** thank you for that, Winston Churchill

26. **Make time for you...**related to Advancing *your* ball, your hopes, your dreams...

27. **Make time for your family and those you care about** This is the ultimate 'give back' in your life. It's invaluable to all of us. Did I say I need to continue working on my own advice? I'm always a work in progress - *the Curve to Infinity*, but always working on continuous improvement.

28. **SWOT Analysis: DO IT**! Objectively evaluate your business by listing its/your Strengths, Weaknesses, Opportunities, Threats. Take action on this list. Constantly check and re-check your business model for relevancy. How are you delivering goods and services? Are you delivering the right goods and services?

29. **Smell the roses** Make time for nature. Release your mind and engage when the opportunity arises. When I was in Southport I never once took it for granted, but I miss it. Go to the beach or mountains or your local park or pond or wherever you go to refresh yourself. Get up from your desk and go.

30. **Appreciate the people in your world, they and you won't be here forever.**

31. **Laugh Some Every Day**: As Jimmy Valvano once said, "Laugh some every day. Cry some every day. If you've laughed some and cried some every day, that's a good day." At least smile. I bet your smile lights up the room. Plus, someone may need your smile that day.

32. **Give back, help others. We are where we are supposed to be.** We should make the most of where we are while we are there, even if we're just passing through. We should help others along our journey.

33. **Run your Own Race, Measure your own curve -- "No Matter the Chatter"**

34. **The sun is setting - what will you regret not doing?** See Marcus Aurelius[31lxxxi]

35. **You get one life, live it.** It's okay to have some fear of and when charting a new course, that's normal, but don't let that fear stop you.

36. **Who's weighing the boat down? Remove dead weight** A Total Quality Management instructor in a course I took (mid 90's) while a manager at Sara Lee Knit Products said, "Identify the concrete heads and remove them." His point: *if part of the boat goes down, it can all go down. Save the boat, save the people.* Don't let someone with a negative, "concrete head" mentality poison your organization. Your team, your organization and you deserve better. Don't be that manager or leader that lets the 5% of bad apples remain, as the rest watch things slowly rot..

37. **Recognize the angels and the miracles all around you every day.** They are there if you pay attention. Sometimes angels come disguised as an annoying person or someone in need.

38. ***Run if you can, walk if you have to, crawl if you must, but never give up*** - Thank you Dean Karnazes.

39. **Travel tip: After 9/11, airport travel became more of a pain than it already was:** If you don't have it, the $85, or whatever it costs, is worth the money for the *Known Traveler Number (KTN)*. If you're status with an airline, it may still help.

40. **Watch your advertising dollars -**I heard that an Editor of a local

newspaper I subscribed to once said during the downturn: "Ha! I'm the only one making money." He meant off the real estate ads that all us real estate agents were taking out in his newspaper. Made me angry!

41. **On Burning marketing dollars:** Related to the above, Zan Monroe, in a GRI Course, made a point about burning dollars by asking people to hold up a $20 bill. He snatched one and set it on fire. The poor sap. He paid the guy back, but he made his point: this is what you're doing if you place ads that aren't well thought out or aren't focused on your target. From my Avery Dennison days, it's called "Target Marketing." I highly recommend Seth Godin's book, *This is Marketing*[32xxxii] for an up to date view on marketing from one of the best marketing gurus of our era. (My son John turned me onto this book - thank you John!).

42. **Be a generalist or be a specialist...** but **decide** what you want to be.

43. **If you are getting into commercial real estate**- you better have an alternate source of income before you get in or get one lined up *real quick like* for those long periods between closings.

44. **If you are getting into commercial estate** consider pursuing the CCIM designation. The networking, and the learning will be worth their weight in gold to you. I'm biased, but it's proven to be true for me.

45. **On making time and juggling schedules**: You can do more than you think you can. I received my MBA from Wake Forest University while managing a 1000-person, 24/7 Distribution Center in Winston-Salem, NC. Three and a half years of night school. I was determined and nothing or no one was going to get in my way.

46. **I bombed a course one time en route to a designation I was trying to achieve (hint: not my CCIM!)**; I admit I was distracted and took it too lightly (no excuses, a bomb is a bomb!), but after I received my results, I was distraught. I had not bombed an exam since my Junior year in high school and then I wasn't trying. I passed it the second time around. I don't give up. I crossed that

finish line but it was a tough exam, but dang it...*My constant life lesson: if at first we don't succeed, try, try again...*

47. **Stay out, this water is shark invested!** Don't come into real estate, you'll get eaten alive.

48. **Come on in, the water is warm:** come into real estate, it's a blast but know what you're getting into.

49. **Sometimes you have to fire your clients.** It's okay, it happens. "It's not for you." "We're not for you." That's the long view and it will payoff for you. This pertains mainly to the real estate industry but certainly can pertain to other industries, businesses as well. Unless the client is Walmart, who was 33% of my business at Hanes and about the same at Avery Dennison.

50. **On unreasonable sellers (or clients):** Related to the above, sometimes, you have to close the book on a listing, shake hands, and say, "I appreciate the opportunity to work for you, but I'm afraid the gap between your expectations and what I think I can deliver is simply too wide. I don't want to over commit and under deliver and have you upset with me. Now that I know what you have and if I have a buyer that is searching for what you have, I will bring them to you." In the words of my colleague, Brian Quinn (BPQ, my original Red Wing Leader), when I was first joining Southport Realty: "Pete, we're not in the museum piece business." Translation: we are in the sales business, and if you have a client who is not reasonable and you recognize you are now going to be in the museum piece business with this client, (the listing just sits forever due to an unreasonable market price) -- move on.

51. **My Best real estate advice?** Buy low, be prepared to hold, for a long time, much longer than you expect...then sell high. Watch your expenses, whether you are a firm owner, independent broker or whatever. The old saying "every Buyer is a liar" is not true, but a few are. Some Sellers will think they are sitting on the last gold or oil reserve in the western hemisphere. Location, Location, Location has morphed into Location, information and analytics...

52. **"Buy land, they aren't making any more of it."** - Mark Twain

53. **"Don't wait to buy land, buy land then wait..."** Brian P. Quinn, Red Wing Leader, thank you for this: I'm convinced Brian could teach a high level sales class if he chose to do so.

54. **"You had a great job, an MBA...Tell me again why you wanted to come into this business?"** Brian P. Quinn when he first met me:

55. **Assumptive close...** sometimes we have to help move people off center (Brian, again).

56. **A hard "no" is much better than a forever maybe...** thank you again veteran land super broker. Actually, it's a glorious thing. (Thank you Greg Cox, CCIM).

57. **It ain't over until it's over** See my Cypress tract example

58. **Cash is king** - having dry powder is a good thing.

59. **Be the old man in the coffee shop**

60. **You can't get a base hit unless you step up to the plate, every day**

61. **Vultures have to eat too,** they have a place in the eco-system, they help clean up the carnage and can get things moving again.

62. **Disclose all material facts...**

63. **On speculation - "Spekalation!" as a family friend who was a financial adviser would call it** Are you buying for income or future appreciation? If appreciation, that is speculation. All good, just know that going in. There is always risk, no matter how wide the bull's eye. We are always throwing darts at a board, but the idea is to try and make the bull's eye as wide as we can.

64. **A wise mentor of mine once told me...** "Pete, some will steal your knowledge they will steal your time and your intellectual capital." (Thank you, Mike Butler). Mike is right, but fortunately for me, it's only been a few. Most people are honest. My Mom thought so, my Dad? Well... Counterbalance.

65. **Your knowledge is worth a lot more than you think.** *A lot more...*

66. **Watch your culture, the environment you create** Turnover is key. If you are a training ground for other firms, um, there is a problem. We rarely lost anyone. It was rare indeed.

67. **"We vote with our shoes"** You've heard me say it a few times now: At Avery Dennison we had a CFO who once said: "We vote with our shoes." It's about the culture and environment we both create and except for ourselves. At Sara Lee Knit Products (Hanes), I had a saying: "We don't lock the gate from the outside." Although, at our flagship plant on Stratford Road in Winston-Salem (no longer there), the top of the fence had spear-like points that pointed the wrong way, inward like a prison, not outward. Our management team had fun with that. Cue the cartoon Dilbert, thank you again, Scott Adams!

68. **Never forget, it's all a people business** As much as some want to avoid interaction with others, most business involves interacting with others. I also always try to operate from a "Hard on the problem, soft on the people" base, as much as that is possible.

69. **Health Lesson learned I hope you can benefit from**: Dad had double bypass two years prior to his massive heart attack, caused by plaque buildup in his calf areas. Make sure your heart patients follow doctor's orders, (ours included a walking program for Dad) after heart surgery. We were ignorant and not militant enough and I'm convinced it took Dad way too early.

70. **Sign up for your first endurance event if you haven't done one,**...Whether it's a 5K walk or any other event, Just Do It! If you want to run a marathon, I highly recommend a few other events first. For instance, maybe set a goal of a 10K and half marathon this year, then a marathon next year. Whatever you choose to do, at whatever level, you'll be glad you did it and you will learn something positive about yourself. *Oh, and I bet you'll do another one...*(Medical disclaimer: consult your physician if you feel the need to do so - he or she may have a reason for you not to do it).

71. **On Pain and Discomfort**: I always love the signs in the workout rooms "Stop exercising at the first sign of Discomfort" ; If I truly adhered to this "mantra" I would never do anything. (my disclaimer here is to follow your doctor's orders please...)

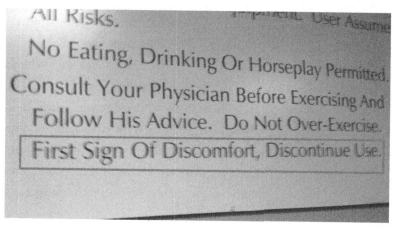

72. **Massage is not for "Sissies"** I thought it was until my first major overuse injury in the sport of Triathlon, then my miracle worker, Ortho Doctor (our Doc on the Dock) prescribed it to me for my recovery from an IT band strain. Thank you, Dr. Allen.

73. **Diversify** In your investments and in your business. Always be thinking about hedging yourself where you can and where feasible. Too many smart people – my finance professors, Warren Buffet, real estate mentors – have told me to do so and whenever I haven't followed their advice, I've been burned.

74. **A "word" (or two) on consultants and coaches**: Call me a healthy skeptic, but I often wonder about people who call themselves 'professional coaches' or consultants, but have never coached anyone or managed anyone, much less been out on the front line or in the arena.

    Be leery of those folks before your hire and spend your dollars on them; interview three of them and ask for results; if they are simply lifetime consultants and have never had line (that is, operational) or P&L responsibility, much less owned their own company, why would you trust their advice and counsel for your precious business?

I had a friend at Hanes, Kris Swamy. Kris was a talented engineer. He was not generally a fan of consultants and the following was his humorous way of expressing it:

Q: *What is the definition of a consultant?*

A: *Someone who takes your watch, tells you what time it is and doesn't give your watch back!*

This would be followed by his mad scientist laugh. A good consultant is worth their weight in gold or are we saying crypto currency these days? But look out for the other fly-by-nighters... The best consultants I have hired keep it simple, focused and give me something I can actually implement, not a three inch thick deck that will just collect dust.

75. **In God we trust**, everyone else better bring *Facts and Data*. (Thank you Claude Pruitt).

76. **Have Faith**...it will get you through when all else fails.

77. **Be your own best friend**, try not to beat yourself up; the world and others are tough enough on us. I stumble on this one at times.

78. **Be positive:** the world is full of negative. Even if you have to reach deep. Fight it. We all slip at times...

79. **Partners:** We should treat independent contractors and employees as the partners they are...

80. **Cross your finish lines. Keep pushing. You can do it, don't let anyone tell you "you can't" and if they do, use it as motivation.**

————

Recommended Reading from my Library: The following are a few of the books I highly recommend:

- *The Seven Habits of Highly Effective People*[33xxxiii] by Stephen R. Covey; Amazing and insightful. I was grateful to Sara Lee Knit Products for putting me through Dr. Covey's seminar, which included reading his amazing book, when I was a young manager in the early 90's. It helped fine tune and hone my leadership and management style and still influences me to this day. It was an amazing journey for me. Now Franklin Covey, the web site of the parent company describes the book as a best seller for the "simple reason that it ignores trends and pop psychology and focuses on timeless principles of fairness, integrity, honesty, and human dignity." Perfectly said. Pick it up if you haven't read it, share it if you have.

- Meditations: A New Translation[34xxxiv] by Marcus Aurelius: Four Star General and 40-year Marine Corps Veteran General James Mattis, who is widely read, once said that if he had to recommend one book for anyone to read, this would be it. I got this one for my son. It's a classic and deserves to be in your library.

- *The Power of Positive Thinking*[35xxxv] by Dr. Norman Vincent Peale; The classic book on faith and positive thinking. More than 5 million copies have been sold for a reason. I took this little paperback on the airplane with me when I was bouncing all over the globe. Some of Dr. Peale's "mantras" would help me fall asleep at night if I had too much stirring in my mind.

- *Millionaire Real Estate Agent*[36xxxvi] by Gary Keller; An insightful read. I read it first when I was getting into the business and then again when I owned a primarily residential firm. Gary's process, insights and detail are right on. Even if you only take a few nuggets away, I bet it improves your business. I recommend this book to new arrivals to the real estate industry and veterans alike, whether residential or commercial focused.

- *The Big Short*[37xxxvii] by Michael Lewis; The inside look on the subprime catastrophe and an exclamation point on why it's important for us to do our own research and having the courage to go against the grain. A Life lesson for me that, no matter what the media or so called "experts" say, no market will run forever, and if you hear the experts saying it will keep going forever, it's time to Sell. The Deutsche Bank trader, Greg Lippman, wearing a T-Shirt that says: *I'm Short Your House* at the Mortgage Bankers Association Meeting is classic. An eye opening, behind the curtain, look at the 2% on Wall Street.

- *Too Big to Fail*[38xxxviii] by Andrew Ross Sorkin; A masterpiece about the mad scramble to keep the largest financial institutions in our land from cratering as we all looked into the abyss that fateful day, September 29, 2008. In my humble opinion, Andrew's book will be read for generations.

- *Lone Survivor*[39xxxix] by Marcus Luttrell; It made me appreciate life even more than I already do and made me appreciate, more than I already do, what our military does for us, including the sacrifices they make for us. Heroes, all of them. The ultimate story of pushing ourselves further than we ever felt humanly possible, of endurance, crossing finish lines and being selfless. Thank you, Marcus. *You are a Hero and a Patriot.*

- *Band of Brothers*[40xl] - by Stephen E. Ambrose; Admittedly I'm an amateur history buff, primarily military history. I'm also an admirer of all who have served or are currently serving for our great country. I gently remind my sons from time to time that "If your Great Grandfather (Ike, Captain Isaac Sheldon French) did not make it through D-Day and the Battle of the Bulge, you would not be here." For me, it's important to remember "where I came from and how I got here" and whose shoulders I am standing on. This book is one of the best tributes to what I believe is truly the Greatest Generation and a great reminder of the sacrifice they made for all of us. Ike, my son's Great Grandfather, signed my copy of the book in 2001 for me. He was an exceptionally good man.

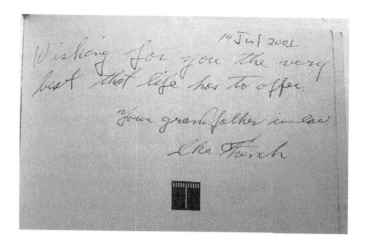

- *Empires of the Mind*[41xli] by Denis Waitley; When Dr. Stephen R. Covey, Pat Riley and Tom Peters all are on the back cover of your book, touting you as one of the best thought leaders in leadership, it must be so. I had the good fortune to see Mr. Waitley speak once and he said "Stop paying so much attention to the guys in the NFL on Sunday, they have already made their fortune, what are you doing to make yours for your family?" Classic, timeless, will endure forever.

- *Ultramarathon Man: Confessions of an All-Night Runner*[42xlii] by Dean Karnazes; This book will inspire you, a true story about some of the ticks or gremlins (hopefully positive) we all have inside us. It's about being motivated by things outside of ourselves and will give you a glimpse into the nuttiness of being an endurance athlete, if you have not actually participated in an endurance event yet; or will help you gain insight into why you do what you do if you have! Dean is the extreme example, the far tail of the bell curve!

- *The Ten Day MBA*[43xliii] by Steven Silbiger; No matter what business you're in and whether you have your MBA or not, pick up this book. It's a great refresher from B-school if you have been, or a thorough and creditable crash course in B-School teachings if you have not been.

- *Next Level Thinking*[44xliv] by Joel Osteen; Joel's book is a journey of faith that helped me shed some of the "garbage" I carried. Prepare to be changed in a positive way by this book. It will definitely help you get to your next level and beyond. (Thank you Mary Soria for introducing me to Joel!)
- *Brokers Who Dominate*[45xlv] by Rod Santomassimo; A very good commercial real estate centric book about the traits that make up a successful commercial real estate broker. Rod tracks several brokers in our industry who exhibit those traits, what sets them apart and frees them to dominate.
- *A Short Guide to a Happy Life*[46xlvi] by Anna Quindlen; A shining example of the phrase "Brevity is the Soul of Wit." Proof that in this day of bloviating, it's okay to make the point concisely and get out. More is often less. (50 pages, but who's counting?)
- *See you at the Top*[47xlvii] by Zig Ziglar: While a manager under the Hanes umbrella, Hanes sent several of us to see a motivational session with former President George H.W. Bush, Zig Ziglar and Dick Vitale. Suffice to say, my teammates and I all left that day giving each other high fives and doing cartwheels down Stratford Road. That day, I became a lifetime fan and follower of Zig.
- *Seussisms*[48xlviii] by Dr. Seuss; thank you KC Conway, MAI, CRE, Chief Economist of our CCIM Institute!; Quick, summarized, great advice on life, leadership, friendship, and on and on. Whether you are a child or 100 years old or any age in between, this will be the book I give any new graduate in my world.
- *This is Marketing*[49xlix] (You Can't be seen until you learn to see) by Seth Godin; One of Seth's others books, *Permission Marketing*, when launched in 1999, from my business school days at Wake Forest, gave me permission not to feel the need to hustle people or use short term sales tactics to win their business. Thank you to my 21-year-old for introducing me to Seth's latest (*This is Marketing*). This will be a classic for years to come and should

be required reading for any business owner or entrepreneur, not to mention any business school marketing student.

- *The Insider's Guide to Commercial Real Estate*[50l] by Cindy Chandler, CCIM, CRE; Cindy is a member of the North Carolina CCIM Hall of Fame and a past President of our North Carolina Association of REALTORS®. Short, concise and right on; a great addition to your library if you are thinking about entering into the field of commercial real estate or as a veteran in the industry, if you want a good reference reminder.

- *The Bible*[51li] by God: pick your version if you haven't already! it won't steer you wrong; It brings me peace.

We are where we are supposed to be, even if we're just passing through.
And we should make the most of where we are while we are here, even if
we're just passing through, helping others along the way.
You may stumble, you may fall, but never give up.
Get up, keep going and cross your finish lines...

CHAPTER 13

MENTAL ENDURANCE AND MAINTAINING BALANCE

"FALL SEVEN TIMES, STAND UP EIGHT..."
--JAPANESE PROVERB

Running, cycling, swimming or any type of endurance related activity is therapy for me. It helps set or reset my "balance." We touched on it briefly a bit earlier(what I alluded to as "teeing" this topic up!): it's not all about the physical. Balance and the *mental side* of our personal equation is just as important if not more so. Some like to look at the water (I do as well!). Some enjoy fishing, reading, going for long car rides. Some meditate. Some fall back to their religious faith (whatever that faith may be), some do not have a religious faith but find strength and balance in other ways. Some may do a collection of several of these things or all of them. Whatever the way, what activity do you proactively engage in that helps set or reset your balance?

I have also realized over the years that in order to achieve "next levels" of performance, whether it was training for a marathon or working on my business, the mental side of me was often the biggest hurdle in my way. I had to overcome the mental side of me to move to the next level. Some call it "thinking positive", Dr. Kevin Elko, a well-known sports Psychologist who wrote the book *True Greatness Mastering the Inner Game of Business Success*[52lii] talks about "finding your quiet."

I became fascinated by the power of mental side of endurance, of doing my best to reach deep and pull the positive out. It's a never-ending journey and it's always a challenge. But I'm convinced it's worth it.

In a book with endurance as a theme, I wanted to touch on the critically important mental side of things, whether in your personal or business life or in endurance sports.

Mental endurance is the art and science of getting and staying positive. Not allowing any room within your being for negative anything. I'm convinced that negativity is evil and a poison. I think we all have some within us; those demons, inner gremlins or whatever you want to call them, some more so than others.

The real estate industry in particular is subject to wild swings, euphoric highs and deep lows, major peaks and dark valleys. If you are not in real estate, your business may be the same...

I heard former Coach of the NFL Carolina Panthers, John Fox, once say, when asked about keys to keeping his sanity as a head coach in the National Football League, "I try not to get too high with the highs and too low with the lows. And every day, I try and be the same guy..."

I'm not a psychologist. I'm not a pastor. I'm not a preacher. I don't push my faith on others, but from experience I am convinced that The Enemy wants us to *bonk*. Not only that, but he also doesn't want us to get back up. He doesn't want us to do good things, for others or for ourselves; he doesn't want us to do good, he doesn't want us to be in a financial or physical position to help others, he doesn't want us to cross any finish lines. He wants you to be a life-time borrower, not a lender. He wants you in debt. He does not want you to have resources to help others. I know this because I've been there before, in my darkest moments, staring into his hell-filled eyes.

Some of you may believe in karma, some of you may believe in God and some of you may believe in none of the above. But whatever you believe in, I'm sure you want what is best for your family and for you. I want that for you and yours too. I know that the mental game, *the war within*, can be a *game breaker* or *game maker* for all of us.

While I'm not a licensed psychiatrist or psychologist, as you know at this point, I've been fortunate to be at the helm of some large manufacturing and distribution operations and a supply chain division for Avery Dennison and have been fortunate to manage and lead many talented manufacturing and distribution employees, managers, tech teams and brokers over my career. I have been led and managed by some incredibly talented managers and leaders. So, while no psychiatrist, my career has afforded me significant experience and observation time of human interactions and the positive and negative nature of people in general so over time I've been able to draw what I believe to be some fairly accurate conclusions.

Whether it's the work world, our personal life or participating in a sport or endurance event, one common trait is the mental side of things – *being positive, staying positive, and believing in it.* We can't just go through the motions. I'm convinced our brain and our inner being are too smart for that. We do have to *believe it.* This trait, of harnessing and maintaining a positive life, positive thoughts is what separates those who create success and separates some from the rest of the pack.

In my experience, it takes little energy and not much creativity to be negative. It takes more energy and some creativity to stay positive. It's hard. It has to be worked on over and over again. Having a positive outlook has to be intentional. Life kicks you in your backside and you want to give up.

I believe there is a War going on that we can't see.

"OK Pete, now you're getting a bit crazy...time for a temperature check. White jacket please Doctor!"

Stay with me here... Those dark forces want to start with our brains and derail us from accomplishing our life's mission, from crossing our finish lines.

Don't let it happen.

Don't let dark thoughts have one inch of your cranial real estate. Don't even entertain it. It's poison. It's a disease. It's a slippery slope.

No matter how bad things get, I've learned that the world is not out to get me. There are good "forces" (in my belief, it is God and his "team") actually for me. Your positive forces want you to advance your ball.

My faith also tells me there is a constant battle going on out there all around us, all the time. I know intellectually I have battles going on inside me as well and I feel like I am generally at peace with myself. That battle can be as simple as getting myself up to go for an early run, knuckling down to complete that long report for a client, making time for someone that needs me and setting aside all distractions to focus on only them. On that last point, I know my loved ones would tell you that's a challenge for me, hey, I'm a work in progress! (My two sons will vouch for this for sure!). All of these are "battles", internal battles we all encounter through the course of our day, week, month and year.

Yes, there are dark or negative forces, I believe that evil is alive and well and roaming the countryside, wanting to distract and keep us from crossing our finish line. Our challenge is to beat those dark forces and smile doing it. Don't just cross the finish line, *give it a stomp when you cross it.*

When I was a young manager at Hanes, I went to a conference in Black Mountain to hear some motivational speakers. One said the first thing he would do when his feet hit the floor each day is run to the mirror, look himself right in the eyes and yell out at the top of his lungs: *WOWWWWW!!!! IT'S GOING TO BE A GREAT DAY ISN'T IT!??*

He screamed this out at the top of his lungs. If you and I were together, I would demonstrate this for you and it would really get on your nerves, that's how loud it was. But it did make me smile (and cringe!).

He said his wife would look at him like he was nuts. I bet she did.

Sometimes, we think positive people are nuts. What the heck do you have to be so happy about, Mister??

But I tried it and guess what? It's hard not to have a smile on your face when you do it. (Author's note: if you do this at the wrong place or time, like say 5am when the rest of your family is still sleeping or you live in an apartment building and you scare the wits out of your neighbors with your carnal cry, some may think you're crazy. But it's okay to have a little crazy in us, right?)

I once had a friend introduce me to his wife at a social gathering. He was a very jovial person and always positive. She came across as negative and a bit rude. As she walked off, I turned to him and said, "So, Tom, what does your wife do?"

Tom said, "She's in the manufacturing business..."

I took the bait. "What does she manufacture?"

Tom said, "Unhappiness..."

Ouch...

The older gentleman behind the desk at the Spears Family YMCA in Greensboro was a blessing to me. His parting words to me every day when I left there around 6am were: "You got the hardest part of your day over with!" Those words, now many years later, are still with me. He made a life-long impact on me. He was a positive angel in my world then and I didn't know it.

We never know when we may have a lasting impact on someone, positive or negative, so why not let it be positive? Why be positive?

Well, for one, it's good for your health. There is evidence, yes, scientific evidence that being positive has broad health benefits.

An article, *Positive Thinking: Stop Negative Self-Talk to Reduce Stress*[53][liii] published by the Mayo Clinic, January 21, 2020 says that positive thinking, ceasing negative self-talk, actually reduces stress. It goes on to state that positive thinking doesn't mean you keep your head in the sand and ignore life's less pleasant situations. Positive thinking or getting to your quiet place or maintaining your mental endurance simply means you approach unpleasantness in a more positive and productive way. You think the best is going to happen, not the worst.

A short excerpt from the article:

THE HEALTH BENEFITS OF POSITIVE THINKING
Researchers continue to explore the effects of positive thinking and optimism on health. Health benefits that positive thinking may provide include:

- Increased life span
- Lower rates of depression
- Lower levels of distress
- Greater resistance to the common cold
- Better psychological and physical well-being
- Better cardiovascular health and reduced risk of death from cardiovascular disease
- Better coping skills during hardships and times of stress

It's unclear why people who engage in positive thinking experience these health benefits. One theory is that having a positive outlook enables you to cope better with stressful situations, which reduces the harmful health effects of stress on your body.

The article goes onto say: *It's also thought that positive and optimistic people tend to live healthier lifestyles. They get more physical activity, follow a healthier diet, and don't smoke or drink alcohol in excess.*

Now, I admit I do enjoy an occasional libation and would, at times in my prior life, overdo it, and heck, I'm a light weight. However, I found it increasingly difficult to run fifteen miles early the next morning if I over did it the night before. My endurance sport world became a built-in bookend or off switch for me. In speaking with some in my world, I realize that I am fortunate to have an off switch.

Several years ago, I asked a friend of mine who battles alcoholism what it was like to come to the realization that he was, in fact, an alcoholic. He put it this way: "Pete, you have an off switch. You can have a few drinks and flip the off switch because you know you're going to go for a long run tomorrow morning... and you know it will be a miserable experience if you don't cut yourself off. Me? I have a few, and then I keep going, pushing through the clouds to the next hemisphere. I have no off switch. That's the difference..."

God Bless him and all who deal with the evil of addiction. I sat there in complete stunned, humbled silence after he said all this. I'm lucky. I realize that. Some others not so much as they are in the grips of addiction.

Running or working out in any form or fashion, is a known stress reliever. That is why I emphasize it gently to anyone I can in my world that will listen, as long as they are physically able to do so (get your doctor's okay!). I call it my *pressure relief valve*. People in my world know I will get grumpy if I don't get up and go. I believe for the most part that our bodies are meant to be in motion.

My father also instilled in me that "if you act enthusiastic, you'll be enthusiastic..." A cherished memory I had with my father is that he actually had given me the poem, *If*, by Rudyard Kipling, who had created the poem for his son, John. And my dad didn't just read it, he had it memorized and would sit me down at night as a child and recite it to me. This beautiful poem came to exemplify positivity and what life is all about for me. Taking the high road, not pointing fingers, taking responsibility for my actions, not letting the world's negativity get me down, crossing finish lines. Rudyard happened to be writing the poem to his son, but to me, it applies to anyone and everyone.

This is the actual poem on the plaque my parents had hanging in my room growing up. It is something I treasure and have tried my best, albeit it not as well as my Dad (Grandpa), to pass onto my sons.

An "If" for Boys

If you can keep your head when all about you
    Are losing theirs and blaming it on you,
If you can trust yourself when all men doubt you,
    But make allowance for their doubting too;
If you can wait and not be tired by waiting,
    Or being lied about, don't deal in lies,
Or being hated, don't give way to hating,
    And yet don't look too good, nor talk too wise:
If you can dream—and not make dreams your master,
    If you can think—and not make thoughts your aim;
If you can meet with Triumph and Disaster
    And treat those two impostors just the same;
If you can bear to hear the truth you've spoken
    Twisted by knaves to make a trap for fools,
Or watch the things you gave your life to, broken,
    And stoop and build 'em up with worn out tools:
If you can make one heap of all your winnings
    And risk it on one turn of pitch-and-toss,
And lose, and start again at your beginnings
    And never breathe a word about your loss;
If you can force your heart and nerve and sinew
    To serve your turn long after they are gone,
And so hold on when there is nothing in you
    Except the Will which says to them: "Hold on!"
If you can talk with crowds and keep your virtue,
    Or walk with Kings—nor lose the common touch;
If neither foes nor loving friends can hurt you,
    If all men count with you, but none too much;
If you can fill the unforgiving minute
    With sixty seconds' worth of distance run,
Yours is the Earth and everything that's in it,
    And—which is more—you'll be a Man, my son!

                Rudyard Kipling

And just in case, you find it hard to read the cursive writing in the above wooden plaque:

If you can keep your head when all about you
Are losing theirs and blaming it on you,
If you can trust yourself when all men doubt you,
But make allowance for their doubting too;
If you can wait and not be tired by waiting,
Or being lied about, don't deal in lies,
Or being hated, don't give way to hating,
And yet don't look too good, nor talk too wise:

If you can dream--and not make dreams your master;
If you can think--and not make thoughts your aim;
If you can meet with Triumph and Disaster
And treat those two impostors just the same;
If you can bear to hear the truth you've spoken
Twisted by knaves to make a trap for fools,
Or watch the things you gave your life to, broken,
And stoop and build 'em up with worn-out tools:

If you can make one heap of all your winnings
And risk it on one turn of pitch-and-toss,
And lose, and start again at your beginnings
And never breathe a word about your loss;
If you can force your heart and nerve and sinew
To serve your turn long after they are gone,
And so hold on when there is nothing in you
Except the Will which says to them: 'Hold on!'

If you can talk with crowds and keep your virtue,
Or walk with Kings--nor lose the common touch,
If neither foes nor loving friends can hurt you,

If all men count with you, but none too much;
If you can fill the unforgiving minute
With sixty seconds' worth of distance run,
Yours is the Earth and everything that's in it,
And--which is more--you'll be a Man, my son!

How about another example most of us know: Honest Abe Lincoln? Born into poverty, he lost eight elections, failed twice in business, had a nervous breakdown, and then was elected President. He epitomized getting knocked on one's keister, picking oneself up, dusting oneself off and pushing ahead.

I believe if we choose to simply focus on the one way to get it done versus the ten ways it can't be done we'd all be better off.

Now, I don't come close to professing to be on par with your pastor or preacher or rabbi, but the bible, in Proverbs 4:23, says, *"More than anything you guard, protect your mind, for life flows from it..."* That's powerful. I agree and believe it to my core.

Our mind is the "central command post" of all we do. If the Enemy can derail you, that is most likely where he will start. To me, this means I have to make a conscious decision, every single day of my life, to focus on positive energy and mindset and give the rest away, not harboring any "garbage" or poison. Getting to my quiet, focused place.

Every day when my feet hit ground, I have to know good things are going to happen.

Gratitude and Attitude. The gratitude I've just been given another day, and the attitude to make the most of it.

That small space (5, 6, 7 inches?) between our ears is so important. Critically important.

I have found that my lowest moments, when I'm running through the Valleys, is when it's the hardest and for me to reach the deepest. But it's also the most critical. This is when the space between our ears becomes so important.

Have you ever noticed how often in life the least physically gifted person or team will win a contest and prevail over a more physically gifted opponent? That is mental fortitude, *mental endurance.*

How do you get out of bed this morning, when the deal you had been counting on for a year fell apart yesterday and you have to make your daughter's tuition payment, your mortgage and pay your utility bills?

If you were right in front of me, I would say "look at me ... if I can do it, you can ... you're not alone. People want you and need you. Your friends and family and others are depending on you. You may be in a valley now, but the next Peak is up ahead, keep pushing!"

There, I just said it to you!

We go where our thoughts take us: up or down. Positive self-talk is real.

In his insightful and very candid book, *Turning the Thing Around: Pulling America's Team Out of the Dumps and Myself Out of the Doghouse*[54][liv] former multiple Super Bowl winner and college National championship head coach, Jimmy Johnson, tells a great story on his approach to being positive.

Some football coaches are superstitious about staying away from their field goal kicker before they make a critical kick, because that side of the sport is known to be such a mental game. The coach typically does not want to take a chance on negatively impacting the kicker.

Coach Johnson, a student of psychology, took a different tact. He wanted to be sure he positively impacted his player. Before his field goal kicker was going into make a critical game-winning kick, he would walk right up to him, look him in the eye, and in a positive way would just say, *"Make that kick."*..he would smile at his kicker and walk off. He was conveying a message: "There is no choice, there is no doubt, I have infinite confidence in you that you are going to make this kick."

I immediately saw the difference and the positive twist between "make that kick" and "you'd better not miss that kick." Yes, huge difference.

The same applies to our business.

I love the commercial where the sales guy, in a white button-down shirt and tie, is in the bathroom, looking at himself in the mirror, getting ready to depart the bathroom for the big sales call. To me, they cast this guy perfectly. He's a rather frumpy looking dude, big hair. And as he looks in the mirror, getting ready to go out and no doubt meet with his prospect, he points at himself and says: *SHOWTIIIIIME!!*

It's hilarious and does a good job of playing on the positive self-talk phenomenon.

Positive self-talk is so important. Especially when things aren't going my way. It's easy for me to be positive when I'm closing deals and running along at an eight mile-per-minute-per-mile pace. It's much more difficult for me to be positive and think about all the things I have to be grateful for when my debt is piling up, I'm not closing deals or have a major deal fall through, or I blow my hip out at mile eight with eighteen miles to go (18.2 to be exact!).

Those are the times when I truly have to focus. It's when we all do. That's what I mean by the *Enemy wants to hit you when you're down*. I'm here to tell you I believe that because I've been there! I know of real "casualties of the interior war" that rages within us at times, and I know some who didn't survive the assault, literally. Man (or woman) down. So, when I say *it's all about saving lives and livelihoods*, I mean it.

Please, if you find yourself at this dark stage, seek help. If not for yourself, for those you love. I'm here to tell you: YOU ARE WORTH IT! And we need you here.

The power of positive thinking is real...

YOU CAN'T BREAK THIS

On that note, as you know by now, I am blessed with two wonderful sons. I touched on this earlier but I want to go into a bit more detail on this now. The following for me is a lesson in life's sometimes unforeseen blessings.

Within the last several years I have had another young man enter my life, who, though not officially my son, has certainly become like a third son to me. We received him when he was age 10. He's now 16 and I've played a small part in raising him since his arrival. His name is Seth.

Seth lost his mother (Becky) to cancer in 2015. One of Seth and Becky's mantras was "You can't break this." And "this" was and is their eternal love for one another, their unbreakable bond. Seth and his mom adored one another; they were absolute ROCK STARS to one another. It was a beautiful thing. Seth was diagnosed with a disease I was not familiar with until I met him: Cystic Fibrosis (https://www.cff.org/What-is-CF/About-Cystic-Fibrosis/). In my learning about this disease, I found two inspirational mantras: *Adding Tomorrows* and *Until It's Done*.

Wow, talk about two mantras that have the word endurance all through them!

When Seth was first diagnosed at age two, the average life expectancy was thirty-seven years old. With advances in treatment, it is now forty-eight years old. If you are not familiar with CF, the daily treatment regime is nothing short of breath taking, not just the medicines that need to be taken each day, but the special vest to help "bang out" the lungs to keep them clear, among other things.

These are things Seth and all CF'ers are accustomed to, but for someone like me to see it for the first time, it is truly jaw dropping. It's also one thing to go through it as a child, but as you move into your teen years and you want to be seen as more like the other kids, it can become more of a challenge. Especially staying on top of the meds (which he has at times "tossed" because he didn't want to stand out).

I am open about the fact that at first, I did not like the idea of him moving in with us. I was negative about it. I thought we were pulling him away from his support network in Elizabeth City, his family there, his friends and his little brother. But Mary (Becky's Mom), who knows the treatment regime and is on top of it, was truly the only one qualified to take Seth in and ensure he continued to receive the proper care. She is also militant enough to ride him like Zorro to ensure he does it every day (I've had a front row seat to it).

The other aspect of this: Becky and Mary, though daughter and mother, were best friends and since Seth's birth, Mary and Seth have had a deep connection. Mary would joke: "Seth is my child…"

Well, sometimes, Life and God have a way of throwing us curve balls. So here was one of mine and I was none too happy about it.

God at times has a good sense of humor and as it turns out Seth has been a blessing for me…If this kid can get out of bed every day with a smile on his face and keep going, *who am I to not do the same?*

Seth is now on a ground-breaking drug, which at the time of this writing, was in pilot phase. We are "fortunate" – but I say it's no coincidence – that Charlotte's CF-certified treatment center with the Levine Children's Hospital was awarded to be part of the pilot program.

Consider that when Seth first arrived in Charlotte, the summer of 2015, he could not run from *here to there* without getting winded or even sick. A couple of years back, not long after he started participating in this pilot drug, he actually won the CF run/walk 5K! It was nothing short of a miracle.

Until it is Done…

We are where we are supposed to be. And we should make the most of where we are while we are here, and help others along the way…

I'll End the Chapter with this:

Taylor Swift got it right in her famous song: *"Hater's Gonna Hate."* Don't listen to the Haters or the negative folks or the naysayers. They will hold you back.

Don't listen to anyone who says you can't do something. Let their words propel you forward to what you want to do, what you want to accomplish. Let it be a hurdle in your high hurdle jaunt. Let it be the fuel to help you *cross your finish line.*

When that type of negativity surfaces, I'm convinced it's the devil (or negative energy if you don't believe in the devil) trying to hold us down, so we can't be a Light to others and help others.

Keep it positive. Take the high road. Smile. Accomplish your goals and dreams. Become a lender and shed being a borrower. Become prosperous and use it to help others. That is my suggestion. Oh... and do so unapologetically.

It's part of the privilege and benefit of living in the greatest country in the world. Others have fought and died so we can do this.

My life has proven out what Henry Ford said:

"Whether you think you can or think you can't, you are right..."

There is a lot to be said for the self-fulfilling prophesy.

Remember, you can talk yourself into or out of just about any kind of performance.

CHAPTER 14

"ONE FOOT IN FRONT OF THE OTHER WILL GET YOU HOME!"

"THE MOST DIFFICULT THING IS THE DECISION
TO ACT, THE REST IS MERELY TENACITY..."
--AMELIA EARHART

"THE IMPEDIMENT TO ACTION ADVANCES ACTION.
WHAT STANDS IN THE WAY BECOMES THE WAY."
--MARCUS AURELIUS

Marcus said it, all the way back in 161AD, and it's still absolutely true today. Marcus was known as the last of the "Five Good Emperors" and is, by most accords, considered a brilliant philosopher.

Well, we are almost home now. How would you answer Marcus if he asked:

What is in your way?

What real or conjured up obstacles are standing in your way of accomplishing a goal? What is preventing you from getting to your next level? Is it the space between your ears? Is it you?

We get in our own way at times, don't we? The saying, "We have met the enemy and they are ours" originated from the War of 1812, in which Commodore Perry reported to William Henry Harrison after the Battle of Lake Erie.

Several years later, 158 years to be exact, it has made me smile to see that Cartoonist Walt Kelly, modified Commodore Perry's quote to "We have met the enemy and he is us." in a cartoon he created in 1970 celebrating the first Earth Day.

Well, I modify them both here a bit further: *I saw the Enemy, and 'twas me.*

Whether it's closing a deal or running a marathon or being there for a loved one, sometimes we stumble across ourselves.

Obstacles happen in life, they just do. They happen to all of us. I have to remind myself of that constantly. The inner battle is a *curve to infinity*, we never truly get there, we only can hope to take positive action and make progress along the way. I try not to confuse progress with motion. I want to be accomplishing, not moving in circles (ye' old definition of insanity...).

At Sara Lee Knit Products, we had a hard-charging, street smart, Executive Vice President of Operations, Julio Barea, who once told a group of us (managers) at the Stratford Road Plant in Winston-Salem, NC:

"You can't get rid of all stress. If you do, you are literally dead. Life and business have inherent stress and how we deal with it separates us from others...Stress can make us better."

Our mistakes, losses, failures, tough times, together can often sharpen us to make us better.

———

THE MARINE CORPS MARATHON (MY SLOWEST, YET MOST GRATIFYING) - ONE FOOT IN FRONT OF THE OTHER...

People have often asked me over the year: "why do you do it? Why do you want to run so far? What do you have to prove?" I sometimes think, *You don't really want me to answer that, do you?*

Dr. George Sheehan, one of our Jedi's in the running world, an iconic philosopher on the sport and author of the classic runner's books *Running & Being: The Total Experience and Going the Distance*[55lv] once said: "He runs because he has to. Because in being a runner, in moving through pain and fatigue and suffering, in imposing stress upon stress, in eliminating all but the necessities of life, he is fulfilling himself and becoming the person he is."

Dr. Sheehan also said: "The obsession with running is really an obsession with more and more life."

Would you agree that sometimes we get to the other side of an experience and look back, shake our head, and say *'Wow'* due to some insight gained? Sometimes we don't know we are going through a blessing when we are encountering it. Sometimes the pain is so great we can't see beyond it to the other side and it's not until later, when we look back, that we realize we were just taught an amazing lesson.

Or how about when we realize we weren't the one actually "doing the action"? I mean, *we were, but we weren't by ourselves.* Like a blur, maybe even a blackout-like moment, out on our feet, we realize later *we were being carried.*

Anyone who has ever trained for a fall season marathon knows this means training in the height of the summer months, which means, depending on where you live, possibly brutally hot temps, even if you are out the door by 4:30 or 5am.

So, did I curse my good friend JimBob for suggesting that we do the Marine Corps Marathon (MCM) in Washington, DC in 2015? No, but I did curse him a bit during my 15, 18, and 20-mile training runs in what turned out to be unusually hot fall weather.

Wonder where the name "JimBob" came from?

Well, Jim Jacquelin was a fraternity brother of my best friend, DeWitt Brown, at the University of South Carolina. Jim is a Philadelphia native. When he came down south for college, he once joked to some of his mates that "all you southern guys have the name Bob after your name, JoeBob, BillyBob..." He was obviously jealous, so the name "JimBob" stuck and it is humorously still with us today. JimBob is back in Philly now and he is jealous of all our Bojangles here, we're hoping at some point he comes to his senses and moves back down to be near us, but that's another topic for another day...

In normal fall weather, we would've had nice, cool fall temperatures in September and coming into October, when the event took place. Specifically, October 25th. We were honored to be participating in the 40th running of the event that ended with 23,197 finishers -- yours truly, barely one of them.

The MCM is one of the largest marathons in the US and the world. It has been voted "Best Marathon in the Mid-Atlantic", "Best Marathon for Charities" and "Best Spectator Event." It is widely known as "The People's Marathon" as it is the largest marathon in the world that doesn't offer prize money. It's also a darn cool way to see our nation's capital and tour some of our nation's most important historic landmarks while running alongside and being supported by the men and women of the United States Marine Corps.

The fall of 2015 turned out to be not so normal temperature wise, which is to say considerably above the normal temperature range, preceded by a summer that felt like we were walking on the sun. *Darn you, JimBob!!*

Yes, it was JimBob's bright idea that we three amigos (DeWitt, JimBob and me) should run the Marine Corps Marathon together.

As technology evolved over the years, it allowed us to stay connected while training using apps, texts, and other means. We became virtual coaches to one another, encouraging, cajoling, having fun and updating one another along our training journey.

For this particular event, we were raising money for *Hope for Warriors*,[56lvi] because we all three are big fans of the military, those who are serving, those who have served and those who made the ultimate sacrifice. We recognize that they all make incredible sacrifices so the rest of us can sleep easier at night under the "blanket of protection and freedom they provide."

The day before the Big Event (Three Amigos: JimBob far right, DeWitt far left, and slow guy in the middle)
HOORAH IS RIGHT!

When we got to event day, other than the traffic in the district and navigating our way down to the start line, I was feeling perfect. It was a cool, misty fall day and, unlike our training run conditions a few weeks prior, perfect running weather. When we sang the national anthem and saw our soldiers parachuting, the feeling of American pride and emotion are difficult to fully convey.

If you have never done it, the rush of game day is unlike any other experience or feeling you will ever have. Those of you who have experienced it will probably agree. It's very difficult to describe but the "game day experience", combined with the realization of the hard work you've put in, the many weeks of training now all behind you, is an adrenaline rush like no other.

Game Day is something we have *earned* and something we should truly enjoy, although admittedly, by the time we hit mile 20, the word *enjoy* is not what comes to mind.

Like many things in my little world, it is an experience over the years I have never taken for granted. As mentioned previously, one of my quips, when looked at by friends or colleagues or relatives like I'm crazy, is *a marathon is just a 20-mile warmup run, followed by a 10K.*

I took off out of the gate and was moving along briskly that morning. At the time, being in my late 40s, 8 to 9 minute miles are what I consider to be brisk. At mile six, I thought *this is going to be my easiest event of all my 20+ years of participating in endurance events.* I felt like I was 18 again. I looked around and enjoyed the sights. I was breathing it all in. I settled into my *Forever Pace.*

LADIES AND GENTLEMEN, WE HAVE REACHED CRUISING ALTITUDE. THE CAPTAIN HAS TURNED OFF THE FASTEN SEAT BELT SIGN AND YOU ARE NOW FREE TO MOVE ABOUT THE CABIN...

Cruising altitude, it was. When I hit mile eight, I remember cresting the Top of the Hill and going under a bridge. I remember looking to my right with a smile on my face. I remember smiling quite a bit during those initial seven miles or so because I was feeling so good. But then, the smile went away. I crossed under the bridge and felt a *POP!.* My mind tells me that I heard the sound, but I don't know that I did. I remember the stabbing pain shooting through my left side like lightning. Never having been stabbed, it felt like what I would think getting stabbed would feel like. I remember thinking *"Oh no, please, not now..."*

Most of us know inherently that marathons are challenging but running with a blown-out hip makes for an awfully long remaining 18.2 miles. By miles nine and ten I had tears streaming down my face. I know, I can hear you: *What a pansy...*

I'm not too proud to admit that I thought the same thing myself as thoughts of throwing the towel in and limping off the course were flooding my mind, streaming through my brain, washing over me like a wave. I didn't have to look at my watch to know that my pace was now almost a snail's pace. I'm sweating now, not just because of my run, but because I'm injured.

———

I had no idea what it was while on the course, and even less of an idea that later, after having recovered, I would be having full hip replacement surgery.

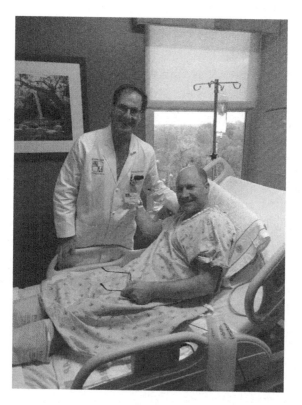

Several months after my successful hip surgery, Mary and I were in the grocery store and ran into my hip surgeon, Dr. Bo Mason, who jokingly (kind of) urged me to walk down the aisle for him. I got a big thumbs up! I was one of his younger patients and they put a new (pilot) device in me that apparently combined the two best devices on the market during the initial pilot program.

They loved having me in their sample population... and... so far so good. I had been experiencing pain, a foreshadowing, for about eight years. My eyes would at times bling open at night due to the pain, the throb.

I remember two months after my surgery, about 3am one morning, my eyes blinked open and I just stared at the ceiling and smiled. *Nothing. No pain. Just like that, it was gone...*

Thank you to one of my heroes, Dr. J. Bohannon Mason, AKA, Bo Mason, my super talented hip surgeon with Ortho Carolina! I'm forever grateful...

———

Back on the course, questions like *how am I going to do this?, how am I going to finish?, what am I going to do?* were flooding my brain.

Rounding the corner around mile eleven, I look up ahead and see a fellow runner, shuffling along. Somehow, I was actually gaining on him. How, I have no idea. As I closed in on him, I realized that his right leg was a prosthetic.

When I got closer, I look up to see the words 'Semper FI' ('Always Faithful') on the back of his shirt. I realized this was a Marine, probably a Purple Heart recipient, and most likely was running with us on that prosthetic leg because battle took his leg from him while he was guarding the gate and our freedom.

That was *"get over yourself, Pete"* moment #1 that morning, the first proverbial bucket of cold water in my face to reach deep and keep moving.

Seeing that Marine made me feel grateful again to be alive, to witness his toughness, his grit, and to consider how deep he had to be reaching mentally to do what he was doing. It humbled me beyond words. Made me feel almost ashamed to even be considering succumbing, much less acknowledging, the pain I was going through...

Gratitude and Attitude came to mind...

But nonetheless, I'm human. And dang, it was painful and it was not going away. Like everyone, I've had my share of injuries and realize that sometimes, during training for example, you hit the wall and have to toss in the towel. No matter how dejected, down or depressed you feel, you have to have the mental fortitude to *shut it down, take a knee, tap the breaks, live to see another day and do no further harm to yourself.*

I knew what I was going through that day was certainly not what our military heroes encounter, far from life or death on the battlefield, but it was especially important to me. This was the finish line of all finish lines I deeply wanted to cross, if not just for the pure symbolism of it and who we were out there running with and for that day.

If you ever have an opportunity to run in the Marine Corps Marathon (MCM), it's a wonderful experience. I have to say it was one of the greatest honors of my life to be surrounded by all those amazing Marines and to think of all they have done and continue to do for all of us. It was humbling. A few tears were shed for sure.

I didn't want to let my teammates down, and in my own mind I didn't want to let those Warriors down who have made the sacrifice for all of us. I felt I would be letting them down if I limped off my own personal little battlefield that day and I couldn't bear the thought of it.

Once again, I could hear Coach Sasser from my mid-August football practice days in the late 80's barking at me in his Drill Sergeant-like yell:

"You're feeling sorry for yourself aren't you!? Then QUIT!!! Stop wasting my time and taking up a locker spot when there are 50 other kids that want to be out here in your spot!"

If you've ever seen Stanley Kubrick's movie *Full Metal Jacket* (1987), Coach Sasser reminds me of Gunnery Sergeant Hartman, brilliantly played by R. Lee Ermey. In addition to Coach Sasser's words, my dad's

"*Get tough, Son...*" was also quietly rattling around the empty chambers of my skull that morning.

I was getting dizzy.

"*Oh crap, I'm gonna pass out.*"

It felt like that moment before I bonk, except I knew I was not bonking.

So, to answer my questions to myself or *whoever* was listening (and yes, I was talking to God for sure asking for his help and strength) of *how am I going to do this? how am I going to get to the finish line?*

I had no idea...

These questions are not unlike those we ask ourselves from time to time in our business when it's a long time between closings. Lord knows, I sure have. If you're in college or if you have a child that is struggling. If you have bills you have to pay or are encountering a life crisis. Or how about you or a family member experiencing a critical health issue? God Bless you and carry you if or when you go through any circumstance like these examples.

At that point, as I'm wallowing further and further into my misery of a run and some of the most excruciating pain of my lifetime, I see another guy up ahead, standing on the concrete curb at a corner, waving a towel. He looks as if he's on a deserted island and he's trying to wave down a rescue boat. He's dressed in full fatigues and looked to be in great shape. He's a Marine and must be a true Drill Sergeant. He sure looked and sounded the part, plus I noticed a few of my fellow runners, who were Marines, snapping a salute to him and he was returning them.

As I came nearer, I could hear him yelling out:

"ONE FOOT IN FRONT OF THE OTHER WILL GET YOU HOME!!!"

It took me a second or two or three but it hit me: *Well, there's my answer.* Simple, straight forward, my God Wink.

That is how I was going to do it.

That was how I was going to cross my finish line.

I put my head down and focused. I would force myself into an out of body experience and as long as I could go, *go I would.* Even if I passed out. That Marine Corps Drill Sgt was my Guardian Angel that day. He was there right when I needed him.

This was the double whammy, *"Get over yourself, Pete"* moment #2, the knock-out punch to my pity party.

And then, as I looked up ahead, there it was, laid out in front of me, the "Wear Blue Mile", as mile twelve to thirteen was known.

The Wear Blue Mile would be the Muhammad Ali haymaker, the pro wrestler coming off the top rope onto my head to end my pity party that morning.

President Ronald Reagan once said:

"SOME PEOPLE SPEND AN ENTIRE LIFETIME WONDERING
IF THEY HAVE MADE A DIFFERENCE IN THE WORLD.
BUT, THE MARINES DON'T HAVE THAT PROBLEM."

The Wear Blue Mile was unlike anything I had ever experienced in my years of participating in endurance sports. Typically, along the route of just about any event I've participated in are people yelling, encouraging, whooping, making loud noises, ringing bells, playing music and everything else you can possibly imagine. It's actually a very welcome distraction and takes your mind off the pain and monotony, sets your mind adrift from the grind.

For the first time that day, I came up to a mile and it was completely silent, almost eerily so. Actually, I don't recall ever in a marathon any mile being that ominously quiet.

I had the humbling experience of once visiting the *Tomb of the Unknown Soldier*, which, of course, is considered sacred ground. This space along the marathon course had that type of feeling, like I was entering Sacred Ground.

Little did I know, *I was.*

At the time, I didn't know about the Wear Blue Mile. (I'm ashamed to say it, color me oblivious). But it didn't take me long to figure out what this mile was all about.

You see, for the first half of the Wear Blue Mile, you look up ahead and see these beautiful pictures (more like large portraits) of our soldiers on the left and the right, all along the way, flanking you, staring at you, their eyes and smiles piercing into you. Most of their professional profile shots were, no doubt, taken prior to going into the field of battle.

It soon dawned on me that these were pictures of *Our Fallen*.

A quarter of the way into mile twelve I could no longer see because of the tears in my eyes, but not due to my pain. Like a gut punch, I was grieving for the Fallen and again was mentally thrashing myself for being so weak in my pain.

Yet, following those pictures of our beloved Patriots, the second half of the Wear Blue Mile has the families of *those Fallen*, of those Patriots I had just seen in the pictures, standing on both sides of the road. There they are with flags waving, wearing blue, and loudly *cheering us on.*

Wait!? Cheering us on? You have got to be kidding me!? We should be cheering you!

That moment has stuck with me and will all the rest of the days of my life. Yes, it applies to endurance sports, to life, and to whatever business you are in:

ONE FOOT IN FRONT OF THE OTHER WILL GET YOU HOME...

Keep it simple, keep moving forward, keep advancing, keep reaching deep and you will cross your finish lines.

This event has become my personal Exhibit A in never having crossed a finish line without help...

You see, when I finished the MCM it wasn't until much later than I realized it wasn't from my own physical strength, mental fortitude, athletic prowess, tough guy skills or whatever-the-heck fleeting thought I had about the "how.".. I realized I was carried.

That realization gave way to me reflecting back on my life and realizing how many times God had carried me...

We've all heard of or read the *Footprints in the Sand* poem. I'd like to share it here:

One night I dreamed a dream.
As I was walking along the beach with my Lord.
Across the dark sky flashed scenes from my life.

For each scene, I noticed two sets of footprints in the sand,
One belonging to me and one to my Lord.

After the last scene of my life flashed before me,
I looked back at the footprints in the sand.

I noticed that at many times along the path of my life,
especially at the very lowest and saddest times,
there was only one set of footprints.

This really troubled me, so I asked the Lord about it.
"Lord, you said once I decided to follow you,
You'd walk with me all the way.
But I noticed that during the saddest and most troublesome times of my life,
there was only one set of footprints.
I don't understand why, when I needed You the most, You would leave me."

He whispered, "My precious child, I love you and will never leave you
Never, ever, during your trials and testings.

When you saw only one set of footprints,
It was then that I carried you."

I certainly don't claim to have written this beautiful poem but, I do claim to be lucky enough to have lived it and experienced it.

I thought about my journey. I recalled the day my Dad died, and I was driving to Charlotte from Southport. I couldn't see the road I had so many tears flowing. Father Barry called me as I was driving. He asked, "Pete, are you driving?"

I said, "Yes, Father Barry, I am..."

"Are you being careful??" The message meaning... "Do you want a double tragedy today, Pete?? Those of us who love you sure don't..."

His question and his phone call that morning woke me up, snapped me out of my fog and back to reality. I had two young sons. I had more life to live. More things to do. *Miles to go before I sleep...*

———

Several times in my life I've realized that God wasn't done with me just yet.

Marcus Aurelius's quote, "The sun is quickly setting on all of our days – don't let time get away, do it now!" is a reminder to me to live every moment, to never take any one day or any one person in my world for granted. Back to the Marine Lt. Colonel's words that day on the beach before our ride with those amazing Wounded Warriors: *Gratitude and Attitude.*

Those weeks later after the Marine Corps Marathon, when it dawned on me that God had carried me, I flashed back to some of the other events in my life: where I was on 9/11, lucky enough to board the right plane, losing my cousin Jeff, suddenly losing my Dad. These memories reinforced for me over and over and over again that no tomorrow is guaranteed...

I realize I am on a journey, at times a reluctant traveler, for sure, but a journey nonetheless, like a river flowing downstream, with no choice but to be a part of that river.

I am where I'm supposed to be...

Often, I look back along my snow-covered path and there was one set of footprints, and they weren't mine. And yes, at some point, I knew I had no choice but to write this book. *I believe there are lives and livelihoods at stake.*

Is someone in your world slogging through the Valley of the Shadow of Death?

My simple and direct message is this: Don't wait. Don't let another day go by without pursuing your dreams. There is no guarantee of the next minute, next hour or tomorrow. I get that it's cliché and many have written it, but it's true and *I've lived it.*

I know we all have our stories. I urge you to tell yours, write your book. Tell it in whatever way you see fit. Let that person you haven't told in a long time know that you love or care about them. Go meet that friend for lunch or coffee.

Offer your helping hand.

Maybe you will be their Guardian Angel.

Maybe they will be yours?

Father Richard, who I introduced to you earlier, our former Army Special Forces member and seasoned endurance athlete, in the heart of the pandemic said "Rise above it all, and answer the call." Amen, Fr. Richard. Amen.

ONE FOOT IN FRONT OF THE OTHER WILL GET YOU HOME...

The Finish line - Jimbob far left Dewitt and me with pursed lips (ha)

———

IT'S ALL ABOUT FINISHING

"DON'T GIVE UP...DON'T EVER GIVE UP."
--JIMMY VALVANO - NATIONAL CHAMPIONSHIP
BASKETBALL COACH, NCSU

As you know, one of my mantras is "Always Training", which to me means that we are always doing our best to improve, always investing in ourselves, always moving forward. No rearview mirrors allowed unless you are using it as game film to improve.

In the end, Always Training leads and is related to: *ALWAYS FINISHING*.

From the movie *Wall Street* (1987), Michael Douglas plays the famous character Gordon Gekko, who, at one point in the movie, turns to his underling Bud Fox (played by Charlie Sheen) and says: "It's all about bucks, kid. The rest is just conversation."

A great line, but with all due respect to Mr. Gekko, in my humble opinion: It's actually *all about finishing – the rest is just conversation.*

The two statements are actually not that far apart.

One key trait I see across all successful brokers, developers, investors, business owners, leaders, and endurance athletes is that they have the discipline to finish, to make sure that everything within their control gets done and over the finish line.

The most successful brokers or entrepreneurs or businesspeople, managers, leaders or athletes seem to have an internal clock, an internal fire that burns. A motivation from within. What motivates these individuals? Is it money? Success? Freedom? Pain? Fear? Who knows?

We all have our own internal motivators or drivers.

It has been said that through our pain, sometimes we find our purpose. We all fall flat on our face sometimes due to our own actions or lack of performance, but more often than not, due to circumstances beyond our control. How do we react? Do we come across as the victim? Or do we pick ourselves up, dust ourselves off, smile (sometimes we grimace) and keep rolling.

In the endurance sports world, we like to compare and contrast goal times, personal records, which is certainly normal. At some point, I transitioned from trying to post my personal record (PR) to simply "finishing", which was always my underlying and ultimate goal in any event. I have always tried to never take finishing for granted...I knew there was always the possibility I may not finish.

The same can be said for me regarding closing a deal: I try to never take for granted any deal will close.

I am motivated by three key triggers: Fear, Pain and Freedom (which includes helping others).

I work my backside off and make sure I take care of what I can control, but beyond that I point up when I cross the finish line with thanks to God and others who helped me along the way, no matter the finish line.

One of my great cycling coaches once said in a class: "You showed up, you finished, you're a winner in my book."

I say the same to you, in whatever you do: *You showed up, You finished. You're a winner...*

My hope and wish for you is many more crossed finish lines in your life.

YOUR AUTHOR CROSSING THE MYRTLE BEACH MARATHON FINISH LINE
(SECOND TIME WAS A CHARM!)

A FEW SELECT MEDALS I WAS FORTUNATE TO BE HANDED
AS I CROSSED THE FINISH LINE IN A FEW OF THE EVENTS
I'VE BEEN FORTUNATE TO HAVE PARTICIPATED IN…

MY ROAD LESS TRAVELED AND A
FEW PERSONAL NOTES

Okay, you did it! You made it to the end with me. The following are just some tidbits, some "bonus" information that I wanted to include. (I can just hear you… "Bonus?!")

Disclaimer: I have not sought, nor received, a Runners World endorsement, but I would like to say a special 'thank you' to them for unknowingly helping me through the years. Little did they know they have been a quiet inspiration and an important part of my support team, helping me realize I wasn't alone. At the very least, letting me know others shared my craziness and my passion for the sport of running (which eventually lead me to swimming and cycling as well!).

The following collage is a collection of emails, etc. sent to me that I have kept from Runner's World *Daily Kick in the Butt*. Many I have posted to my social media, with some in my world thanking me for the "positive" shout out for the day. In my humble opinion, these all certainly apply directly to endurance sports, but they also directly apply to the endurance sports of life, business and real estate. Heck, I think if you just keep these nearby, focus and put them into practice, you will cross some finish lines you never thought you could cross.

By the way, Fred (you'll meet him in a bit) thinks the Endurance Collage ROCKS!

As you have probably gathered by now, my mom, dad and sister (Kathleen) represent the core of my SAG team in life. I realize how lucky I am to have and to have had that in my life. Yet another thing I don't take for granted and for which I am grateful!

From these three, my team expanded out to Uncle Paul and Aunt Denise, Aunt Debbie and Uncle Anthony, Uncle Joe and Aunt Sandra, my cousins Jeff and Natalie and, of course, my grandparents, Pete and Irene Frandano, and JD and Boots Pool. My sister and I have discussed our loving family network over the years as have Mary and me. I also know I would not have made it on this journey without Mary. *All I know is This* (this is also the title of my *Endurance Life Song*, please check it out on my website. www.frandano.com!); my SAG team has carried me...

I've tried my best to pass this tradition of loving support onto my sons, although, I know I have at times fallen there also. It's a journey I will never give up on. As you have probably surmised, I am also incredibly grateful for those two as well.

My sister and I concur that we are truly fortunate, incredibly lucky to have experienced this type of love from a father and mother who were always there for us. We know it's unique and I wanted to share just a bit of it with you in two letters I have included in the following pages.

A father to a son and a mother to a son, both very different, from very different backgrounds, different points of view, different "coaching styles", different motivational styles, but together, the base it created and the perspective – well, I know I'm lucky and my friends often pointed out how lucky I was over the years (thanks guys!).

ENDURANCE COLLAGE

During the writing of this book, I got up from my desk at one point to go find the eulogy I had written for my dad's service but I could not find it. Instead, I found a treasure trove of what seemed to be an endless basket of handwritten and typed letters from my parents. Mom could type. Dad could not, but his penmanship was quite good and his detail impressive! They came from that era where people actually sent letters to one another (remember those days?) and I was fortunate to be the regular recipient of such missives from Mom and Dad.

Mom would always draw a little smiley face and/or happy stick figure person on her envelope, which is where my man, **Fred**, comes from, my *Positive Endurance Man.*

I felt God gave me another God Wink with two letters I found almost instantly when searching for dad's eulogy. The letter from my mom was right on top of the stack, in the goofy/silly envelope with the smiley face in the middle of the "P" in my name.

The two letters were written to me upon Mom and Dad's arrival back to Charlotte, shortly after they dropped me off at Appalachian State University. (I loved Appalachian State University and Boone, NC. It has been an important part of my life. Thank you again, Joe Ward, then Director of Admissions, for taking a chance on me!)

Once you have taken a look at these two letters, I think you will understand the counterbalance mom and dad were for one another and to my sister and me. My mom, our cheerleader for life, late in her life suffered from pre-dementia, but we didn't realize how much so until Dad had passed. At that point, we realized how much Dad was, to use a baseball vernacular, shading from centerfield to leftfield to help cover for Mom.

Not too long after my Dad passed, I was at a lifelong family friend's house, the Fowlers, to celebrate a baby shower for my cousin, Natalie. My mom had gotten there ahead of me.

I walked into the Fowler's house and made my way to the kitchen where a dear friend, Lynne Rhinehardt, greeted me enthusiastically, hugged me, then pulled back, put her hands on my shoulders, eyes slightly wide, and in a voice very low and quiet said, "Peter, Take care of your mother..." Then, she nodded up and down intently.

Mom had apparently been very confused about the oven and a few other things and I think that was the first true indication that she was beginning her downward spiral.

When Mom was diagnosed with stage 4 Lung Cancer, her pre-dementia seemed to make her almost oblivious to what was going on with her, other than being in quite a bit of pain, which was heartbreaking.

Mom lived to the age of 70, too short for us, but as I said in her eulogy, *we have a cheerleader in Heaven now*. Mom longed to see the Caribbean one last time before she went to Heaven, so in good 'ol Miracle-like fashion, God gave us a window of opportunity about a month or so prior to her passing. The docs said, "If you are going to go, now would be a great time to do it." and so, we did. We returned; and a few weeks later, I was with Mom when she passed.

But it wasn't that easy. There is always a bit more to the story. I have to mention another guardian angel in my life, a good friend and neighbor. I would not have been there at the moment Mom passed onto the "purly gates" had it not been for my neighbor, Dennis Whittaker.

My sis had received the call that night from another angel at mom's senior housing home, Legacy Heights. The quiet, sweet Jamaican accent on the other end of the phone when my sister answered the call around 1am, August, 1, 2014 said, *You better come, your mother needs you..*

My sister called me, but I didn't answer, sleeping right through the call. A bang on the door alarmed Mary and she nudged (elbowed!) me and I went downstairs. It was pouring rain. I look through the door and see Dennis, my next door neighbor, soaking wet. The rain was coming down sideways at that point. My sis had called him and he had hopped up, run over and, thankfully, banged on the door until I got there.

I jumped in the car, rushed to Legacy Heights, and was holding Mom's hand as she labored her final few breaths. I swear she was blinded by the light because she squinted as she looked through me. It's as close as I think I've ever come to Heaven: looking into the face of someone who was looking into Heaven.

Thank you, Dennis!

I tucked these letters here in the back of the book so as not to invoke any feeling of obligation, but I wanted to share them with you as they give a bit of a glimpse into that love, that base from which I was fortunate to operate, one that has been part of the fuel that has powered me through this Endurance Event called *Life.*

333

August 13, 1984

My Dear Son,

It's the night before you leave for college...and I don't know exactly what to say to you.

Shall I tell you how much you were wanted before you were conceived? Shall I tell you how hard Dad and I, with God's help, tried to conceive you? Shall I tell you our unbelievable joy when we saw your face for the first time? Or how we counted your fingers and toes to make sure they were all there?

Perhaps I should tell you that you have brought us unending joy over the years...your first toddling steps, your adventurous curiousity about every aspect of life and of the living, your thrill with your new sister, your scrapes with... and your love for...your many friends, your pursuit of learning and your admiration (and dislike) of your various teachers.

Dad and I have watched you grow day by day, for over 19 years. We have laughed with you, talked with and to you, preached to you, counselled you, cried with and for you, worried about you, nagged you, hounded you, hugged you, kissed you....but, most of all, we have loved you with our whole beings. You are the best of the both of us.

How lucky and blessed we are to have a son like you!

Now you are going out on your own. It's frightening to know that I can't watch over you 24 hours a day. How will you ever manage to live without me? Honestly speaking, you will manage very well.

You have a spirit that says "survive"...a spirit that says "succeed"...a spirit that says "be happy". A God-given spirit.

Since the moment of your conception, I have felt that God touched your life. In moments of crisis, I have turned to Him and said, "He is Your son...watch over him and help me to do Your will." And within the last year, you have had a religious experience which showed you that you are a son of God. I pray that you will cling to that experience, and that belief, as you continue through your life's journey. Remember that I turned to you last Sunday...our last Sunday before your college life...and told you that the following should be your theme song:

"Be not afraid. I go before you always. Come,
follow Me, and I will give you rest.

You shall cross the barren desert, but you shall
not die of thirst.
You shall wander far in safety though you do not
know the way.
You shall speak your words in foreign lands and all
will understand.
You shall see the face of God and live.

Be not afraid. I go before you always. Come, follow
Me, and I will give you rest.
If you pass through raging waters in the sea, you
shall not drown.
If you walk amid the burning flames, you shall not be
harmed.
If you stand before the pow'r of hell and death is at
your side, know that I am with you through it all.

Be not afraid. I go before you always. Come, follow
Me, and I will give you rest.

Blessed are your poor, for the kingdoms shall be theirs.
Blest are you that weep and mourn, for one day you shall
laugh.
And if wicked men insult and hate you all because of Me,
blessed, blessed are you!

Be not afraid. I go before you always. Come, follow
Me, and I will give you rest."

It's not easy to hold on to your faith and your morals when
you go to college. There will be many people who will tempt
you to do wrong, or who will tease you if you go to church
regularly. But I trust you to do what you know is the right
thing. You have never been easily swayed by others...in fact,
you usually are the one who sets the good example for others.

It's with mixed feelings that I turn you over to freedom.
There is a great deal of pain in letting go...but also a
great deal of pride. I am proud to know that you are ready
to move on to bigger and better things. I am proud to know that
you are excited about your future and confident of your success.
I am proud that I have helped raise a son who is ready for life,
and all its joys and sorrows, ready to tackle the world, ready
to grow academically, emotionally, spiritually, and socially.
In short, I am proud of YOU, Pete.

You are facing some of the very best years of your life. I want you to enjoy every moment, absorb as much knowledge as you can, experience new people with new ideas, learn to cope with daily freedom (and the responsibility it brings), and have a wonderful time doing it all.

You will be on your own, for the first time. But, in reality, you will never be on your own -- not as long as Dad and I exist. We will always be here for you, ready to listen, to hug, to help, to guide, and most of all, to love without reservation. You can always count on us to be there for you...never *hesitate* to come to us in moments of joy or pain, confusion or elation, success or setbacks.

I think I've "done good". I'm very proud to say that you are my son. And I want you to move on with God's love...and especially with mine.

GO FOR IT...and be happy.

With all my love,

Mom

From Dad:

Wednesday
8·13·86

Dear Pili,

By the time you read this letter you'll be all squared away as a member of the Freshman Class at ASU. Wow! You did it and I'm very proud of you. A very new, interesting and challenging part of your life begins. All of your decisions will be your own. No one will be around to counsel, guide or advise you regarding the many alternative choices you will have to choose from. I am sure that you will make the right ones for you and for your future.

As we've discussed this is an extremely important time. Not only are you embarking on a totally unique, new experience, but, equally important, you are setting the stage for your future. You have before you every opportunity to be successful, happy and fulfilled. Please remember that each day in your life is very important and must be planned and lived so as to maximize your opportunities for future happiness & success. It is still very important to set specific, precise, attainable, near term and long term goals for yourself. In the business world we also talk about two different sets of goals - reasonable goals - ie, those you feel you can readily achieve, and ② stretch goals - ie, goals which are possibly attainable but will require a number of different sets of circumstances to fall in place. For example a reasonable goal might be to obtain a C+ or better average in your courses first semester. A stretch goal might be to obtain a B or B+ average. And so on. You might want to set up class attendance and church attendance goals as well as campus involvement goals. Extra curricular activities should be planned for and intramural sports. Don't put yourself in a position where you will look back with regret over the things you did not try to do. Make lists of things that you want to accomplish and set out to accomplish them, for desire one. Keep in mind that driving to reach goals is as important as attaining the goals. Actual attainment of goals which have been well thought out and strongly pursued will leave you with a wonderful feelings. Somebody once said "it's not whether you win or lose, it's how you play the game that's important."

Keep the "big picture" in mind. Don't let minor set-backs cause you too much concern. Life is full of successes and failures and your personal growth will be largely determined by how well you deal with "triumph and disaster and treat those two imposters just the same". I hope that you take the plaque (I forgot you're already there so I'm going to put it in your boxes) "If" with you because as time goes by it will be useful to reflect on the words contained in it. They are meaningful, relevant and important to understand.

I could not write this letter and complete it without telling you how much you will be missed. Your love, cheer, goodness, humor and caring has made me and mom very proud and happy to have you as our son. Kathleen doesn't say too much, but we know by some of the little comments she has made that she will miss you so very much, too. It's going to be very lonesome not having you around. But, that's life, and part of your growth. I hope you understand our interest in what's happening (happened) in your life. Now and always we are concerned about your physical, emotional and psychological growth. We want you to be happy and successful. If you are, then we will be happy, too.

Just remember, we're as close as your phone. While I know you want to make your own choices and decisions, sometimes you might want to "bounce something off" old dad. Always know that I want you to feel free to do so. As uncle Paul said, "You are the first born of the first born. You're on the carrier of a torch of love, knowledge and accomplishment which you will someday pass to your children and they to theirs. So, strive hard to make that torch shine brightly and the "best" will be yours and everything that's in it and, which is more, you'll be a man, my son." Good luck on this part of your journey through life.

With the deepest love any
father can have for a son,

Dad.

A bit verbose aren't they? I say again, I am an extremely fortunate son and a truly fortunate man...

WHAT ARE THE THREE THINGS? THE ENDURANCE LIFE CHART

In the spirit of keeping it simple and not losing the forest for the trees, this is my executive level summary in anticipation of your question:

So, Pete, what are the 3 Things I should take away from your book?

And what an outstanding question it is!

WELCOME TO THE ENDURANCE LIFE CHART

Whether running your business, a marathon or your personal life, within this chart lies the essence of running from Peak to Peak. The Endurance Life Chart will help you cross your finish lines and lead to a more fulfilling life.

Behold below, the infamous *Endurance Life Chart*... seems to be a lot going on, right? Actually, it's pretty simple. Let's take a look at the structure.

WHAT ARE THE 3 THINGS ???
The Endurance Life Chart

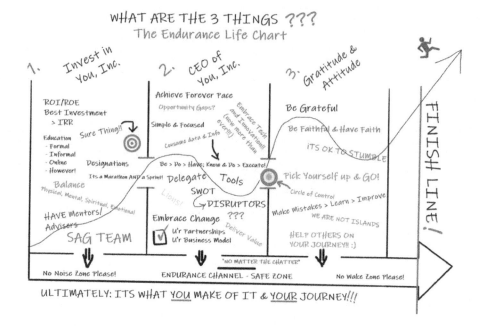

These are the 3 Things, made up of what look to be silos, but they are not silos. Silos typically stand alone and are isolated. These are more like chambers that flow in and out of one another and they are not stagnant. They are alive. If you think of yourself as *You, Inc.*, with you as the **CEO**, then you are well on your way.

The 3 Things are:

1. Invest in You, Inc.
2. CEO of You, Inc.
3. Gratitude and Attitude

Let me touch on each briefly.

1 - INVEST IN YOU, INC.

Invest in yourself - it all starts here. Investing in yourself is the best investment you can make. It's the closest "thing" we can get to a *sure thing bet*. Investing in **You, Inc.** does what I call "widening the bull's eye." Whether reading a book or some other publication or writing a book or an article. Whether formal or informal education, online class, tapping into mentors, maintaining Balance of the 4's, (physical, mental, social/emotional and spiritual) or whatever you are doing to broaden and deepen you, it's all an investment in **You, Inc.**

2 - CEO OF YOU, INC.

You are the **CEO of You, Inc.,** ; have a plan, keep it simple, weed out the crap. Check and have a plan to re-check your business model for relevancy. This has always been important, but in this post COVID-19 world, it is *more important than ever.*

Part of the CEO's job is to spot or recognize disruption or have team members that send up smoke signal warnings on the horizon.

In business school, one of the great tools we were taught in our strategy classes was called SWOT Analysis, most believe "invented" by Albert Humphrey (Stanford Research Institute) in the 1960's:

- Strengths
- Weaknesses
- Opportunities
- Threats

SWOT analysis is a tool/process/framework to help a person or entity lay out the strengths, weaknesses, opportunities, and threats to a business.

SWOT ANALYSIS

	Helpful to achieving the objective	Harmful to achieving the objective
Internal origin (attributes of the organization)	Strengths	Weaknesses
External origin (attributes of the environment)	Opportunities	Threats

Somewhat related and interconnected, from his outstanding and classic strategy book, *Competitive Advantage*, author Michael Porter taught us about the *Five Forces*. This is essentially a tool or framework or process for analyzing the competition (or threats) of a business:

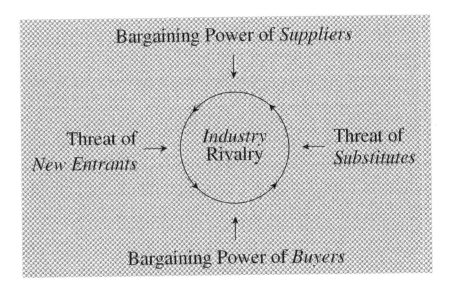

Both of the processes/systems above are the CEO's tools to help spot and take advantage of disruption, no matter the industry, business, or opportunity.

The CEO may have someone (or a team) execute the above but ultimately, the responsibility for ensuring the ball is advancing falls directly in the CEO's lap. Part of the CEO's job at times, is like a forward scout, to go up on the ridge, climb a tree, get in a helicopter or do whatever she/he needs to do to gain a glimpse out toward the landscape ahead. Of course, this is not literal. Your helicopter may be in the form of those around you, information sources, people with dissenting views or research you gather.

If you are a one-person, sole proprietorship, then you are the team. Whether CEO of a Fortune 500 Company or a sole practitioner, we are each CEO's and we need to be able to spot disruption, recognize it and ride the wave.

I have a saying:

WHEN STANDING ON THE BEACH, IF YOU LOOK OUT AND SEE
THE TSUNAMI COMING, THE TIME FOR RUNNING HAS LONG
SINCE PASSED. YOU BETTER BE A STRONG SWIMMER...

Some like to use disruption as a fear tactic. "Watch Out! Disruption is Coming!"

Disruption is nothing to fear. And no, it's not one thing, it's three things. It's not just *coming*.

Disruption, in just about any industry: 1) has been coming, 2) is here at our doorstep, and 3) is going to keep coming.

What do we do about that? Do we roll over and hunker down? Or ride (surf) the wave? Turn it into an opportunity? Yes! I call them *Opportunities for the Vigilant...*

The CEO needs to maintain focus and have the strength, courage and conviction to make tough decisions. As the CEO, we may have to be ruthless at times, in terms of guarding our time and advancing our ball. Hopefully, not at the cost of others, but the hard/cold fact is that in our everybody-gets-a-trophy society, there are winners and losers, so why not win and take some folks along with you over the finish line? The CEO recognizes they have to help themselves first before they can help others. The CEO, as captain of the ship, also realizes at times that in order to save the entire ship, hard sacrifices have to be made.

As the CEO of You, Inc., life, distractions, noise will come flying at your head and you'll be ducking, bobbing and weaving. We need to have a filtering mechanism, a screen, and be disciplined to keep moving forward... *no matter the chatter.*

3 - GRATITUDE AND ATTITUDE

Faith, giving and receiving help. This is the philanthropic component of **You, Inc.**

I'm grateful and thankful. I try to maintain my faith, even when I stumble, picking myself up, trying to help others along my journey, making mistakes and learning from them.

This is the realization that every finish line I have crossed in life, whether in business or a marathon or life in general, I had some help along the way. Yes, I exerted my own energy and effort, but someone, somewhere, *helped me along the way.*

This is also the humbling realization that *you can't do it all by yourself and you're not an island.*

This important aspect is linked to the CEO who recognizes, realizes, and accepts that there are going to be winners and losers in any market or business, and that sometimes there won't be enough lifeboats or lifejackets to go around. There weren't enough during the Great Recession and most likely there won't in our post-Pandemic world, so why not win and be a lifeboat for others? Winning without guilt...It's not a bad thing at all.

———

In our *Endurance Life Chart*, the section across the bottom of the chart shows the *no noise zone* and the *no wake zone*. In these spaces we are below the turbulence, below the choppy waters above, below the business cycle (represented by the upward and rolling line).

When we have done the job of filling those silos with a few things that are important to us, we will minimize the noise, the turbulence, the business cycle impacting us. We always cycle, but we can define our life and set it as a fortress for ourselves and others to withstand the cycle. To *cross finish lines.*

I have filled up the silos with *stuff* that means something to me.

Think of those items within the silos as hints. I suggest you fill them with *stuff* that means something to you. I have put a blank copy of the Endurance Life Chart at the end of this section for you to fill as you see fit!

And how about 3 of my life lessons?

IT'S YOUR LIFE, LIVE IT

I'm living proof that if you want to make a change in your life, you can make it – no matter the stage of life. I was thirty-five when I made my change, after almost 14 years in the Fortune 500 world. If your personal business model needs changing or   modification, and you need to move to another business or even make a life change, I know it's easier said than done, but *you can do it.*

IN ALL YOU DO, REMEMBER THAT YOU ARE THE CEO OF YOU, INC.

We have a personal responsibility to do the best we can. We have a personal responsibility to be accountable to ourselves and others, and to make our mark on the world and help ourselves and others along our journey. We are the *CEO's of our lives.* We choose our partnerships, where we spend our time, what our business models are. We have one precious life, so live it...

HELP OTHERS ALONG YOUR JOURNEY

Mother Teresa said *"If you can't fee a hundred people, then feed just one."* Short, simple, A lesson in: *Brevity is the Soul of Wit.* I agree with the good Sister.

———

YOUR ENDURANCE LIFE CHART

(to fill in as you see fit…)

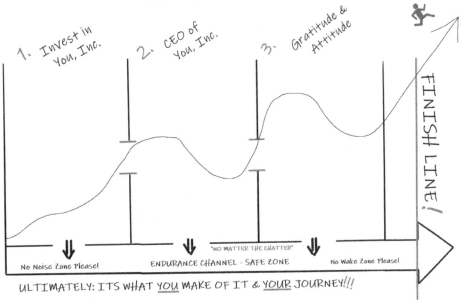

WHAT ARE THE 3 THINGS ???

The Endurance Life Chart

1. Invest in You, Inc.

2. CEO of You, Inc.

3. Gratitude & Attitude

FINISH LINE!

No Noise Zone Please!

ENDURANCE CHANNEL - SAFE ZONE

"NO MATTER THE CHATTER"

No Wake Zone Please!

ULTIMATELY: ITS WHAT YOU MAKE OF IT & YOUR JOURNEY!!!

Check out Fred in the upper right of the chart. Like us, he is pushing hard to reach the top of the next peak, ever encouraging, always helping us to remember to keep it positive and keep looking up.

Life and business always cycle.

The choice of what we do about it within the cycles is completely up to us.

———

MEET FRED

We all have Giant Heroes in our world, one of mine is Fred. He's my Positive Endurance Man, or my PEM, for short. He is my reminder to stay positive, keep it simple and keep pushing.

Where did my PEM come from you ask?

When I went off to college, my mother, my biggest life cheerleader, would send me letters and she always drew a little stick figure or smiley face with a message like "Wheee!" or "Hey there!" or "I miss you!" or "I love you!" on them. Amazingly simple, but very powerful, and it always brought a smile to my face. Her little stick figures were soon associated with joy and positive feelings, so he became a reminder and a symbol of encouragement for me.

And the name *Fred?*

A lifelong friend of mine, Eric Wilhelm, would always use the name "Fred" in sentences to make folks laugh. My mom picked up on it and loved it, so I guess you can say, it stuck. Fred is more than a superhero to me, he's a Giant Hero. With your help and mine, Fred will help feed the hungry and help house the homeless.

MEET FRED!

(HE'S MY PEM: POSITIVE ENDURANCE MAN)

At times, Fred (via my mom) has provided me with much needed perspective. And from my time in the arena, during the long war, I certainly needed that.

Then and now: *Lives and Livelihoods are at stake...*

When I started out writing this book early in 2019, I worried about this statement being seen as overly dramatic.

I no longer worry about that... May God Bless you on your Journey.

———

ACKNOWLEDGMENTS:

If anyone ever tells you they wrote their book in three hours, don't believe them (unless it's a "short story" in which case there may be some hint of truth there!).

Everyone on the list below has touched my life in some way. This is my "thank you" list. I did my best to include the folks who have been instrumental in my life, either directly or indirectly. In some cases, it may have been sharing their precious time, experience, and wisdom with me. In other cases, it may have been a positive influence on me when they didn't know they were a positive influence or were a positive motivation for me without even knowing I was "watching." (No, I'm not a 'creeper' as my son would call it)

When you look back over your life, you realize how many had a hand in helping you along the way. I'm sure I have missed someone below so my apologies in advance but I did my level best on my thank you list. This list is made up of friends, family, colleagues, teachers, a few clients and, of course, mentors and coaches.

And to my sons, John and Joe, thank you for making me the *luckiest dad in the world.*

I want to give a special thanks to the team who helped me assemble this book, who bore with me and helped me get it the way I wanted it. If you ask Mary, she may tell you I wrote this book at 3am every night, which is probably not too far off the mark.

Part of the reason I partake of the endurance sport fruit is to blow off steam – on top of everything else it does for me. It definitely acts as a pressure relief valve. My small circle knows that if I have missed a work-out (rare, I have to be next to death or injured) I get a bit grumpy. So, given the time of day I wrote most of this book, if you read something that makes you think I have flipped my cray-cray switch, please allow me to hide behind my three o'clock in the morning excuse. Thank you all for supporting me and, more importantly, for putting up with me.

Thank you to all of the following good folks (and to those friends, family and colleagues I've missed who have impacted my life) from the bottom of my heart, and every one of them will most likely know why they are on this list.

If not, I invite them to call me or email me and I will tell them personally!

John Frandano
Joe Frandano
Pete Frandano (Dad)
Bobbie Frandano (Mom)
Kathleen (Frandano) Franek
Jeff Pool
Joe Pool
Natalie (Pool) Crockford
Sandra Pool
Paul Frandano
Denise Frandano
Debbie Piccillo
Anthony Piccillo
Peter and Irene Frandano
JD and Boots Pool
Mary Soria
Beth Hardin
Dr. Bill Hardin
Melinda Koenigsberg
Pamela Frandano
Robert French
Jean French Turner
Seth Soria
DeWitt Brown
Dave White
Jim Jacquelin
Grant Barger
Mark Folk
Leslie Sheppard
Blake Sheppard
Rachel Franek
Adam Franek
Andy Sheppard
Kate Sheppard
Ike and Francis French

Rob Franek
Gracie Crockford
Hallie Crockford
Mike Crockford
Ray Jones
Dr. Bill Davis
Father Frank O'Rourke
Father Ed Sheridan
Dr. Jack Meredith
Dr. Ronald Copley
Kevin Sisson
Kim Macaulay
Eddie Blanton, CCIM
Tony Rickard, CCIM
Cindy Chandler, CCIM, CRE
Hector Ingram, MAI
Steve Candler
Mike Barr, CAE, RCE
Andrea Bushnell, Esq.
Jeff Siebold, CCIM, MAI
T. Cooper James
Jerry Rowland
Hanes Walker
Bill Wilder
Bill Snipes
Wilson Sherrill
Ben Styers
Ray Bowling
Jerry Shremshock
Jim Boyd
Willard Bullins
Joe Larkin, CCIM
Tom Wilhelm
Pete Herran
Dr. Joanne Allen

Rob Pressley, CCIM
Sledd Thomas, CCIM
Eric Wilhelm
Richard Hefner
Aubrey Prescod
Jean Baker
Jean Brown
Alan Holden
Rob Cheek
Howard Bissell
Beverly Keith, CCIM
Charlie Ellis, CCIM, CPM
Bo Proctor, CCIM, CPM
Tem McInville
Jim Davis
Claude Pruitt
Jim Schenck
Mitch Smith
Ed Stack
Rob Vaughn, CCIM
Karen Mankowski, CCIM
Drew Showfety, CCIM
Steve Rich, CCIM
Danna Mathias
Chad Whitley
Mike Butler
Brian P. Quinn
Jerry Fitzgerald, CCIM
Pappy Corbitt
Bob "Bubba" Lewis, CCIM, SIOR
Andy Dinkin
Trevor Kong
Steve Hills
Dr. Joe Peele
Joe Ward

Kirk Davis
Coach Glenn Sasser
Ralph Falls
Jordan Washburn
Tony Martinette
Frank Efird Sr.
Frank Efird Jr.
Dr. Ron Pannesi
Brent Cawn
Nat Shaw
Joe Hamner
Brett Rhinehardt
Bo Rhinehardt
Pat Plettner
Derek Flynt
John and Lynn Rhinehardt
Andy Pressley
Fred Dula
Jim Perkins
Roy Thompson
Bo Corley
Joe Figard
Joe Fazzari

Judge Chase Saunders
Sam Cornwell
Dr. Dennis Whitaker
Doug Sawyer, CCIM
Dr. Stan Harris
Maria D'Marco
Greg Cox, CCIM
Jack Carlisle
Scott Stover
Cynthia Walsh, RCE
Pam Hayes
Brian Deutsch
Skeet Harris, MAI, CRE
Bryan Butler
Will Leonard
Reggie Clark
Charles Fulcher
Simon Coulson
Francesca Fazzolari
Jay Chambers
Bill Allen
Dr. Bo Mason
Dr. Domenic Palagruto

Lou Baldwin
Jay Astoske
Kim Anne Russ
Mary Anne Russ
John Russ
Jay Taylor, CCIM
Carol Lineberry
Theresa Salmen
Joanna Edwards
Margaret Martin
Jerry Adams
Dr. Ralph Fox
James Milner, CCIM
Father Richard Sutter
Margaret Bishop
Wayne Faulkner
Geoffrey Curme
Mike Gauldin
Mike Petkauskos
Jim Kane
Rick Hood
Cliff Ray, CCIM

ENDNOTES

Chapter 1

1[i] https://www.amazon.com/Big-Short-Inside-Doomsday-Machine/dp/0393338827

2[ii] From the FDIC's (Federal Deposit Insurance Corporation) website: On Friday, June 8, 2012, Waccamaw Bank, Whiteville, NC was closed by the North Carolina Office of the Commissioner of Banks, and the Federal Deposit Insurance Corporation (FDIC) was named Receiver. No advance notice is given to the public when a financial institution is closed. (It didn't take long, I can't imagine the pressure Jim was under, nothing personal ever in these kinds of "battles").

3[iii] To explain the concept of "loss share agreement", the following is from the FDIC website: Under loss share, the FDIC absorbs a portion of the loss on a specified pool of assets which maximizes asset recoveries and minimizes FDIC losses. Loss share also reduces the FDIC's immediate cash needs, is operationally simpler and more seamless to failed bank customers and moves assets quickly into the private sector.

Typically, what would happen is the "conquering bank", tapped by the FDIC to come in and vulture over the fallen bank, would cherry pick the good assets and leave the scraps to the government and the taxpayers.

Chapter 2

4[iv] War Room meeting occurred at our Division HQ in Winston-Salem every Monday morning. Directors of manufacturing or their appointee would show up and they would go through all of the numbers from the previous week's production and delivery performance. Line managers mixed in with Ivory tower staffers, it was corporate America at its finest and Willard had a particular disdain for staffers making a $100,000+ per year that had no direct reports and in his mind no real responsibility other than riding herd on his and others performance...through my career, I grew a similar disdain for folks who's only job I perceived to be was to Monday Morning Quarterback we managers (coaches) and those of us who were actually responsible for managing large facilities and people to cross performance goal finish lines...Most good managers, and Willard was a damn good one, defended his people/team members to the point of defiance and like any great coach, Willard would take the hit if his team didn't make the goal and would pass our credit to others if they did make their goal. Willard "only" had a 2 year Associate's degree but he was a rising star and was super street smart and charismatic...He would play the "I'm the lowly 2 year Associate's degree guy from Wytheville Community College running circles around these MBA's" card with a smile on his face...and I love it....It was a quick perspective check for me to not judge folks by their academic pedigree.

Chapter 5

5[v] Navy SEAL admiral Shares Reasons to Make Bed Everyday:
https://www.google.com/search?q=make+your+bed+every+day&oq=-
make+your+bed+every+day&aqs=chrome..69i57j0j46j0l5.3286j0j7&sourceid=-
chrome&ie=UTF-8#kpvalbx=_COjjXoOoNu2ZwbkPhuuo6Ac47

6[vi] https://www.womensrunning.com/
training/10-ways-marathon-training-humbles-me/

7[vii] https://www.webmd.com/cancer/lymphoma/diffuse-large-b-cell-lymphoma#1

8[viii] CAMA stands for 'Coastal Area Management Act' and in summary regulates things like construction setbacks (i.e. where you can construct a property) which by CAMA guidelines is "measured landward from the first line of "Stable-Natural" vegetation'. This basically sets the important guidelines regarding where one can build in proximity to the water line (in this case, the Atlantic ocean) and the important vegetation that often acts as a natural and protective buffer to the shoreline; the guidelines (not a choice, but required by law) are set up to help preserve the environment and there is a practical point of not allowing the overzealous to build any closer to Mother Nature than one would want to in a sane state of mind with encroaching oceans and all. My experience has been that Mother Nature at times can be quick to come down on our heads and she does not discriminate in her fury. In North Carolina, the purpose of CAMA is to protect the unique natural resources of the North Carolina coastal areas. There are 20 CAMA Counties in North Carolina which are subject to the CAMA rules. Areas of Environmental Concern (AECs) are the foundation of the CAMA regulations.' This stemmed from the Coastal Zone Management Act of 1972 which was an Act of Congress passed in 1972 to encourage coastal states to develop and implement coastal zone management plans.

Chapter 6

9[ix] NCNB, which later turned into NationsBank and then eventually the amazing Behemoth called Bank of America; this company and its ensuing "war" with then First Union helped build and grow Charlotte into what Mr. McColl would call the "banking epicenter of the south."

10[x] https://www.investopedia.com/terms/b/bankruptcy.asp

Chapter 7

11[xi] https://jeffreypfeffer.com/books/the-knowing-doing-gap/

Chapter 8

12[xii] For more on Site To Do Business click here:
https://www.stdb.com/

13[xiii] https://armyandnavyacademy.org/blog/
why-discipline-is-beneficial-for-young-men/

14[xiv] "Yes, but are they happy? Effects of trait self-control on affective well-being and life satisfaction
https://pubmed.ncbi.nlm.nih.gov/23750741/

15[xv] Included with permission by Cindy Chandler, CCIM, CRE, The Chandler Group

16[xvi] https://www.amazon.com/Insiders-Guide-Commercial-Real-Estate/
dp/1475437269/ref=sr_1_1?ie=UTF8&qid=1489111104&sr=8-1&keywords=the+insider%27s+guide+to+commercial+real+estate"

17[xvii] https://www.forbes.com/sites/carolinehoward/2013/03/27/
you-say-innovator-i-say-disruptor-whats-the-difference/#340932a96f43
18[xviii] https://www.investopedia.com/terms/m/mooreslaw.asp,
19[xix] Empires of the Mind: Dennis Waitley page 70

Chapter 10
20[xx] https://www.runnersworld.com/nutrition-weight-loss/a20851510/
the-science-behind-bonking/

Chapter 11
21[xxi] https://www.amazon.com/Marathon-Ultimate-Training-Programs-Marathons/
dp/1609612248
22[xxii] https://www.amazon.com/Triathlon-Training-Michael-Finch/dp/0736054448
23[xxiii] https://stillnessbook.com/
24[xxiv] The Importance of Vacations to Our Physical and Mental
Health - why Presidents (and all of us) need vacations. By Dr. Susan
Krauss Whitbourne; June 22, 2010: Psychology Today: https://
www.psychologytoday.com/us/blog/fulfillment-any-age/201006/
the-importance-vacations-our-physical-and-mental-health

Chapter 12
25[xxv] Thank you for that, George Bell; I served with George on the then NCAR
now NCR (North Carolina Association of REALTORS®, and George at one time
oversaw our forms committee . He used that term with our NC Exec Team one
time when we were going through a forms revision and he was explaining some
things to us in layman's terms.
26[xxvi] frandano.com
27[xxvii] https://www.amazon.com/Brokers-Who-Dominate-Traits-Producers/
dp/0983834903
28[xxviii] https://www.amazon.com/dp/0684856360?tag=amz-mkt-chr-us-20&asc-
subtag=1ba00-01000-org00-win10-other-smile-us000-pcomp-feature-scomp-wm-
5&ref=aa_scomp&pldnSite=1
29[xxix] https://www.t360.com/rankings-reviews/swanepoel-mega-1000/
mega-downloads/
30[xxx] http://homepages.se.edu/cvonbergen/files/2013/01/The-Abilene-Paradox_The-
Management-of-Agreement.htm_.pdf
31[xxxi] https://www.amazon.com/Meditations-New-Translation-Marcus-Aurelius/
dp/0812968255/ref=pd_lpo_14_img_0/132-4705702-9819840?_encoding=UT-
F8&pd_rd_i=0812968255&pd_rd_r=1ddcd256-6f6e-4588-8145-eaf9e3f-
598d4&pd_rd_w=fh5mo&pd_rd_wg=cmrZo&pf_rd_p=7b36d496-f366-4631-
94d3-61b87b52511b&pf_rd_r=S3956M5G5SR48N6P8MBY&psc=1&re-
fRID=S3956M5G5SR48N6P8MBY
32[xxxii] https://www.amazon.com/This-Marketing-Cant-Until-Learn/dp/0525540830
33[xxxiii] https://www.amazon.com/Habits-Highly-Effective-People-Powerful/
dp/0743269519
34[xxxiv] https://www.amazon.com/Meditations-New-Translation-Marcus-Aurelius/
dp/0812968255/ref=pd_lpo_14_img_0/132-4705702-9819840?_encoding=UT-
F8&pd_rd_i=0812968255&pd_rd_r=71aaf122-fd25-4a55-a012-f04ea1b-
3d26e&pd_rd_w=19WPC&pd_rd_wg=08nkk&pf_rd_p=7b36d496-f366-4631-

94d3-61b87b52511b&pf_rd_r=Z4QRE4HCY08WZ9GCMQEQ&psc=1&refRID=Z4QRE4HCY08WZ9GCMQEQ

35[xxxv] https://www.amazon.com/Power-Positive-Thinking-Norman-Vincent/dp/0743234804

36[xxxvi] https://www.amazon.com/Millionaire-Real-Estate-Agent-About/dp/0071444041

37[xxxvii] https://www.amazon.com/Big-Short-Inside-Doomsday-Machine/dp/0393338827

38[xxxviii] https://www.amazon.com/Too-Big-Fail-Washington-System/dp/0143118242

39[xxxix] https://www.amazon.com/Lone-Survivor-Eyewitness-Account-Operation/dp/031632406X

40[xl] https://www.amazon.com/Band-Brothers-Regiment-Airborne-Normandy/dp/1501179403/ref=sr_1_2?dchild=1&keywords=band+of+brothers&qid=1591553731&sr=8-2

41[xli] https://www.amazon.com/Empires-Mind-Lessons-Succeed-Knowledge-Based/dp/0688147631

42[xlii] https://www.amazon.com/Ultramarathon-Man-Confessions-All-Night-Runner/dp/1585424803

43[xliii] https://www.amazon.com/Ten-Day-MBA-4th-Step-Step/dp/0062199579

44[xliv] https://www.amazon.com/Next-Level-Thinking-Powerful-Successful/dp/1546010521

45[xlv] https://www.amazon.com/Brokers-Who-Dominate-Traits-Producers/dp/0983834903

46[xlvi] https://www.amazon.com/Short-Guide-Happy-Life/dp/0375504613

47[xlvii] https://www.amazon.com/SEE-YOU-AT-TOP-Anniversary-ebook/dp/B0047T78TQ

48[xlviii] https://www.amazon.com/Seuss-isms-Guide-Those-Starting-Already/dp/0553508415

49[xlix] https://www.amazon.com/This-Marketing-Cant-Until-Learn/dp/0525540830

50[l] https://www.amazon.com/gp/product/1419540564/ref=dbs_a_def_rwt_bibl_vppi_i0

51[li] https://www.amazon.com/bible/s?k=the+bible

52[lii] True Greatness: Mastering the Inner Game of Business Success https://www.amazon.com/dp/0814433383?tag=amz-mkt-chr-us-20&ascsubtag=1ba00-01000-org00-win10-other-smile-us000-pcomp-feature-scomp-wm-5&ref=aa_scomp&pldnSite=1

53[liii] https://www.mayoclinic.org/healthy-lifestyle/stress-management/in-depth/positive-thinking/art-20043950,

54[liv] https://www.amazon.com/gp/product/1562827251/ref=dbs_a_def_rwt_hsch_vapi_taft_p1_i0

55[lv] https://www.amazon.com/Running-Being-Experience-George-Sheehan/dp/1623362539

56[lvi] https://www.hopeforthewarriors.org/

ABOUT THE AUTHOR:

Peter A. Frandano, CCIM, GRI, MBA has a combined 30+ years in the Fortune 500 and real estate arenas and is a proud alumnus of the University of North Carolina Chapel Hill and Wake Forest University's Graduate School of Business. As a former Fortune 500 Logistics/ Supply Chain Exec who bounced all over the globe for quite a few years, Pete decided post September 11, 2001 (9/11) to jump out of that arena to pursue his entrepreneurial dreams in the real estate industry and more time with his family. Though Pete has had the good fortune to coach and consult with many great colleagues over the years, Pete prides himself as being a front line, *in the arena* guy. Pete focuses his time in the real estate industry in the commercial sector, specializing in transactional brokerage, valuation and consulting. Pete was co-owner of a full service real estate company (Southport Realty) in beautiful coastal southeastern, NC and returned to Charlotte in 2014 where he now divides his time between the city and the coast. Pete has been President of River Sound Inc., a real estate consulting firm since 2005. Pete takes great pride in having been called a "thought leader" by industry peers and has been fortunate to be recognized by his peers in leadership in the industry. In 2012, he was humbled to be awarded the coveted REALTOR® of the Year Award by his peers for his service with the Brunswick County Association of REALTORS®; Pete served as the 2011 President of BCAR and was the 2017 President of the nationally recognized and award winning North Carolina CCIM Chapter. Pete has also served as a member of the Board of Directors for the

REALTOR® Commercial Alliance of Southeastern, NC (Wilmington), The Charlotte Regional Commercial Board of REALTORS® (CRCBR), and as a Board member and Regional Vice President for the North Carolina Association of REALTORS®; at the national level Pete has had the opportunity to serve in various capacities including Board Member and industry Legislative roles. Thanks to his clients and his peers, Pete has been fortunate to be recognized as a Top Performer by the CCIM Institute and is honored and humbled to be an immensely proud member of the North Carolina CCIM Hall of Fame. Pete is proud to be a small business owner and entrepreneur, a seasoned and enthusiastic endurance sport athlete, a team player, and has been the grateful recipient of a great deal of help along his journey. He enjoys nothing more than helping others run from peak to peak, to cross their finish lines. Pete is a big believer in the American Dream and because of his sons, has been honored with the best two words he could ever be called: *Coach and Dad.*

Picture taken by your author of the Yacht Basin, Southport, N.C.
For me, it represents our country and all of us…enduring,
overcoming and crossing finish lines!

Ok, I admit I fancy myself as an amateur photographer. That picture reminds me of all that is good about our country and our great state. To me, it represents all of us enduring, overcoming and crossing finish lines!

Made in the USA
Columbia, SC
27 March 2021